KING EDWARD VIII

His Life and Reign

Photograph by Hughes & Mullins, Ryde.

1896. *Prince Edward at the age of* $2\frac{1}{2}$ *years with his great-grandmother,*
Queen Victoria.

KING EDWARD VIII

His Life and Reign

by

HECTOR BOLITHO

Author of *"Albert the Good," "Victoria the Widow
and her Son,"* etc.

1937

EYRE AND SPOTTISWOODE
LONDON

First Edition March, 1937
Second Edition March, 1937
Third Reprint March, 1937
Fourth Reprint March, 1937
Fifth Reprint March, 1937

**Made and Printed in Great Britain for
Eyre and Spottiswoode (Publishers), London**

To J. S.

Contents

CHAPTER   PAGE

I. THE CLOSE OF VICTORIA'S REIGN. BIRTH AND BOYHOOD OF EDWARD VIII   3

II. CORONATION OF KING GEORGE V. HIS CHARACTER. PRINCE EDWARD OF WALES. THE DUCHY OF CORNWALL   17

III. A STUDENT IN FRANCE   25

IV. OXFORD   31

V. GERMANY   41

VI. THE WAR   47

VII. A SOLDIER IN FRANCE   55

VIII. WAR ON ITALIAN FRONT   65

IX. THE END OF THE WAR   77

X. CANADA AND THE UNITED STATES   85

XI. THE BARBADOES, HONOLULU AND FIJI   97

XII. NEW ZEALAND   103

XIII. AUSTRALIA   113

XIV. LIFE IN ENGLAND. RETURNED SOLDIERS   125

XV. KING GEORGE AS A FATHER   133

XVI. INDIA   143

XVII. SOUTH AFRICA   167

XVIII. THE TRANSVAAL   181

XIX. ST. HELENA, THE ARGENTINE AND CHILE   189

XX. WORK AMONG THE POOR   197

XXI. LIFE IN ENGLAND: AVIATION   207

XXII. KING GEORGE'S JUBILEE. THE PRINCE'S FRIENDS   229

Contents

CHAPTER   PAGE

XXIII. DEATH OF KING GEORGE V   241

XXIV. THE REIGN OF EDWARD VIII   253

XXV. THE KING AND THE PRIME MINISTER   263

XXVI. THE ABDICATION   279

      APPENDIX   291

      INDEX   297

List of Illustrations

1896. PRINCE EDWARD AT THE AGE OF $2\frac{1}{2}$ YEARS WITH HIS GREAT-GRANDMOTHER, QUEEN VICTORIA

Frontispiece

FACING PAGE

THE PRINCE WITH KING EDWARD VII   6

PRINCESS MARY, PRINCE EDWARD AND PRINCE ALBERT AS CHILDREN   8

KING GEORGE V (WHEN PRINCE OF WALES) WITH HIS THREE SONS   12

THE PRINCE OF WALES AS A MIDSHIPMAN   14

1911. THE PRINCE OF WALES IN HIS INVESTITURE ROBES   22

1914. THE PRINCE OF WALES LEADING HIS COMPANY OF GRENADIER GUARDS IN FULL SERVICE KIT ON A ROUTE MARCH   50

NOVEMBER, 1915: KING GEORGE V VISITS THE WESTERN FRONT   72

1918. KING GEORGE VISITS THE FLEET AT ROSYTH, EDINBURGH, NOVEMBER, 1918   80

THE PRINCE OF WALES LEAVING FOR AUSTRALIA AND NEW ZEALAND   100

1920. THE PRINCE OF WALES IN AUSTRALIA: PERTH, JUNE, 1920   122

1920. THE PRINCE OF WALES WITH QUEEN ALEXANDRA AT THE CHRISTENING OF LADY PATRICIA RAMSAY'S SON   136

1924. THE PRINCE OF WALES AND LORD BADEN-POWELL AT WEMBLEY   160

List of Illustrations

FACING PAGE

1927. THE PRINCE OF WALES'S VISIT TO THE EAST END: THE PRINCE AT PELL STREET CLUB, CABLE STREET, E. 1   200

THE PRINCE OF WALES RIDING AT THE BEAUFORT POINT-TO-POINT   216

THE PRINCE OF WALES, WITH PRINCESS ELIZABETH, RETURNING FROM CROTHIE CHURCH DURING A VISIT TO BALMORAL IN SEPTEMBER, 1933   218

THE PRINCE OF WALES READY FOR A FLIGHT   220

1933. THE PRINCE OF WALES AT AN UNEMPLOYED CAMP NEAR SUTTON COURTNEY, BERKS   226

1923. THE PRINCE OF WALES IN CANADA, RIDING ON THE BAR U RANGE RANCH   232

1935. THE PRINCE OF WALES AT ASCOT RACES   238

1936. KING EDWARD VIII AND QUEEN MARY ARRIVING AT THE CENOTAPH ON ARMISTICE DAY, 1936   256

1936. KING EDWARD VIII'S VISIT TO SOUTH WALES: INSPECTION OF THE PEN-Y-GARN HOUSING ESTATE, NOVEMBER 19, 1936   268

MRS. SIMPSON   272

1936. KING EDWARD VIII BROADCASTING TO THE BRITISH EMPIRE FROM BROADCASTING HOUSE   286

KING EDWARD VIII

His Life and Reign

Chapter One

THE CLOSE OF QUEEN VICTORIA'S REIGN. BIRTH AND
BOYHOOD OF EDWARD VIII

And Melancholy mark'd him for her own.—
THOMAS GRAY.

Chapter One

THE CLOSE OF QUEEN VICTORIA'S REIGN. BIRTH AND BOYHOOD OF EDWARD VIII

*I*N the summer of 1897 the Duke and Duchess of York went to stay with Queen Victoria. She was delighted by their visit. "Every time I see them I love them more and respect them greatly," she wrote in her *Journal.* "Thank God! Georgie has got such an excellent, useful and good wife." There was much to talk about to her grandchildren while they were staying at Windsor. Their eldest son, David, was now three years old, and he was running about the lawns of White Lodge, lively as a rabbit.

The Queen had ruled the land for sixty years, and the century she knew was coming to its end. When she ascended the throne in 1837, England had been a fair agricultural country. Now it was given over to industry: factory chimneys had risen on the edges of the fields, and steamers moved down the once placid rivers, laden deep with manufactured goods. In the 'thirties the talk in the inns had been of crops and of beasts. Now, when the day's work was over and when Englishmen sat over their tankards of beer, they talked of inventions and of new machines. The smocks of the farm worker had given place to the overalls of the mechanic and the artisan.

How remote the tranquil evenings with Prince Albert must have seemed to Queen Victoria in 1897 as she dozed over her papers: the games of whist and the sentimental ballads which they used to sing at the pianoforte, away back in the 'forties. There was so much to remember and marvel over in the long years of change and discovery. The gas-lamps at the gates of the Castle had been a novelty in the early days, when she used to drive down with Prince Albert from smoky London. Soon the rooms at Windsor were to be wired for electric light and she had been able to speak over the telephone with Lord Salisbury in his room in London, twenty miles away. A few weeks before she had written in her *Journal:*

> " At twelve went down to below the terrace near the ball-room, and we were all photographed by Downey by the new cinematograph process, which makes moving pictures by winding off a roll of films. We were walking up and down and the children jumping about."

The time had almost come for her to leave the quickening world. She was very tired, and when the papers arrived in the red despatch boxes from Whitehall she had to fortify her sight with belladonna before she could read them. Her secretary used special broad nibs to write his reports for her, and the sheets of paper were dried in a little copper oven beside his table so that the ink should be thick and black, to save her eyes.

She was a little old woman, nearing death. But there were wonderful signs to comfort her as she was wheeled from room to room in her rolling chair. Three years before she had driven over to White Lodge to see her first English great-grandchild. " After tea," she wrote, when she had returned to Windsor, " I went to see the baby, a fine, strong-looking child."

Prince David was born in June, when the walls of White Lodge were hidden behind masses of magnolias. The house, which was set in Richmond Park, was not vast and grand. It had been built by George I as "a place of refreshment after the fatigues of the chase." The elegant words might still have been used to describe its amenities in June of 1894, when the Prince was born.

Queen Victoria went to White Lodge again in July, when

The Prince with King Edward VII.

her great-grandson was christened. The carrying cloak
which she gave him was made from her own wedding veil.
Again it is in her *Journal* that one reads of the day. "The
dear fine baby," she wrote, "wearing the Honiton lace robe
. . . was brought in . . . and handed to me. I then gave
him to the Archbishop and received him back. . . . The
child was very good. There was an absence of all music,
which I thought a pity. . . . Had tea with May, and afterwards we were photographed, I, holding the baby on my
lap, Bertie and Georgie standing behind me, thus making
the four generations."

When Prince David was almost eighteen months old, his
brother, Prince Albert,* was born at Sandringham, and
eighteen months after this time his only sister was born.
White Lodge was now too small to hold the growing family,
and the Duke and Duchess divided their year between
Sandringham and London.

Of the many stories told of the ex-King as a little boy,
there are two which allow us to see the lines along which
his character was to grow. One afternoon the two Princes
had to listen to a long story, told to them by an old man.
Prince Albert yawned, without shame, and his older brother
nudged him and whispered, "Smile." The other story
shows us the first young sign of the compassion which
became one of the guiding forces of his life. One day when
he was talking to Lord Roberts of the time when he would
be King, he said that he would "pass a law against cutting
puppy dog's tails" and prevent "them" from using bearing
reins on horses. "These are very cruel," he said.

Queen Victoria died in January of 1901, when the Prince
was almost seven years old. He went down to Windsor, in
his sailor suit, and he stood above the tomb of Charles I,
in St. George's Chapel, while his great-grandmother's
coffin was lowered into the vault.

Queen Victoria had not wished to be buried with her

* Now King George VI.

7

wicked Hanoverian uncles, and the next day her relatives followed her coffin on its last journey to the mausoleum at Frogmore. Light snow fell as they walked down the slope "as it had fallen two hundred and fifty years before, when the Cavaliers carried the coffin of Charles I into the dark, silent chapel at Windsor."

A new age began and a new monarch ruled in the Castle which Pepys had described as the "most romantique" that "is in all the world." Up to this time the Princes had not been steeped in the history of their family. A few romantic stories had gathered about White Lodge, but Windsor held the record of our kings from the time of the Conqueror. When King Edward VII went to live in the Castle, his son and his daughter-in-law opened Frogmore, a quiet, unassuming house in the Park: a house set in an English water-colour scene of ponds and lawns, daffodils and singing birds.

English boys of twelve years are not very different in their aims and dreams. At the age when the warpath of the Red Indians and the hazards of capture by cannibals fire the average imagination, boys are happily free from introspection and they have a good appetite for mischief. Prince Albert was more prone to adventure and pranks than his older brother. Prince David was shy and this shyness stayed with him until the war came, to wear it away. His life was simple and his education was hard. His father was heir to the Prince Consort's stern sense of duty, and he believed in the thoroughness of tutors and the cautionary air of schoolrooms.

Prince David had a friend and champion in the new King. When he was very young he had been taken in great awe to see his great-grandmother at Windsor. Queen Victoria had been a matriarch in whose presence children spoke in whispers and walked on their toes.

Now that King Edward ruled in the Castle, everything was different. His mother's apathetic afternoon teas gave place to gay evening parties. Sir Sidney Lee tells us that

Photograph by Elliott & Fry.

Princess Mary, Prince Edward and Prince Albert as children.

"the best and most interesting personalities in the country were to be found at the Court of King Edward VII, whatever their birth and upbringing." The King had not lost his love of fun in gaining his crown, and, as Prince David grew older, he turned to his grandfather more and more, with the strange and secure confidence which exists between older people and their grandchildren. King Edward had also been the object of a rigorous educational scheme and he knew, with all his heart, the perils of authority and the pain of censorship. One day, at Sandringham, when King Edward arrived, his grandson rushed out, like a wild thing, past family and servants. He kissed his grandfather's hand and then kissed him again and again on the cheek. The King was his escape from the discipline which was wisely maintained at home.

When Prince David was ten years old his grandfather gave him a party at Buckingham Palace. The Prince received his guests so solemnly that King Edward described it all as "infernally bumptious." It seemed for a moment that the dignity of princes was appearing too early in the boy, especially when, at another children's party, he made a short and grand speech. He had been given a sword, and somebody advised him in a whisper to say "Thank you." He climbed on to a chair and said: "Thank you for giving me such a beautiful sword. I shall always keep it and remember this night."

There was respect but little fear in the young Prince's love for his grandfather. One day a seamstress called at York House. Prince David opened the door and called to her: "Come in, there is nobody here . . . there is nobody that matters, only Grandpa."

The Prince began his London life in York House in St. James's Palace. Few of the street scenes of London are more enchanting than the view of the gates and the turrets of the palace when you see them from the descending slope that leads from Piccadilly. The façade of St. James's is a sixteenth-century dream, surviving in busy twentieth-century London. Within the old walls earnest secretaries and quick-footed messengers are about their business. While he was a boy in St. James's Palace, Prince David was given his first glimpse of State affairs. He saw the boxes which came every day from Whitehall, and he peered around the corner at the ambassadors and commissioners who came to see his father. Sandringham and Frogmore had given him a dream or two, but York House gave him realities. He could hear the whir of traffic from his bedroom window and he could see the chimneys of Westminster, with their moving flags of smoke. He could hear the click of soldiers' heels in the courtyard and the metallic thud of rifle-butts upon the flagstones. He learned to play with his first sword; he drilled his brothers and he enrolled even his sister into his games of war. The soldiers who guarded his father's palace were as magnificent to him as they were to the grubbiest Cockney boy meandering past with his thumb in his mouth.

When he was thirteen years old Prince David went to Osborne as a naval cadet. Any other boy might have felt that he was embarking upon an adventure as he steamed over Southampton Water, among the ships that smelled of Colombo, Hong-Kong and the Indies. But there was a tutor at Prince David's elbow to remind him of his purpose.

Fifty years before, Queen Victoria's "marine villa" had been the pride of the Isle of Wight. The Italian façade of Osborne had looked out upon a garden inhabited by marble Dianas and bronze sea monsters, with cupids riding upon their backs. Bay-trees had formed a guard of honour down the path which led to the sea, and near by had been the gigantic cedar under which Queen Victoria used to take tea with her ladies or talk over the troubles of the world with her ministers. Wych elms and pines grew between the house and the beach, and a clock in the tower told the time to the four corners of the park, marking the hours with a lazy, melodious bell. Life at Osborne had been elegant and safe in the 'fifties, but the Victorian picture was torn from its frame when Prince David went there as a cadet in 1907. The shawls and teacups of his grandmother's day had been packed away and the cedar was lonely on the lawn. Long, dull buildings marred the grace of the old gardens, for King Edward had given his mother's house to the nation, and the noise and bustle of the naval college had chased the Victorian ghosts away.

When the Prince had been at Osborne a week or so a young cadet asked him: "What is your name?"

"Edward," answered the Prince, for this was his name to the world.

"Edward what?" he was asked.

"Just Edward, that is all," he said.

His princely responsibilities meant little or nothing to the other cadets, and he was soon drawn into the normal life of Osborne. He was given the nickname of *Sardine,* for no apparent reason, and his slightest offence against the ethics of his contemporaries was punished by guillotining him in the dormitory window, as a cruel and boy-like reminder of what had happened to Charles I, whose prison had been at Carisbrooke near by. Once the Prince revolted against the traditions of the college. When senior cadets entered a room it was usual for the despised juniors to retire and leave them in possession. Prince Edward obeyed the law at first. He stepped into the gutter when his betters passed him in the street, and he ran out of common rooms when they appeared at the door. There came a time for faint protest. One day, instead of hurrying out of the presence of the seniors when they appeared, he sauntered slowly away. One of them grabbed him and said: "You are the Prince, are you? Well, learn to respect your seniors." A bottle of red ink was poured down his neck and he left the room.

The historical lessons of the Isle of Wight could not have

been encouraging for Prince Edward. At every point he was reminded of his inheritance. If he went to Osborne House he could see the white marble busts of his ancestors, arranged in niches along the corridors; in the neglected gardens he could see the miniature fortifications among which the Prince Consort had taught his sons to be soldiers. Everywhere were signs of discipline. The incessant voice which whispered in his ear was of duty. The word enveloped him and there was no escape.

Although Prince Edward's training was the same as that of the other cadets, he sometimes stepped out of the mundane picture. One day, twenty-four battleships, sixteen armoured cruisers, forty-eight destroyers and more than fifty other vessels moved across the Solent in celebration of the visit of the Tsar of Russia. Three days afterwards Prince David was allowed to show his illustrious cousins over the naval college, and in the afternoon the rooms of Osborne House were opened for them. Prince Edward answered the Tsar's questions, he talked with the gentle little Tsarevitch, and he walked with the Tsarina, who, it was said, already seemed to wear her fate in the sad expression upon her face.

As the Prince learned more of the life of the sailor he came to a new field of understanding with his father. Prince George, who once said, " In the Navy we have a motto, ' Keep your hair on '," had not outgrown the bluff heartiness of the wardroom. Even when he was King, one of his chief delights was to talk with the friends of his seafaring days. He watched his son with daily concern as he trod in his footsteps. There were letters from York House almost every morning, and during the Prince's weeks of leave, father and son found much to talk about. At little more than Prince David's age King George had been the youngest cadet in *Britannia*. The fierce light of inheritance had not yet beaten upon him, for his elder brother was still alive. He had been able to enjoy the spells of careless ease

Photograph by W. & D. Downey.

King George V (when Prince of Wales) with his three sons.

in his ship, without any worry about the prospect of a crown. He had been a boisterous cadet, not above putting marline spikes in the bed of a First-lieutenant. Prince David's life at Osborne was not very hilarious. He was more prone to self-analysis than his father had been, and he carried his responsibilities seriously. Once he took his place in the chorus, wearing a wig and dress, when the college produced *H.M.S. Pinafore*, but somebody who saw him as " a sister, a cousin or an aunt " said that he wore a wistful and unhappy expression. Even in the gay atmosphere of amateur theatricals he was not able to shake himself free of his shyness.

Osborne contributed to the Prince's knowledge and no doubt made him more aware of the intricacies of human nature. But the machinery of the College system did not change the main lines of his character. That the Prince learned something while he was a naval cadet, and that he remembered what he had learned, was shown some years afterwards when he was in America. He visited the Ford Motor Works, and the proprietor was *surprised* because his " royal guest had such an intimate knowledge of engineering." Major Verney, who recalls the incident, says that the Prince had not forgotten Osborne, the " grease on his face " and the " steel filings in his hair."

From Osborne the Prince went to Dartmouth. He worked hard, completing his five years of training, and he passed his examinations without favour. Whenever he went to London people said that he was growing "to be just like his grandfather." The friendship between the King and his grandson had grown with years, and the guileless stories of childhood gave place to serious talks as they walked together at Balmoral. In Scotland, Prince David was able to shoot with his grandfather and to talk with him more peaceably than in London. It was during one of these summer holidays beside the Dee that the Prince met the Emperor and the Empress of Germany. It has been said that one day, when Prince David was walking away, King Edward turned to the Emperor and said: "There is the last King of England."

In May of 1910 King Edward died at Buckingham Palace. The nine years of his reign were over, and the Prince, now a boy of sixteen years, went once more to Windsor. Again the rulers and princes of Europe came to England and walked in the funeral procession to St. George's, where King Edward and Queen Alexandra had been married forty-seven years before. The gay and prosperous interlude of King Edward's Court ended. He had ruled the land in a time of richness, self-indulgence and social upheaval, and he handed on a changed kingdom from that which he had inherited at the beginning of the century. The new King had a different and more terrible rôle to play, and it was well, as we have learned, that he inherited his grandfather's sober character and moral courage to sustain him in the years that lay before him.

Prince David was now heir to the throne, and he was soon to be known as Edward, Prince of Wales. On the twenty-fourth day of June he was confirmed in the small private chapel at Windsor. His father, his mother, Queen Alexandra, the Empress of Russia, his aunts, his uncles and the Prime Minister celebrated his admission to the Sacrament by singing "Fight the good fight." It was a sign that his boyhood had ended.

In August of 1910, three months after his grandfather's death, the Prince sailed away in *Hindustan* as a midshipman. All the old authorities in his life were left behind. He enjoyed his first holiday, although a new governor was sent with him to add to the ordinary discipline of the ship. The Prince was supremely happy during the tour, which lasted two months, and he left *Hindustan* with a stab of regret. "Not the smallest exception or discrimination has been made in his favour," wrote the naval authorities when the cruise was over. "The Prince of Wales has taken

The Prince of Wales as a Midshipman.

part in every duty that appertains to the working of a great battleship, and has cheerfully and efficiently discharged the less agreeable as well as the most agreeable of his tasks. The day before yesterday, for example, he was bearing his share in 'coaling ship,' and you know what that means. He has worked hard in the gunroom and at drill, and has, among other things, been associated with the landing of small armed parties. Throughout the whole period of his training on board he has been an extremely hard worker, and has struck all those about him, high and low, as what we call 'a live thing.' It was obvious that he liked the life, and earnestly endeavoured to do credit to himself and to those entrusted with his tuition in various departments. Everybody in the *Hindustan* will be sorry to lose so good a comrade and so intelligent a ' man.' I say ' man ' advisedly, because he has shown application and aptitude beyond that which might have been reasonably expected. He was a thoroughly hard worker, and is in many respects ahead of his years."

The Prince's career as an active sailor came to an end. He said good-bye to Dartmouth with a pretty gesture. He restored to the Corporation the silver oar which they had formerly held as "a symbol of the rights of the Bailiwick of the water of Dartmouth." His first public speech was brief, and his voice showed that he was nervous.

The friends and the circumstances of the Prince's life changed once more. Osborne and Dartmouth faded into history, and with them the friends he had gathered about him. Oxford was before him, and he had to adjust his life and change his society accordingly. It was the inevitable fault of his training that his background was for ever changing. People crowded in on him and then they departed, making him feel that life was a whirl in which no person and no scene was stable. This disadvantage must always be remembered in the Prince's favour by those steady and docile people who live upon the rock of certainty. Most people have the opportunity of living in a chosen community, and those who join the Services or who go to universities carry some of their friends with them from one sphere to the next. The Prince never enjoyed this privilege. Nothing seemed permanent to him except the responsibilities of his inheritance. He made his friends at Osborne, but they went to sea while he stayed ashore. He sailed in *Hindustan*, but he left the ship's company to go to Oxford. He was unable to enjoy the influence which growing friendships would have been for him. The lessons in personal loyalty which he would have learned through friendship seemed to pass him by. In considering the years of his education it is important and just that one should remember the many changes of which he was the victim, and understand, therefore, why it was not easy for him to remain loyal to a central purpose in the development of his mind and character.

Chapter Two

CORONATION OF KING GEORGE V. HIS CHARACTER. PRINCE
EDWARD OF WALES. THE DUCHY OF CORNWALL

*An age touched by the spirit of Hope
inevitably turns to the young, for with the
young lies fulfilment.* -LORD MORLEY.

Chapter Two

CORONATION OF KING GEORGE V. HIS CHARACTER. PRINCE
EDWARD OF WALES. THE DUCHY OF CORNWALL

KING GEORGE was crowned in June. The Prince knelt
before him, took off his coronet and said: " I . . .
do become your liege man of life and limb and of
earthly worship: and faith and truth I will bear unto you,
to live and die, against all manner of folks." When he had
kissed his father's cheek the King leaned forward, drew the
Prince nearer to him and kissed him in return. We are
told that he was seriously conscious of the importance of
the Coronation, and that when one of his younger brothers
became mischievous in the carriage on the way to the
Abbey, the Prince disposed of him beneath the seat until
he promised to behave more sedately.

King George's character and interests were to bring many
changes into the thought and policy of his country. He was
to become the greatest of the essentially *English* sovereigns,
combining some of the qualities of Alfred the Great with
the domestic virtues of George III, who was also " pure
in life, honest in intent," and for whom the heart of
Britain beat kindly " because according to his lights he
worshipped Heaven." The changes which came with King
George must be considered, for they were an important
influence upon his son's character. With King George the
last drop of German blood was drained from the Royal
Family; no man could have been more English. His
opinions, his prejudices and his habits were those of an
English squire. He hated wearing the robes of great occasions and liked best to tramp through the park at Sandringham in tweeds. He had been bred in Norfolk, and the

19

great Lord Leicester himself had not loved its earth more than the new monarch. King George declared his own insular loyalty when he said that he regretted the time he had spent in Heidelberg "learning their beastly language." This Englishness was his own creation. Queen Victoria began her reign with natural love for Germany, which was fostered by her family ties and her idolatry for her husband. In the closing years of her life this love for the Germans soured, and she wrote in 1870 that it was "merciful the beloved Prince was taken, for had he lived" she "could never have prevented him from joining the German armies." As she grew wise she came to dislike the aims of Bismarck and then of her strident grandson. One of her ladies wrote of a day when she "pitched into" her daughter, the Empress Frederick, for being too Prussian in her notions. But Queen Victoria enjoyed her experiments in foreign diplomacy, and she liked her prestige as matriarch of all the Courts of Europe. King Edward brought a change into European friendships. He closed his heart against Germany from the time of the Schleswig-Holstein invasion, when his wife's country was menaced by the aims of Prussia. The division between mother and son was bitter then.

Some years after, when the Emperor William left Sandringham after a visit, King Edward turned to his guests upon the doorstep and said: "Thank God he has gone." He disliked his nephew and the Prussian spirit which he exalted. His gay nature as well as his prejudices caused King Edward to give his heart to the French, as opposed to the *ernstes Deutsches Gefühl* of his father.

None of these European affections disturbed King George, and he came to the throne with no compelling interests beyond those of his own Empire. He was ill at ease with the "foreign" outlook, and this limitation became his strength. Living and thinking within his kingdom, he was not harassed by ambitions among the nations. He set a new standard of behaviour for himself and his people and he pursued it, with his grandfather's single-minded determination, from the beginning to the end. The King favoured respectability and he was embarrassed by the rich vulgarity of Edwardian society. He was intolerant of mischievous gossip, which had been the delight of social life in the twenty years preceding his reign. He kept early hours and he was abstemious. King George was a good man, and his religion lay in his conscience. Glimpses at this inner power which guided him were rare, but he once revealed his simplicity of faith when he said to one of his cousins: " I become very unhappy about the young people in the country. I feel that they do not say their prayers." Such were the motives which guided him as a sovereign and a father.

Now and again during his life King George allowed himself to be lured into pageantry, much against his will. He did not mind the long, monotonous hours of labour over his desk, but he shunned ceremonies and disliked the panoply of kingship. When the glory of the Coronation had passed he divested himself of his grand robes and returned to the sober clothes which suited his character. Now it was the Prince of Wales who took on the old glamour of princes. When he walked across the greensward of Carnarvon Castle, to be invested as Prince of Wales, he might have been a legendary figure straying through the scenes of one of Scott's novels. Carnarvon is not as old as Windsor, but its roofs have tumbled in and its towers yawn open to the sky. There is no life about these old walls, within which Edward the First offered his son to the Welshmen to appease their discontent. Carnarvon is a ruin now, with one great wall facing the sea and another casting shadows over the inland stretches where the Romans made the camp of Segontium a thousand years ago. The Prince of the twentieth century walked here. Dressed in his velvet surcoat and white breeches, he seemed to be a messenger from the dark centuries, bringing his

Herald and Arch-Druids and Druids at his heels. He was the nineteenth Prince of Wales, but he was the first to speak to the Welsh people in their own language, described by themselves as "the language spoken in Heaven." He was conscientious from the beginning, and it was a graceful gesture for him to learn a few phrases of Welsh so that he could say to them: " Mor o gan yw Cymru i gyd" (" All Wales is a sea of song "). His young, fresh voice gathered strength as he conquered his shyness. " The great title that I bear," he said, " as well as my name David, all bind me to Wales." In the language of the records, he was " presented before the King in his surcoat, cloak and mantle of crimson velvet, and girt with a belt of the same; when the King putteth a cap of crimson velvet, indented and turned up with ermine, on his head, as a token of Principality, and the King also putteth into his hand a verge of gold, the emblem of government, and a ring of gold on his middle finger, to intimate that he must be a husband to his country and a father to his children."

The King's eldest son bears many titles and honours, and of these two are of importance to him as heir to the throne. The eldest son of a sovereign is Duke of Cornwall the moment he is born. The title is his by virtue of his position as heir. He also receives the badge of three feathers, wrongly called the Prince of Wales's feathers, as a sign that he is the Sovereign's eldest son. The King is not *obliged* to make his heir Prince of Wales, although this has always been the custom. The title Prince of Wales is not hereditary, but is the subject of a new grant under each new King and is conferred at the will and discretion of the Sovereign. The illusion about the badge of three feathers belonging to the Prince of Wales has continued for many centuries. It is a legend which surprises all the more because the first prince who ever used them in their present form, Edward VI, was never even created Prince of Wales. King George was at liberty to make any of his sons Prince

1911. *The Prince of Wales in his Investiture Robes.*

of Wales, had he wished to ignore tradition, but he could not have taken the badge of three feathers from his heir.

Although the Duchy of Cornwall was formed to enrich the eldest sons of kings, for almost half the time since its creation the Duchy has been in the possession of the Crown —when there have been no princes to enjoy it. There are records which show that Queen Mary bought herself " silks and velvets " with the Duchy revenue. The two most exciting chapters in the Duchy history were provided by Cromwell and George IV. " His cursed Highness " sold the Duchy lands to private individuals, but they were easily bought back again during the Restoration. George IV shattered the Duchy's security by signing a bond which gave Coutts' Bank the right to all its revenue during his lifetime. Thus a banker became Duke of Cornwall in all but name. It must be added, in the King's favour, that much of the money was spent on works of art and gold plate which now adorn Buckingham Palace and Windsor Castle.

While King Edward VII was a minor, Prince Albert governed the affairs of the Duchy, and, with his usual care, he lifted the shaky estates into safety. When his son was old enough to use the riches of the Duchy as his income a fortune had been saved for him, and Prince Albert had nursed the finances so cleverly that they produced an income of about £70,000 a year. Prince Albert brought one amazing change into the policy of the managers. He built seventeen buildings of flats in the Kennington estate, which belongs to the Duchy. Each flat had its bathroom. This was in 1847, when bathrooms were rare even among the rich, and before there was one in Windsor Castle. It was this policy which has endured to this day.

King George was the first monarch who made the tenants of the Duchy care for him personally as a landlord and not only as a King. On Dartmoor to this day there are older people who will tell you of when he went to see them and of the spontaneous speech in which he called them "my friends."

It was not until he returned from his Empire tours that King Edward VIII was drawn into the detailed interests of his estates. He decided to devote more money to rebuilding schemes, although at that time his income from the Duchy was about half what was paid to King Edward VII and to King George when they were Princes of Wales. The ex-King's unselfishness in regard to the Duchy is not fully realised. He developed the schemes introduced by his father, and in the years 1909-14, no less than £300,000 were poured back into the estates for rebuilding and improvements. The Duchy continues to prosper, for its own good as well as for the Crown. The Labour Council in Kennington smiled upon King Edward VIII and declared him to be one of the best landlords in the kingdom. The Home Farm in Cornwall, the oyster fisheries, the experiments in stock-breeding and the rebuilding of the residential areas were solid proofs of his ability to govern the vast lands under his control.

Chapter Three

A STUDENT IN FRANCE

I travelled among unknown men,
In lands beyond the sea;
Nor, England, did I know till then
What love I bore to thee.
                    WORDSWORTH.

A STUDENT IN FRANCE

THE vitality of the ex-King always amazed and sometimes alarmed those who watched his progress. Mayors of small towns were walked off their feet because of his exuberance, and faithful servants have sometimes found their physical endurance long spent while he went on, eager with questions, prying into corners and storing his astonishing memory with fresh information. He inherited this fierce enthusiasm from his mother. Queen Victoria was also blessed with tireless zeal and stamina; she was never tired and she pooh-poohed draughts and rain. Her ladies used to moan over the cold of Balmoral and they often shivered in the frigid sitting-rooms, clinging to the circle of the fire while the Queen sat at the far, frozen end of the room over her game of patience. Her love of carriage exercise in heavy rain and her shocked protest when she found fires lighted in the bedrooms of her ladies caused many a sad letter to be written late at night by one or other of the members of her Court, who poured out her misery to a trusted sister or friend. Queen Mary has been equally tireless all through her life. After a long day of duties she has always been able to approach some new and sudden plan with the vigour of the morning. One day, in London, she was driving back to Buckingham Palace after opening a new building somewhere in Campden Hill. There had been engagements in the morning, and her lady-in-waiting might have been forgiven if her thoughts moved towards her sitting-room and her tea. As the Queen left the building she said that she wished to drive back along a new way. There was a part of London she did not know. They travelled through miserable slums, and in one street the Queen saw a number of men sitting on a staircase outside a house. She wished to know why they were there, and somebody was sent to enquire. The answer was terrible. The men were waiting, in turn, to occupy a bed upon which they could sleep for a penny an hour. The Queen drove on. The day did not pass without a practical attempt to change the miserable lot of the men she had seen, and within a little time the right machinery was set to work and the horror of the slums was removed. There was no sentimentality—only the practical decision which removed a blemish in the life of London, without ostentation or fuss.

This untiring eagerness and interest in the burdens of humanity first stirred in the Prince of Wales during the months after he left Dartmouth, when he began to work among social institutions. But his first view of his responsibilities was brief, for the next step in his education was being prepared for him. He was to go to France to polish his languages. From the moment the Prince of Wales arrived in Paris his charm earned the good opinion and favours of the French people. He was among "foreigners" for the first time, and the experiment benefited him because every man he spoke to and every scene which was spread before him was examined through a note of interrogation. He embarrassed people by his incessant questions; his eagerness unlocked all doors.

One's thoughts travel back to 1903, when the Prince's grandfather arrived in Paris, during one of the dark seasons when Englishmen were unpopular with their fickle neighbours. He arrived in Paris in the morning and found the crowd "sullenly respectful." Somebody had shouted, "Vivent les Boers!" at him as his carriage rolled past. One of his suite murmured, "The French don't like us," and he answered, "Why should they?" He waited until the evening to make his first gesture of friendliness. He went to a theatre and he was greeted coldly. Sir Sidney Lee tells us that while the King was standing in the lobby of the theatre he "espied a great and charming artiste whom he had seen act in England. Holding out his hand, he said: 'Oh, mademoiselle, I remember how I applauded you in London. You personified there all the grace, all the *esprit* of France.'" The words were loud enough to be overheard, and the pretty compliment of the evening became the breakfast-table gossip of Paris next morning. The French discovered "that the King of England was determined to be the friend of France."

Prince Edward of Wales went to France in a less troubled time. He was dynamic and charming, although he was still almost irretrievably shy. The people of Paris, who gathered at the station to see him, asked no more than this. His frank smile won their applause. The important weeks of his visit to France were spent at the château of the Marquis de Breteuil, a beautiful house which looks out over a well-bred garden with valeted shrubs and stone vases. In a book of snapshots taken at the time of the Prince's visit to Breteuil, one catches occasional glimpses of the Marquis himself, a straw hat on the back of his head, sitting on the edge of a table; another of the Prince, looking very English, with his hat worn at a respectable angle and a carnation in his buttonhole. If photographs are to be believed, the discipline was not too heavy upon him at Breteuil, for even his English tutor unbent and was photographed, looking gay and human, in a little boat. We find the Prince at Maintenon: a slim boy with his hands raised in the air, preparing to dive into the water. And then, triumphantly, the Prince on the terrace, with the fourth roebuck which he had shot while in France.

A French scholar had been called in to assist in the Prince's education, and the choice of M. Maurice Escoffier was a stroke of good fortune. There is a charming snapshot of him, with cigarette, gallant beard and a hat worn at a rakish angle to assure us that he did not make his instruc-

tion alarming. The Prince's energy was surprising, even to
the busy French. At this time he began a diary, in the
manner of his father and his great-grandmother, setting
down almost every incident and impression of his days.
One naturally knows nothing of these pages, but there are
further snapshots to show him enjoying himself at picnics
in the hills or walking through the scenes of the country.
From Breteuil he went south, and we see him watching the
life on board a French cruiser. He photographed the statue
of King Edward at Cannes, Marseilles from the hills, the
door and the cloisters of the church at Arles and stretches
of the Italian coast. He went far and he came home with
a fresh store of impressions and information. There was
only one depressing note, from the public point of view.
Before he left Paris he was painted by François Flameng.
The portrait appeared in the English newspapers in celebration of the Prince's return. People were distressed to
find him frowning, as if the weight of his young life were
already too much for him. It seemed that he was taking his
responsibilities almost too seriously and being deprived of
the mischief and delights of being young. His face was
melancholy in repose. England had no wish to exact such
a debt from him before his time.

Chapter Four

OXFORD

When all the world is young, lad,
And all the trees are green;
And every goose a swan, lad,
And every lass a queen;
Then hey for boot and horse, lad,
And round the world away;
Young blood must have its course, lad,
And every dog his day.
CHARLES KINGSLEY.

Chapter Four

OXFORD

THE Prince of Wales tried to lose his frown when he went to Oxford. He was less manacled by rules than any other royal undergraduate had been, and he had much to be thankful for in his freedom. King Edward VII had matriculated as a nobleman, and he had not been allowed to live in college. His parents had sent him up to Oxford with warnings and rules that might have been framed for a penitentiary. He was allowed to "wear nothing extravagant or slang," and he was to avoid "foolish and worthless persons." He had been allowed to read a novel only "as an indulgence," even if it was by Sir Walter Scott. He had not been allowed to smoke. He had to wear a special gown when he attended debates, and everybody rose as he entered a lecture room. He ate his meals with his staff, in his own house. Queen Victoria and Prince Albert had built every possible wall between him and his temptations, which had already manifested themselves. They were haunted by their fear that he would walk in the way of his Georgian great-uncles, and this anxiety drove them to extremes of caution. The royal parents of the last three generations have often been criticised for the way in which they have trained their heirs, but it is not easy to realise or understand the unique problem of a monarch who is forced to equip his son to take his place. The responsibility is unnatural and tremendous. Estrangement between parent and son seems to be inevitable. In 1901 the leader writer for *The Times* summed up the difficulties which harass an heir-apparent.

33

"There is no position in the world more difficult to fill than that of Heir-Apparent to the throne. It is beset by more than all the temptations of actual royalty, while the weight of counteracting responsibility is much less directly felt. It must be with a feeling of hopelessness that a man in that position offers up the familiar prayer, 'Lead us not into temptation.' Other men may avoid much temptation, but the heir to a throne is followed, dogged, and importuned by temptation in its most seductive forms."

Oxford had changed when Prince Edward went there as an undergraduate at the age of eighteen. Germans and Americans had brought a more cosmopolitan note into the life of the old University, and the Rhodes Scholars who mingled with their English contemporaries talked of life in New Zealand and of sheep-farming in Australia. As the Warden of New College had said, Oxford became "part of the great world."

King George's discipline for his sons was always strict, and his natural kindliness was confused by his sense of duty, but he did not repeat the mistakes of the Prince Consort when he sent his eldest son to Oxford. He allowed the Prince to live as an ordinary undergraduate. If the Prince had not already been enriched by experience at Osborne, service in *Hindustan* and study in France, the sudden freedom might have unbalanced him, for he was still very young. He was the superior of his contemporaries in experience of life and of people. It is pleasing, in tracing the story of his time at Oxford, to note the growth of his poise. He was fickle as a sportsman, and he did not plod on with any one form of exercise. Hunting, shooting, tennis and golf each held his devotion for a time, for he was inclined to experiment with new diversions. He had not liked riding when he was young, but, under the influence of Major Cadogan, he soon found pleasure in hunting.

The Prince began his Oxford foxhunting career in February of 1914 with the South Oxfordshire Hounds, and on the first day, as if conscious of the occasion, hounds killed five foxes. The Prince played Association football for the Magdalen second eleven, and he beagled with the New College, Magdalen and Trinity pack. He shot a little, though not with his father's zest, and he began soldiering with the O.T.C. These energetic diversions kept him busy, but not at the expense of his life within the College. The unique character of social life at Magdalen must be remembered if one is to appreciate the democratic influence which surrounded the Prince. In other colleges clubs and societies were inclined to become cliques because no member could join them except by election. This was not the rule at Magdalen. Undergraduates could join any society they wished, without election, and they therefore shared each other's interests more readily. A writer in the spring number of *Oxford*, 1936, recalled this aspect of the King's life in the University, and added: " It is well to have this picture in mind, otherwise to say that His Majesty took a full part in the general social life of the College would not mean as much as it actually did."

After some months had passed Oxford accepted its royal undergraduate without fuss and surprise. Tourists gaped at him and visitors were shown the windows of his rooms in the cloisters. The " frozen music" of Magdalen's lovely tower became a secondary attraction when Americans were able to look across the cool green lawn of Magdalen towards the old wall behind which the heir to the throne was studying, or practising his banjo. When the guide was able to lure them away to the quiet of Addison's Walk and to the rails of the deer park, he completed their delight by telling them that the park had been fenced off and stocked so that the Prince could enjoy a little stalking before breakfast.

A contemporary wrote in *The Times* of the Prince as an undergraduate:

" We found that he was in no way different from any other undergraduate, except that he looked rather more youthful than most. . . . Oxford took, perhaps, a fortnight before it settled down entirely and got over the novelty of having a Prince of Wales going in and coming out daily. There were tiresome photographers and reporters, and a tendency for crowds to collect at likely places for him to pass. But his fellow-undergraduates did not take long to learn the necessary lesson. Members of Balliol signified their opinion of an inquisitive crowd by pouring water from the upper windows on their heads."

When winter came the tourists had flown, and the Prince was no longer a curiosity to the people of the town. He walked among the silver-brown walls of the colleges and he rode out in the morning, an eager, restless figure, moving against the winter trees and liquid blue sky, just as any other undergraduate might walk or ride.

The student who wrote of the Prince in *The Times* said:

" Everything was made easy for him to take an immediate place in college life and interests. And he plunged at once into an almost bewildering catholicity of interests and amusements. He was entertained and gave entertainments in return, and those present found that, though he was at first rather shy, he was a delightful addition to a dinner-party, most attractive in the quiet and humble part he took in the conversation, but full of humour and with opinions at once decided and sane. His laugh and smile are perhaps particularly attractive."

As his shyness passed, the Prince took the initiative in making friendships, and the adventures which ensued all added to his knowledge of human nature. One evening he picked up his banjo and wandered around the cloisters of Magdalen to call on a friend. Major Verney tells us in his book that the company which he found in his friend's room included a "rampant, tearing Socialist from the Midlands who had commenced life in a nail factory at the age of eight, educated himself—and arrived at Oxford at the age of thirty-three, with a red tie." A test for the Prince's charm had come. "He picked up a glass of beer from the table and said, 'Here's luck, everybody,' and then played a tune on the banjo." When the Prince had returned to his rooms the nail-maker rose to his feet and said to those who remained: "'I'll give you a toast.' He raised his glass and said: 'The Prince of Wales, God bless him!'"

The Prince's banjo was the first of a number of musical instruments to which he was devoted. He was an indulgent musician, because he gave his heart to the banjo, the ukelele and even the bagpipes. Many people suffered during these interludes, and his diligent practice upon the banjo, at all hours of the day and night, was such a pain to his neighbours in Magdalen that they organised a protest beneath his window. He won the day, for he produced bagpipes and drove them away, with their fingers in their ears. Some years afterwards he diverted his talents to the ukelele, and he confessed in a public speech that if he had taken "a single day longer to learn *Clementine*" he believed that he would have "been murdered" by his staff.

The Prince was not over-sentimental as a youth, and he never allowed his kindliness to lead him into false feeling. When he was still young he was able to guard himself against these dangers. He was stubborn when necessary, and when his time at Oxford came to an end he had enough will-power to cope with the thick-skinned and the pompous. Servants and little people were safe with him, but humbugs were likely to suffer at his hands.

One turns to a story of his first visit to South Africa to show that there was an iron will to guard his sympathies.

One day he stood in front of ten or twelve thousand children while they were singing a hymn. Major Verney has written: " There was a quality about it that was deeply stirring, almost sacred. . . . As the last notes of the hymn died away in the sunlit air there followed a pause, tense and breathless. It was dramatic and full of feeling. In the middle of it a woman rushed up to the Prince and thrust an autograph book at him. 'Won't you please sign your name in this for me, sir?' she gushed. Prince Edward stared at her for a few seconds, then he spoke: ' No, I will not sign your book.' "

In the less exciting fields of scholarship Prince Edward was not brilliant. The Dons sometimes grumbled with disappointment because their royal pupil did not eat up the intellectual meal which they had prepared for him. He seemed to be devoted to the present and the future and to be lacking in veneration for the past. He did not sit back in a deep chair to listen to the lordly language in which they told him the story of his inheritance. He usually sat on the edge of the chair, anxious to escape and make his own history. He was not unlike his grandfather in this impatience with the past. When King Edward VII was faced with the antiquities of Egypt, he "treated the pillars and sculptures with well-bred courtesy," and Dean Stanley, who was with him, was so depressed over his failure as a tutor that he wrote: "I cannot bring myself to pour out words into unwilling or indifferent ears." Gladstone also complained that King Edward VII knew "everything except what is written in books." The President of Magdalen made a similar comment on Prince Edward when his time at Oxford was ended. "Bookish he will never be," wrote the President, who had planned the Prince's curriculum. He was not to learn through lectures or the printed word. He belonged to the generation which was destined to bear the burden of the Great War. It was well, no doubt, that he turned to human nature and contacts with his neighbours rather than to books for his lessons. He did not accept the example and views of his elders with blind obedience, nor did he willingly inherit their prejudices. He began to frame his own philosophy, through experience.

The President of Magdalen said that the Prince would never be a "British Solomon," but he wisely added that this was "not to be desired." "The Prince of Wales will not want for power of ready and forcible presentation," he said. "All the time he was learning more and more every day of men, gauging character, watching its play, getting to know what Englishmen are like, both individually and still more in the mass."

Thus armed, the Prince of Wales came down from Oxford and prepared to face the world.

Chapter Five

GERMANY

*. . . there was never a rumour
Of asking Hohenzollerns for a sense
Of humour.*

SIR OWEN SEAMAN.

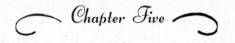

Chapter Five

*I*N the spring of 1913 the Prince of Wales went to
Germany. The links between the two countries were
already weakened. Every now and then there was
feverish talk of war, but the generation which governed
and prospered in England in 1913 was slack and confident,
and when the Emperor spoke of his "shining armour," and
when he paraded the finest army in Europe and boasted of
the second navy of the world, Britons warmed themselves
at the fire of their own smugness and accepted the re-
assurances of the pacifist press. King Edward VII had never
been hoodwinked over the ambitions of the Prussians, nor
had he been gentle in telling the Kaiser what he thought
of the boasts of Germany. When King George was about to
visit Berlin as a young man, King Edward had written to
the Kaiser: "In sending my son to Berlin . . . I intended
it as a personal mark of my affection and friendship towards
you, but after reading the violent accusations which have
been made in the Reichstag against England I think it
might be better for him not to go where he is liable to be
insulted."

A lull came to the anger and suspicions between the two
countries in the spring of 1913, and the journey made by
the Prince of Wales could not have been more gay and
friendly. The choice of his tutors was once more fortunate.
Major Cadogan went with him, to represent the best
characteristics of an English soldier. Major Cadogan was
also more dependent upon experience than books for his
learning, and no better guide could have been chosen.
Professor Fiedler had been appointed German tutor to the
Prince. He was a scholar who had not grown less human

in the process of learning. The Prince once described him
as "a jolly old chap," but he was more than this. He soon
became so fond of his pupil that he was able to show him
the most gracious and cultivated side of German life, without the fierce glare of Prussian enlightenment. More and
more as these years of adolescence passed, the heir to the
throne made one hope that unselfishness was to be one of
the chief traits in his character. His deference for his tutors
was almost embarrassing. The best beds were for them
because they were older; the comfortable chairs and the
least draughty corners. This consideration was one of his
chief characteristics until the strange changes which came
before his abdication, when he seemed to turn against his
own kindly instincts.

The joy of this German holiday is best understood while
looking over a book of snapshots which the Prince made
while he was abroad. There are photographs of him on the
edge of pine forests, on the terraces of grand German
castles and standing on parade grounds. One sees him in
a white peaked cap at Friedrichshafen and walking with
Count Zeppelin. This was a great year in the conquest of
the air. Pegoud had "looped the loop," and Lord Fisher
had appealed to Mr. Churchill: "For God's sake trample
on and stamp out protected Cruisers and hurry up Aviation." The Prince was already excited by the prospect of
flying, and he watched the experiments in Germany and
talked to Count Zeppelin with delight. He went to Stuttgart and stayed with two of the most charming of his cousins
in Germany, the King and Queen of Württemberg. They
closed their eyes and their hearts to the plans of the
Prussians, and there was no hint of "shining armour" in
their hospitality. But the peaceful scenes of their palace
were no more than an interlude. The Prince saw also a
river of helmets shining in the sun during a field day at
Stuttgart; he saw infantry sweeping across the ground and
a squadron of aircraft resting on the snow.

Perhaps the horrible portent of these scenes escaped him. When he went to Germany again in the summer he photographed old women dozing over their baskets in the market-place at Nürenberg, and laughing flower-girls beneath their umbrellas. His camera was always busy, catching his cousins at work and at play. Sometimes they stood in starched groups, conscious of their uniforms. But there were the older ones, who were not restless with ambition. There were his "Aunt Augusta" in her bath chair, his "Uncle Adolphus" at Neu-Strelitz, and his "Auntie Elie" in a stiff silk dress of her time. He shot wild boar in the park and he drove one of his aunts in an automobile. The most picturesque part of his journey was when he came to Thuringia, his great-grandfather's country. He went to the palace from which the old Duchess had waved her handkerchief to Prince Albert in the winter of 1839, crying, "Albert, Albert!" as he drove away to be married in England. Every acre of this lovely country was steeped in the history of the Prince's family. He flew into the silver air over Gotha, to look down upon the forests in which his great-grandfather had shot, and over the dusty Thuringian roads, with their borders of apple-trees. It was the old, cultivated life of Germany which embraced him during these visits to country places; the sweet and gentle life which was slowly withering away under the heat of Prussia's pride.

The Prince dined in Berlin with the Emperor before he returned to England. His grandiose cousin was impressed. When the dinner was over, the Emperor said of his guest: "A most charming, unassuming young man such as one would expect from such a family—but a young eagle, likely to play a big part in European affairs because he is far from being a pacifist."

As he grew older the Prince's energy increased. In route marches with the O.T.C. he smiled when others were limp. At Oxford he ran to his lectures, and in the ballroom he was always the last dancer to leave the floor. During his visit to Germany in 1913 two officers were delegated to guide him for part of his holiday. They were motoring one day when the Prince became restless. He asked the driver to stop the car. He felt stiff, he said, and he wished to walk home. One of the German officers meekly explained that fifteen miles lay between them and "home."

"Never mind, I can manage that distance all right," he answered.

The officers had to follow, in the cause of good manners, but only one of them faltered at the Prince's side at the end.

One more story comes from Mr. David Williamson, writing of the Prince's holiday in Norway. "His tirelessness in ski-ing was most noticeable. He went long expeditions at Fjnse day after day, and the distances he covered were far greater than the average man cares to go. On one occasion two well-known army skiers went for a trip. About two hours after their departure the Prince followed, and met the officers returning. They lunched together on the contents of their haversacks, and then the return journey began. The Prince and his friends soon eclipsed the officers, ski-ing at great speed, and he had been busy answering letters for some time before the arrival of the other members of the party."

Chapter Six

THE WAR

. . . a new mistress now I chase,
The first foe in the field;
And with a stronger faith embrace
A sword, a horse, a shield.
RICHARD LOVELACE.

Chapter Six

THE WAR

ON a warm day of June, 1914, "a hot and dusty khaki-clad youth," gripping his rifle, went up to a civilian who was standing on the All Arms Bridge which spans the Basingstoke Canal at North Camp. He frowned at the landscape before him. Then he smiled at the stranger and asked him which of the several spurs before him was Furze Hill. A reporter from the *Daily Chronicle* was standing near by, and he wrote the story. The scene was Aldershot, and the O.T.C. were in training. A "battle" had been arranged between Cambridge and Oxford, and the Prince of Wales was in charge of the scouts of his corps. "The civilian unceremoniously gripped the youth by the sleeve of his jacket and swung him round to follow the direction of his outstretched finger. He was ignorant of the fact that he was holding the Prince of Wales, who, as a lance-corporal, was in charge of the scouts of the Oxford University Battalion of the Officers' Training Corps.

"They were seeking to get into touch with a hostile force of the Cambridge University Corps on the Fox Hills. The Cambridge force had heard of the march of the Oxford men and had prepared a trap for them, the object being to 'annihilate' the Oxford men as soon as the decoys on Tunnel Hill had brought them into the trap. Thanks to the skill of their scouts, led by the Prince of Wales, the Oxford force were able to turn the tables on their opponents. At the foot of the Fox Hills the Oxford scouts got into touch with the Cambridge Cyclist Corps. . . . The information was promptly conveyed to Colonel Stenning, commanding the Oxford force, and he kept clear of the trap."

The Prince's first training as a soldier was as simple as his life as a young sailor had been. He did all the disagreeable duties as well as the pleasant ones. His sensibilities were not spared the experience of an issue tin wash-basin and a bell tent, which he shared with five other cadets. Nor was his digestion spared the strain of army rations.

In no sense was the Prince nursed through his training, and he displayed his eagerness when he said to the musketry instructor one day, when he had been asked to name the parts of a rifle bolt: "I'm hanged if I remember, but I'll soon learn."

The problems of the Prince's education increased, for King George realised, perhaps too seriously, that the training of his heir was one of the most frightening of his responsibilities. As a father, King Edward VII was always careful that there should be "no noise or fuss of directions" in training *his* sons. King George viewed his duty as a father more sternly than this, and his affectionate care of his son was mingled with watchfulness and the unbending code of duty which guided his own life.

The Prince of Wales had been a sailor for a little time so that he might know the ways of the sea. He was modest as to the amount of learning he had gathered in the Navy. "I hold the very high rank of Admiral," he said some years afterwards, "but I would never advise anyone to sail in a ship in which I had charge of the navigation." Now he was being trained as a soldier, with the help of enough learning from the Dons to allow him to take his place in intelligent society. He was an Englishman, with an Englishman's sober devotion to sport. Yet he was to be a cosmopolitan, with the grace and language to carry him into favour with foreign Courts. He had to mind the dignity with which to walk valiantly among princes and yet keep the free unselfconsciousness with which to attract the affection of his people.

The plans for the Prince's training were shattered in

1914. *The Prince of Wales leading his company of Grenadier Guards in full service kit on a route march.*

1914, and two months after the "hot and dusty khaki-clad youth" stood on the bridge over Basingstoke Canal, war was declared between England and Germany. The dreadful summer passed, and when winter came London was used to the melancholy scenes of stretchers arriving at Victoria, of ambulances, of parks changed into training-grounds, of darkened houses and the menace of raids from the air. The Prince of Wales went into training with the first battalion of the Grenadier Guards, and at Warley or on the parade ground of Wellington Barracks, the "hot and dusty khaki-clad youth" was turned into a soldier. The war grew in magnitude and became more horrible. The glamour passed and the long monotony began. The Prince's heart thumped the same battle tunes as those of his father's people. The pathetic ecstasies and the new hates of war pressed in about him, and, in common with the millions, he felt that his duty lay in active service. He went to Oxford and saw the Belgian soldiers lying in their cots. He spoke to them in their own language, and, with the deepening of his compassion, there grew also a wish to go to France with his battalion. The days of training at Warley came to an end; the date of sailing was fixed. At the last moment the Prince was told that he would not be allowed to go. It was his second disappointment, for only a few months before, when he said that he wished to return to the Navy, the Admiralty had refused the responsibility of turning any warship into such a glorious target for the enemy. Lord Kitchener was working at the War Office at Whitehall. It was his restraining hand that kept the Prince back.

One morning early in October of 1914 the Prince of Wales, wearing the uniform of a subaltern, hurried up the vast marble stairs of the War Office and asked if he could see the Secretary of State for War. He found Kitchener sitting in the famous oak-panelled room which looks out into Whitehall and towards the arches beneath which the Life Guardsmen were mounted upon their horses.

Kitchener and the Prince sat on opposite sides of the great table, and they called each other " sir," the one voice calm and strong, the other eager and young. Kitchener had always been fond of the Prince, and he had said how striking it was to see " King Edward's most attractive traits . . . reproduced in the youthful Prince of Wales." The subaltern pleaded, but Kitchener would not change his mind.

" What does it matter if I am shot? I have four brothers," asked the Prince of Wales.

Kitchener answered: " If I were certain that you *would* be shot, I do not know if I should be right to restrain you. What I cannot permit is the chance, which exists until we have a settled line, of the enemy securing you as a prisoner."

Sir George Arthur has told us that Kitchener clung " tenaciously to the theory that death on the field of battle can never be matter for lament, but that capture—however unavoidable—spelt triumph for the captor and some indignity for the captured." This was the theme of Kitchener's argument, and the Prince walked out of the War Office with no more satisfaction than Kitchener's assurance that he would be allowed to go to France only when there was a settled line.

The Prince found little sympathy for his cause. Most of the officers with whom he had trained at Warley were devoted to him. One of them has said that when the Prince's shyness had passed he was an influence for happiness and a stimulating companion. Their sympathy with him was silent, and they had not encouraged him when he moaned over Kitchener's decision. He was alone in his disappointment, and he turned to an old friend of his grandfather's, Sir Dighton Probyn, and entreated him to plead with Kitchener. In the room at Marlborough House, where the Prince had played with his grandfather when he was a little boy, he pleaded with his grandfather's friend. Sir

Dighton said afterwards that tears came into the Prince's
eyes as he begged to be allowed to go to France.

A month passed and the Prince went to Kitchener again.
The Field-Marshal was still certain of his decision, and he
only repeated his promise that when there was a stable
line the Prince would be allowed to join his battalion in
France. A few days afterwards Kitchener was able to keep
his word. Within forty-eight hours after the first battle of
Ypres he made arrangements for the Prince to sail. The
Prince hurried off to Marlborough House with the good
news. Sir Dighton Probyn described the scene in a letter
to Sir George Arthur. "I saw the dear . . . Prince of
Wales yesterday. He came to wish me good-bye—and it
really was delightful to see the change that had come over
him since he had last been in this room. On the last occasion he really *cried* with sorrow at the idea of 'being dis-
graced,' and he said he was not being allowed to go to the
war. Yesterday his face beamed with joy. Do let Lord
Kitchener know this."

At half-past twelve on the morning of November 12 the
young soldier leapt up the stairs of the War Office two at
a time to say good-bye to Kitchener before he left for
France.

Chapter Seven

A SOLDIER IN FRANCE

Their deed, from age to age,
Shall voice and verse engage,
Swelling the splendid page
Of England's story.
ALFRED AUSTIN.

A SOLDIER IN FRANCE

THE family ties and associations between the Prince of Wales and the countries of Europe were slight. The Empress Frederick was dead, and there was little sympathy between the English Court and her son. The family links with Bulgaria had been severed, and the strange case of the Russian Royal Family, living apart from their subjects, had little in it to appeal to English thought. An English princess had once attended a reception while she was visiting Russia, and as she was standing near to the door, she had seen a servant hurry in to tell a Grand Duchess that her coachman had been frozen to death while waiting on the box of her carriage. All that she had said was: " But how am I to go home?" When this story was brought back to England it served only to emphasise the gulf which existed between the English Court and survivals of eighteenth-century monarchy in Europe. The phrase *The English Royal Family* had now come into fulness of meaning. In the old days of Queen Victoria's diplomacy there had been many relationships with Europe to be considered because of marriage or tradition. These had passed by 1914, and when war was declared, the people had no need to look anxiously towards Buckingham Palace, wondering which way sympathy might stray. The King and his family were the sponsors of Britain's causes and they were the shrine of Britain's loyalty. Theirs was almost the only solid power among the shifting tides of government and opinion during the war. Statesmen rose and fell and generals were changed, but the influence of the King was permanent. There was no cleavage of feeling and loyalty in the Prince of Wales when he crossed to join his regiment in France. Nothing mattered to him but his own adventure and the valour of his father's people.

Up to this time King George had not suffered anxiety from having a member of his family in danger from the enemy. Now he became one of the anxious parents in a country at war. His son went to France under the personal direction of Lord Cavan, and all the King said to him was: "I want you to look after him." Lord Cavan's task was not easy, for the Prince threw himself into his new life with so much energy that those who watched him were continually alarmed. As early as February the officers of his regiment used to say: "A bad shelling will always produce the Prince of Wales or Llewellyn Jones." Jones was a raw-boned Welsh chaplain who had met the Prince on the road one day outside Armentières. Llewellyn Jones was walking when the Prince stopped his car and "gave him a lift." Jones did not know until afterwards that his friend was the Prince of Wales. Sometimes the Prince's energy ran away with his discretion and he caused unnecessary anxiety to those in command. Sir Charles Monro has written of a morning when he was told, rather early, that the Prince was missing. He had left for the front trenches with his old company of Grenadiers without orders. The General asked for his car and followed. "When he came abreast of the company he beckoned to the Prince, who somewhat reluctantly came to the side of the car."

The Prince mumbled as he came near to the General. "I heard what you said, Prince," said Sir Charles—"'Here is that damned old General after me again!' Jump into the car, or you will spoil my appetite for breakfast."

The Prince's inherited energy made him impatient. He had arrived in France before the dulness of war had set in. The peasants were still "stripping their gardens to pelt our soldiers with flowers as they passed," and the Tommies were still giving away their badges and buttons as souvenirs, so that they had to tie their clothes on with string. The Prince hurried away from these zones of picturesque safety. It would not be right to insist too much upon his courage, for he did what was expected of him. But in the light of his later relationship with his people, before his abdication, it is important that we should note how closely he tried to identify himself with the conditions of battle. A private wrote of him: "He is among the keenest and hardest soldiers." One day he was in a house which was "rocking and shaking all night under the constant detonation of bombardment." It is in these letters of soldiers to their relatives that one finds the simple pictures of his life in France. "The Prince is always in the thick of it," wrote a private in the Coldstream. "Only last night he passed me when the German shells were coming over. . . . I hope, please God, he will come home safe and sound without a scratch." One day the Prince brought a German officer down in his car. When the prisoner was handed over an Irishman wrote: "Never saw anyone look so well as the Prince of Wales. He is simply full of vim and has a real weather-beaten look, and is as wiry as a cat." In brief, the Prince was "a handful" to those who were responsible for him, and they often became impatient with his impetuousness. He would not accept authority blindly, and his revolt against the discretion of the old was significant. He belonged to the new generation which was to stand strangely alone when the war was over: independent, and inclined to resent all fetters.

The Prince would walk six miles alone, before breakfast, as if the demands of the day were not enough for him. One day Sir Philip Gibbs forced his way through some brushwood on a slope to reach the crest of a hillock. He saw two Generals and several staff officers on the hillside. Two other figures climbed the slope and joined them. One of them arrested his attention. "Who was that young officer, a mere boy, who came toiling up through the slime and mud, and who at the crest halted and gave a quick salute to the two Generals? He turned, and I saw that it was Edward Prince of Wales; and through the afternoon, when I glanced at him now and again as he studied his map and gazed across the fields, I thought of another Edward Prince of Wales, who, six centuries ago, stood on another field of France."

The Prince's service was scattered over many areas. In January of 1915 he was A.D.C. to Sir John French at St. Omer, and in February and March he was attached to the Second Division, under General Horne, at Bethune. In April and May he went to the First Corps, and then, after brief leave in England, he went back to the Guards Division.

In April of 1915 the Prince came back to England for a few days to carry a despatch from Lord French to Lord Kitchener. " I am sending another despatch by the Prince of Wales," wrote Lord French. " May I appear at your breakfast-table at 8.30 a.m. on Wednesday, the 14th? I can get over late on Tuesday. I am telling the Prince of Wales to tell the King I can go to see him on Wednesday if he wishes to see me, but I have asked him to tell no one that I am coming, and I am sure you will also keep my secret. I don't want the P.M. or Winston or anyone but you and the King to know I am in London. I will bring maps and copious notes and tell you everything, but I don't want to have anything in writing. I am in strong hopes of a great advance. I hope you agree in all this. A wire in answer will do; put ' Yes ' or ' No.' "

On the evening of his arrival in London with the despatch, the Prince dined with Lord Kitchener at St. James's Palace. The little party was robbed of any official air by abandoning uniforms in favour of dinner jackets, and it is an interesting reflection on the sturdy discipline of Kitchener that he served no wine to his guests. The King

had banned alcohol at Buckingham Palace for the duration
of the war, although this total abstinence was against the
advice of his doctors. Kitchener likewise dismissed wine
and spirits from his table in York House, and from 1915
until the day of his death the rule was not broken.

Kitchener was very happy to see the change in the young
subaltern, the increased poise and self-confidence. He said
afterwards that he felt that he had given the Prince the first
big adventure in his life. This time Kitchener played the
rôle of listener, and he encouraged his guest to tell a host
of stories of his months in France. The Prince went to
Windsor when the dinner was over, to see his father, and a
few days afterwards he returned to France.

Although the Prince enjoyed the society of the great
people during his service in France, his youthfulness and
his love of company often guided him away into the less
grand company of junior officers and men. One persistently
traces his grandfather's character and tastes in him: the
wish to know everybody, the natural taste for cosmopolitan
society and the impatience in the presence of pompous or
magnificent people! Already he seemed to turn away from
conventional society, as if it bored him. One day he went
to the Hôtel du Grand Cerf, which had been spared when
the Rue de la République was bombarded. It happened
that M. Marcel Laurent, the French novelist, saw him and
wrote a pleasant account of the scene.

"In the common dining-room" Marcel Laurent found
a party of British officers at luncheon. He wondered if they
were really officers, for their khaki uniforms showed no dis-
tinguishing marks. "They are conversing in low tones, and
do not break off in their talk at the appearance of a soldier
who, pipe in mouth, advances towards them and stands
listening to them. He, too, is distinguished by no ribbon,
no officer's stripes, no badge, no insignia. He is not tall,
very slender; he would even appear a little frail if his firm
carriage did not undeceive one. The peak of his cap drawn

low over his forehead, a crook-handled walking-stick hanging from his arm, his wrists protected by warm woollen mittens, he pleases by his graceful bearing.

"Is he a junior officer, this young man, eighteen at the most, blue-eyed, fresh-cheeked, clear-complexioned? One guesses him to be a recruit of the previous day, but where will one meet a more youthful voluntary recruit?

"He goes away for an instant, he inspects a large grey automobile which is standing before the door, and he returns, still standing, talking and laughing, with his companions. Someone says: 'No, it is not a party of British officers, or this soldier would speak to them at a greater distance.'

"However, the meal over and the bill settled, the travellers get their things together, betake themselves to the car, consult a map slipped behind a sheet of glass, and take their places. The young soldier of eighteen jumps in and takes the wheel; then, as the motor drones and moves off, the hotel proprietor, knowing something of the secrets of gods and kings, certain of no longer committing an indiscretion in raising an august incognito, points to the unassuming fair young man who, pipe in mouth, is driving the grey automobile: 'His Royal Highness the Prince of Wales.'"

Early in 1916 the Prince went into training with the first battalion of the Grenadier Guards at Calais. But he was impatient with training, and news from Egypt made him wish to go farther afield and see the campaign in the Near East. The King was anxious when the plan was suggested to him, because the submarines added an awful danger to ships crossing the Mediterranean. Again it was Lord Kitchener who sponsored the Prince and encouraged the King to allow him to go. The secrecy in which he made the journey is a tribute to the silent service, for even the destroyers *Acorn* and *Sheldrake*, which escorted the light cruiser in which he crossed from Marseilles to Alexandria, were not aware that they were guarding him. The officers of the escort were surprised when, in the safety of Alexandria Harbour, the Prince signalled them his thanks.

The Prince met Australian and New Zealand soldiers for the first time in Egypt. Their vitality and frankness were the first influences which came to him from the far-away countries of the Empire. After he had bathed with them in the Canal, near to Ismailia, eaten with them and shared their jokes, he was a Little Englander no longer. A new interest came into his life, and he wished to understand the life of the new countries. A fresh theme had begun for him, and it was to grow in strength and equip him for the mission which was given to him after the war, when he became his father's greatest ambassador among the people of the Dominions.

There was business for the Prince while in Egypt. He was entrusted with the drawing up and writing of a report on the Suez Canal defences. He went as far as Khartoum, and then he set out on his journey home again, with the long report, written in his own hand.

As the days in Egypt passed, those who were with the Prince saw a change in his manner. His journey away from England and the affairs of Europe no doubt gave him the perspective he had always lacked, and the result of this was increased confidence in himself. The historical monuments and ancient appeal of Egypt did not draw him into the past. It was already apparent that his heart and mind were with his own century. One is reminded of the journey which King Edward VII made over the same country in 1862, and the likeness between grandfather and grandson is sharpened when we turn back to Dean Stanley's letters, in which he recorded his failure to interest Prince Albert Edward in the " tumble-down old temples." The scene in Jerusalem also might have had the Prince Edward of this century as its central figure instead of his grandfather. Dean Stanley wrote of the evening when Prince Albert

Edward went to his tent to ask for the names of all the places he had seen so that he could write them down in his *Journal*: "The Prince paused at the door of the tent as he was leaving, and, turning to Dean Stanley, he said, in his most engaging manner: 'You see that I am trying to do what I can to carry out what you said in your sermon . . . Gather up the fragments.'"

The wish of the twentieth-century Prince was much the same. It was through his sense of duty that he tried to learn, but he expressed his real feeling for the past when he hit a golf ball from the summit of one of the Pyramids. The voices of his own time were more stimulating and important to him than the voices of the dead centuries. He was spurred to interest in the building of a new empire, through meeting Australians and New Zealanders on the banks of the Canal, but the memorials of old empires were one with the dust into which they were crumbling.

Chapter Eight

WAR ON ITALIAN FRONT

Happy is England! I could be content
To see no other verdure than its own;
. . . . Yet do I sometimes feel a languishment
For skies Italian, and an inward groan
To sit upon an Alp as on a throne.

KEATS.

Chapter Eight

WAR ON ITALIAN FRONT

THE Prince was refreshed by new interests when he sailed away from Egypt. He had enjoyed his brief experience of the raw-boned Australians, and through their physical bravado and their frankness they had given him his first lesson in the colonial point of view. He has never turned from candour when it was within the bounds of good manners, and he liked the people of the new country, who dealt in neither compliments nor idle words. He was bored by the report which he had to prepare on the Suez Canal, feeling that the mission was invented to give him a reason for going to the Near East. But the time in Egypt had not been wasted; he had seen a new country and he had met new men; his horizon was now widened, and from this time he talked of Australia with growing interest. When he arrived in Egypt he had seemed tired and disgruntled, but he left for Italy in May with his old spirit alive once more. This was well, for he was on the edge of an interesting adventure.

The King of Italy sent the royal train to carry the Prince from Spezia to Udine, then the Italian Headquarters. They were to be together for four days, on the Austro-Italian front. The simplicity of their meeting and the frankness which soon made them talk like father and son prompts one to turn back to the story of two of the Prince's ancestors who were received in Rome in vastly different circumstances. At the same age as his great-grandson, who was now travelling towards Udine in his drab khaki uniform, the Prince Consort had been to Rome and he had sat with the Pope, talking sedately of Etruscan art. King Edward VII had also visited Rome when he was young. King Victor

Emmanuel had been at Windsor a little time before, and he had shown Queen Victoria a photograph of his royal children, with the exclamation: " Ah, this is nothing; you should see my other family." She was so alarmed that she wondered whether it was wise for her impressionable son to go to Rome at all. He left for Italy with many cautions, and, taking no chances, Queen Victoria instructed Colonel Bruce to be at hand even when her son went to see the Pope. " God knows" what they might pretend had been said by the Prince if Colonel Bruce were not present as a witness.

Neither Etruscan art nor Queen Victoria's fear of the " purple papal people" disturbed the pleasure of the meeting between King Emmanuel and the Prince of Wales in 1915. The friendship between the House of Windsor and the House of Savoy scorned the doubts of the 'fifties, and it did not anticipate the rifts of 1936. The Italians still sang " In guerra con tutto il mondo, ma in pace con l'Inghilterra " (" With all the world war, but peace with England ").

Only three years before, during the Turko-Italian War, the King of Italy had abandoned hostilities as the *Medina* passed through the Mediterranean on the way to India with King George and Queen Mary on board. The official record of the *Medina's* voyage says: " The next five days were smoothly spent in crossing waters that were troubled in another way, for Their Majesties were now within the zone of war between Italy and Turkey; but it was remarkable testimony of respect to the British Sovereign that, although the *Medina* might at any moment have been within earshot of a sea fight, both belligerents agreed that the passage of the King should be completely peaceful, and they made their dispositions accordingly. . . . The navy . . . did no less honour to the royal travellers. The mariners' lights along the coast . . . were all temporarily relighted as Their Majesties passed by."

An eminent British soldier who served with the Italian

forces has described the simple life which King Emmanuel led with his troops. During all the years of the
war he never left his soldiers except for his annual leave of
two weeks. "The King would receive his visitors in a tiny
bedroom—the visitor sitting on the only chair, the King
on the end of the camp-bed. Books were his only luxury.
This simple monarch, who collects coins with as much
eagerness as King George collected stamps, brought none
of the paraphernalia of royalty with him to the front. The
stories of his simplicity were always stirring smiles among
the British officers who knew him. Once, when he had to
spend a night in the open, the officer accompanying him
showed the King a small attaché-case and said that it contained all his luggage. 'I have done better than that,' said
the King, producing a small parcel wrapped in an old
newspaper. He would spend the day in the trenches, un-
recognised, dressed as a private, and hold councils with his
Generals in the evening."

The Prince was given a small cottage within the war
zone. The unhappy strain which came to the friendship
between Italy and England in 1935 must awaken regret in
us when we look back upon the simple scenes of 1915. A
little time before, Queen Mary had been told of King
Emmanuel's daring, and she had charged a British officer
going to Italy to ask him to be more careful. The King's
answer was like the plea of the Prince of Wales to Lord
Kitchener. "The Queen is very kind—very kind. But what
does it matter? I am but one link in a chain, and if I am
killed there is somebody younger and more able to take my
place. But thank the Queen. She is very kind."

The same British officer has said of the meeting between
the King and the Prince: "They were all the time warning
each other not to take risks. The King was afraid of the
Prince's daily habit of going too near to the Austrian lines.
When the Prince went back to Italy again in 1918 to stay
with the King, he broke away from all warnings and control

and flew over the Austrian trenches. The aircraft were stationed near to the front, and on a hot, sunny day the Austrian airmen would fly up into the sun's direct rays and swoop down, with the protecting light behind them. On such a day the Prince flew off with Barker, the Canadian airman, and they went over the Austrian lines. The King was perturbed and almost angry at the bravado of his guest. But he was equally indiscreet, and one day he went up to the lines himself and sat down under a tree to eat his luncheon. A shell exploded and carried the tree away while the King was resting, after his meal was ended.

The Prince of Wales came back to England having made a new friend. The line of Cymbeline rang true for him. " Let a Roman and a British ensign wave friendly together."

In May of 1916 the Prince was attached to the Fourteenth Corps at Lovie Château, again under Lord Cavan. He remained with them during June and July, moving with them to the battle of the Somme. The war had now got into his blood. His experiences on the scattered fronts had made him wiser, but they had also bereaved him. His friend Major Cadogan had been killed early in the war. During the battle of Loos in the autumn of 1915 he had come grimly near to death himself. He arrived at a village and left his chauffeur in the car while he went up to the lines. When he returned the car was smashed and the driver was dead at the wheel. He was an old retainer and he had been a servant to the Prince when he was an undergraduate. The Prince gathered the man's belongings into his handkerchief and carried them back to Headquarters.

Through these experiences the will and the knowledge of the Prince were increasing towards the time when he was able to say: " In those four years I mixed with men. In those four years I found my manhood." In this search he did not become more docile, nor was he more inclined to accept judgments of his elders without question. He tried to stand upon his traditions as upon a hill and not to be engulfed by them. Perhaps he suspected the ancestral voices which had prophesied war and was already listening intently for the voices which were to speak of peace. His thoughts were his own, but his actions were enough for us to judge the way these thoughts were straying. The Emperor of Germany was wrong when he said that Prince Edward was "far from being a pacifist." He was not a sentimentalist over man's need for self-protection, but he did not forget the lesson of his four years on service. In 1929, when he spoke at the British Industries Fair, he said that he hoped for a day when, " if two nations want to fight, there will be some power which will say, ' Move on!' the same as a London policeman would say if he found two men fighting in the street."

The Prince's impatience with his superior officers did not abate. General Maude said that the Prince was always "anxious" to be with him when he went to the front trenches, and another officer who was asked to watch him sighed with relief when the Prince was transferred. "Thank Heaven he's going," he said. "This job will turn my hair grey. . . . He insists on tramping in the front lines." In the history of the Welsh Guards, Major Dudley Ward writes of an occasion when the Prince "came up to the line and the guns started to drop shells all around him, so that he and General Gathorne-Hardy had to double across to some pill-boxes in the Grenadier lines."

Two more pictures of the Prince's war service are important to us in a search after the growth of his character. A soldier who was present during King George's accident in 1916 tells one of them. The King was inspecting the Flying Corps at Hesdinguel Airdrome, and after riding down the company he turned to inspect a new machine. Without any warning the men gave three cheers. "The King's horse, which had up to this time taken no notice of the cheering, suddenly reared up and slipped backwards, falling on the King."

It was the Prince who stayed with his father during the awful drive back to the château at Aire, anxiously watching the King's face growing paler and paler. When the King was safe in bed the Prince hurried back to England " to report all details to Their Majesties the Queen and Queen Alexandra." The same officer has said that " the older staff officers and officials who were at Aire were greatly impressed by the way the Prince grappled with the situation, anxious but excited, efficient although he was deeply sympathetic." The other story is of his compassion. One day he went to a hospital, where he was allowed to see only the more happy and presentable patients. He knew there were others, and he asked to see them. These were men in another ward who had been deformed by their wounds. He spoke to them, and when he came to the end of the ward he was asked not to go into the next room, where there was a man misshapen beyond recognition. The Prince insisted. He went into the room and found a man, horribly torn, lying upon the bed. He leaned over the bed and touched the soldier's cheek with his lips.

When the war passed the Prince of Wales was one of the few of our leaders who did not turn from its ugliness. His care for the wounded was a passion with him, when it had become little more than an expensive duty to others.

One service which has grown out of the Prince's experiences in France is the Toc H movement. The story of the birth of Toc H is well known. Talbot House, named after the Prince's Oxford friend, was first opened in December of 1915. It was in Poperinghe, and the Guards Division came to the salient in the spring of 1916. The Prince had been withdrawn from his own regiment, and he was now with the 14th (Lord Cavan's) Corps Headquarters. In April he went to Talbot House for the first time, and after this he visited Mr. (Tubby) Clayton many times and became interested in the work he was doing. Mr. Clayton has said to the author: " The Prince's natural

72

November, 1915.   King George V visits the Western Front.
The Prince of Wales on the extreme left and King George and General Joffre on the extreme right.

shyness and reserve no longer impeded him. He had in 1916 won a place of his own in the esteem of all ranks in or near the line; he knew what he could do, and did it with a cheerful tact and most unfailing energy. He learned to love the wayside conversations, and he found men most refreshing. To him a pair of shoulders in a tavern, a laden figure picking its way up a duckboard track, a man upon a road or a soldier writing home meant someone to be talked to as he passed. And what he said was never strained or formal. This was the beginning of his development as a conversationalist, and now I think he is the most accomplished conversationalist in the world. Think of the hundreds of people to whom he speaks, people with strong prejudices. They may be social, political, intellectual or racial prejudices. A phrase askew in the Prince's conversation would be a disaster; a friend of England lost and perhaps an enemy created. And yet, with this art which makes it possible for him to talk to almost anybody on the subject which interests them, he is never merely 'all things to all men.'

"It is not generally fluidity which makes his talk so versatile. It is because of his undimmed, never-wearying attempt to find out facts, which he sorts discerningly and puts in his astonishing memory. From this store the facts have an odd habit of popping out at the right moment, months or even years later. All sorts of conditions of men thus become attached to the Prince with a kind of loyalty and appreciation which is essentially personal and has nothing to do with his unique position."

The purpose of Toc H in peace time is to conquer hate. This aim appealed to the Prince, and when Mr. Clayton remodelled Toc H to suit the needs of the young, after the war, the Prince gave his name and his support to the plans. In 1919 Toc H was poor and its future was dim and uncertain. But it was doing work which no other society attempted. The war was ruthless in combing out the ardent and sincere social workers from the sentimental bunglers, and the Prince soon became aware of Mr. Clayton's disciplined sincerity. He said that the Scout movement gave a stimulus to the life of the very young and that the War Associations guarded the old soldiers. In between, Toc H found a new field of influence. Mr. Clayton has told the rest of the story. "The Prince has led the building of Toc H, and he guided it in many overseas developments. He has visited houses of Toc H in every part of London, in Birmingham, Manchester, Sheffield, Newcastle, Halifax, Hull, Southampton and as far off as Buenos Aires. On his way back from Melton he has twice turned aside for a friendly glimpse of the house at Leicester. He has lit every lamp from his own, and never missed a chance of showing kindness to great or tiny meetings."

The Prince's unusual fervour over the work of Toc H touches one of the mainsprings in his nature. "All problems at bottom are human problems," he once said. "I have often called upon Toc H to serve. I call upon it now to serve with its mind as well as with its hand. Understanding comes not from the heart only, but from the head."

As far as is humanly possible, Toc H aims at the death of prejudice and the fostering of opinion. The Prince's enthusiasm over this law of living, which was revealed to him in France, caused him to nurse Toc H from the day when it was a struggling thing, with no money in the bank, to its present power, spread over the world.

The war ended, and the Prince came back to England. Four years before the King had allowed a young man to face the hazards of war, much against his will. Now a man came back in place of the boy: a man who was to be identified with all the strange changes born of peace. The war created a wide gap between the generations, and it was exemplified in the differences of character in King George and his son. Fathers who belonged to the old generation and sons who had been through the anxiety and unsettling

74

experience of France lived in different worlds, and many soldiers returned from the war to find that they were uncomfortable living among people who did not understand them. Even when heroics faded and the mundane affairs of living came into order once more, the difference persisted.

From the time of his return to England the Prince of Wales chose an independent way. It led him far from the traditions of his father's Court. He resented the old order, and conventional society did not amuse him. Like his grandfather, he found pleasure in a small coterie of friends, chosen for their amusing qualities rather than for their position or their intellectual gifts.

In time, the dwindling ranks of society resented the originality of his choice of friends. He seldom went to stay in great country houses, where he might have met and known his contemporaries, and, as independence increased, he was almost stubborn in his habit of turning his back upon the conventions of polite society. The Prince was not alone in this reaction. In the restless years after the war, when the life of restaurants swelled and the old-fashioned notions of home life were neglected, the young of every class liked to boast of their independence and to fly in the face of convention. It was not consoling to be told that this was an inevitable state after war. It did not make King George's problem as a father any less menacing, nor could it console him or any other parent in the land for the fact that the young were lost to the old as no generation had been before.

If the Prince of Wales disappointed his father and those ranks of society which expected their Prince to be their leader, there was another field in which the heir to the throne performed unique service. His judgement sometimes erred, but his compassion brought the poor close to his heart. The final battle of his life as King was to be between his heart and his judgement, and it was to be his judgement that failed. But it should be remembered by those historians who come to our problems in later years that King Edward's final renunciation of his crown must be judged in the light of the years when he lived a restless, uncertain life: a life which gave him little chance of developing those serene qualities of mind which might have guided him into higher spheres of moral conquest when the hour of his temptation came.

If King Edward failed in the high offices forced upon him as a sovereign, he did not fail as Prince of Wales. The pain and humiliation of his exile must always be remembered as the tragic end of a great mission among the poor people of his father's kingdom. His compassion guided him to nobleness among them, and that compassion was already strong in him when he returned to England in 1918 and began to identify himself with the stark and uncertain life of a people who were trying to recover from the disaster of the war.

Chapter Nine

THE END OF THE WAR

> . . . and horror
> Drifted away . . . O but everyone
> Was a bird; and the song was wordless; the
> singing will never be done.
> SIEGFRIED SASSOON.

Chapter Nine

THE END OF THE WAR

ALTHOUGH the area of Queen Victoria's Empire was almost doubled during her reign, it was to Europe that she looked for her interests rather than to the new countries of the south. Her Ministers inclined to view colonial problems as a nuisance, and as late as 1902 there were complaints from the permanent officials in Whitehall, who were "a good deal bored . . . with Colonial Premiers in general and Mr. Seddon* in particular." Queen Victoria had allowed her eldest son to open a bridge across the St. Lawrence in 1860, and in the same year Prince Alfred had laid the foundation-stone of a new breakwater in Cape Town. Her effigy had been made in snow by her loyal subjects in the west of Canada, and the main streets of colonial towns had been named after her. But Queen Victoria's thoughts and affections were too closely tied to Europe for her to comprehend the problems of her own Empire. King Edward, who was the the first sovereign to use the title of King "of the British Dominions beyond the Seas," broke down some of these prejudices when he came to the throne. But it was not until his son, Prince George, toured the world that an English prince was able to understand the aims of the Dominions and Colonies. King George's final command over the hearts and fidelity of his people in the Dominions had a tangible beginning. Perhaps he guessed at the survival of Englishness in the countries at the bottom of the world when, on going down to his first breakfast in Australia, he found a wreath of roses around his plate, placed there, his hostess told him, "for Sunday morning and in memory of England." His journeys as a

* Premier of New Zealand.

79

cadet allowed him to gain at least a hint of the colonial point of view. When he returned to England after his second tour of the Empire, he revealed the convictions which had come to him in the speech which he made at the Guildhall. He had sensed the perils of widening the gulfs between the parent England and her colonial children. "The old country must wake up," Prince George had said, "if she intends to maintain her old position." When he became King, when the torments of war and the chicanery of diplomats drew his attention to Europe, he did not forget the lesson of his journeys to the young countries. His almost inhuman capacity for storing knowledge was centred on the Empire, no matter how often his Ministers talked of the old enmities of Europe. The Lieutenant-Governor of Western Australia said* in 1934 that of all the officials he had met in London, none knew as much of the life and industry of his part of Australia as King George. The detail and certainty of his Sovereign's knowledge astounded him.

It fell to Prince Edward of Wales to complete this bond between Britain and her Dominions, not by appealing to old sentiments, but through practical interest which has never weakened since he made his first journey to Canada after the close of the last war. Perhaps his encounter with the Australians in Egypt first made him realise that the strength of his father's Empire depended more on friendship with the new countries than by meddling with the old feuds of Europe. The theme of interest in the Dominions persisted, and it grew. When news of the Armistice came to him he was in billets with the Canadian Corps. The Armistice was to be declared at eleven o'clock next day, and he hurried to Mons and arrived in the market-place in time to hear the clock strike the hour: the hour when "horror drifted away." He took his place in the scene and he saw the aircraft flying back to Mons after firing the last shots of the battle. From this time his interests were

* In conversation with the author.

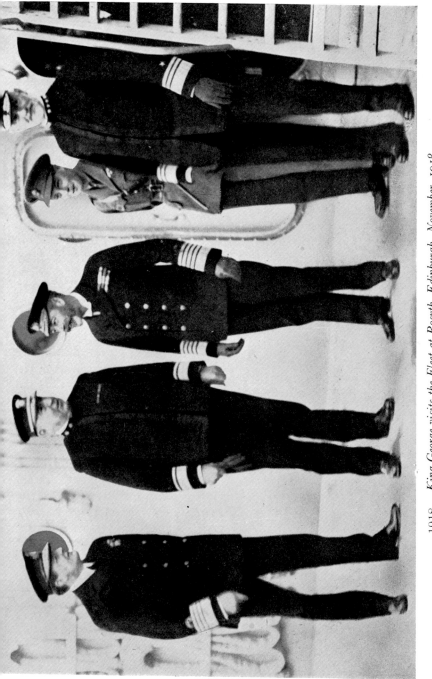

1918. King George visits the Fleet at Rosyth, Edinburgh, November, 1918.

Left to right: Admiral Beatty, Admiral Rodman (U.S. Navy), King George V, The Prince of Wales, Admiral Sims (U.S. Navy).

diverted to the positions controlled by Dominion soldiers. He was attached to the Australian Corps Headquarters at Ham, and in January of 1919 he was attached to the New Zealand Division at Leverkusen. No other soldier had seen the war from as many angles, but the abiding impression which he brought back to England was of the part played by the soldiers of Canada, South Africa, Australia and New Zealand. He had shared the emotions engendered by the Armistice with them, and when he returned to London and made his home in York House it was of the countries of the Empire that he thought. There was no need for him to depend upon sentimentality in attaching himself to what was to become one of the great causes of his life. He was among the first of the country's leaders to see that the Empire could be bound together as an economic unity, independent of the rest of the world. This great vision may not have been clear to him in 1918, but he was already beginning to see it upon the horizon.

While the Prince's Empire journeys were being arranged he had to become a Londoner again. He was allowed the privilege of his own house and establishment. He was a man now, with his own public engagements and his own staff. He slowly imposed his identity upon English people to whom, before the war, he had been merely the eldest of their Sovereign's sons. Up to 1914 King George and Queen Mary had guarded their heir from too much limelight. The sons of kings are in greater danger of being spoiled by adulation than the sons of other people, and King George was haunted by the dreadful possibilities of allowing Prince David to appear too often in public when he was a boy. The Prince had driven through the streets for the Coronations of his grandfather and his own father, and he had captured the stage for his investiture at Carnarvon. But for the most part he had been kept in the shade, and his growing personality had not arrested public attention before 1914. The first time he emerged from this dimness was when he appealed for funds in aid of National Relief.

He began his speech in a nervous, hesitating voice. For two or three minutes it seemed that he would fail, but his sincerity burned brightly behind his indecision, and he spoke so fervently towards the end that the women who listened to him took off their jewels and the men emptied their pockets in aid of the fund. This was a little beginning to his popularity.

When the war ended and when the mass of people no longer had the trenches as a focus for their emotions, they turned to find new altars. The Prince of Wales soon became a public hero and a lion. He became also a romantic figure, like a prince of old. When he paused to help an old soldier, to be kind to the sick or to aid charitable objects, he satisfied the public craving for peaceful chivalry, to take the place of the filth and misery of war. The Prince's photograph was in every house. "God Bless the Prince of Wales" became a popular anthem, and the newspapers, fumbling for grand words with which to describe him, called him Galahad. At first he was not made dizzy by this praise. He tried to escape from the flattery and cheers. But no man except one formed through obscurity and disappointment could have withstood the temptation to vanity when all the world had set out to make him vain. Although the Prince did all that was asked of him, his modesty was slowly shaken. Every day he moved among cheering crowds; every speech made before him was a compliment. His slimmest platitude was printed in big letters in the newspapers. It is little wonder that he fell into the harmless conceit which afterwards grew dangerously, so that it destroyed his self-judgement and made him over-assured; which made him lose all capacity of knowing the difference between wild popularity and calm esteem.

Nevertheless the Prince worked hard and he assumed more and more of the duties which were part of the penalty of being heir to the throne. King George did not make the mistake Queen Victoria had made in keeping the affairs of State back from her son. She thought him indiscreet, and he had to wait until he was fifty-one years old before he was allowed to know all that was happening between his mother and her Ministers. King Edward did not repeat the error. "Let my son know, but no one else," he often said when a document or despatch was placed before him. As far as was consistent with his prestige and duty as a constitutional monarch, King George followed his father's plan, and he slowly admitted his son to more and more of his confidence.

In his new home within St. James's Palace, the Prince of Wales built up the structure of his independence. His will became his own, and he made every attempt to govern his household according to his own wishes. The manhood which he had discovered in France urged him to make his life according to his own standards. These standards were distressing to his father and to older prelates and statesmen, but they seemed to be in harmony with the aims of the mass of younger people. Sick of war and broken by its miseries, they became merciless with humbug, suspicious of the guidance of the old, and cynical about many of the lessons they had learned at their parents' knee. The disillusioned and independent young believed in the Prince of Wales, and from this time he was able to stir the public conscience. On Peace night the thousands of people who pressed against the railings of Buckingham Palace were not satisfied with seeing only their King and Queen. They would not go home until the Prince came out to speak to them. On that night he became a Londoner and the Prince of his father's people. Uncertain of most things, they believed that they were justified in being certain of him. As much trust in heroes as was left to them was given to him, with all England's heart.

Chapter Ten

CANADA AND THE UNITED STATES

*I came to a new world in which men lived
topsy-turvy lives. They bathed in the sea at
the hour when Englishmen slept; they spoke
always of the future, whereas Englishmen
usually speak of the past. But they were
mighty men, these whose bodies were
browned by Colonial suns and whose
thoughts turned to originality and enterprise.*—PHILIP STONE.

CANADA AND THE UNITED STATES

MANY Englishmen fail to understand the people of the Dominions and Colonies. They take the loyalty of the new countries for granted, but they make little effort to foster these emotions or even to deserve them. On the eve of the war there were gaps between the life and thoughts of Britain and her Dominions. The early settlers had been bound tightly to England. The books on their shelves had been English, and the pictures on the walls of their wooden houses had been landscapes of Sussex or Cornwall, the Cheddar Gorge or the view of Westminster across the river. Letters exchanged between brothers and sisters kept the old loyalties alive. But when a new generation tilled the colonial earth, they were merely the cousins of their relatives in England, and letters were no longer exchanged between them. The parents of this new generation of Australians and New Zealanders had understood the jokes in *Punch*; the pompous squire, the Cockney wit and the Scottish ghillie were all tangible to them, but not to their sons. The younger colonials created their own humour out of the life about them. They caricatured their own types—the squatter, the aboriginal, the Red Indian and the Maori. They no longer whistled "John Peel" and "Widdecombe Fair." They had their own songs and their own muscular poets. Their diet changed. Pineapples and grapes were on the working man's table in Australia. They put stuffing into mutton and called it colonial goose. In New Zealand the townspeople ate oysters as nonchalantly as their forbears had eaten winkles. They evolved their own slang. All these apparently superficial changes were important, for gradually it meant that England and the new countries no longer spoke the same language.

By 1914 the gap in habits and interests was wide, and when the Australian came to England, like a son coming home to pay his respects to his grandparent, he was not wholly acceptable to the English. He was shown the Houses of Parliament and he was allowed to walk on the lawns of Buckingham Palace. To the subdued Briton, he seemed to be raw. The Australian was still loyal in his heart, but he visited England as a healthy child might call upon a grandfather who was losing his faculties. The Englishman responded by patronising the " colonial." When England was a Roman colony, Sallust wrote: " Poor Britons, there is some good in them after all—they produce an oyster." The Englishman had his revenge for this slight by thinking: "Poor Australians, there is some good in them after all—they produce sheep."

The war came in time to recapture and strengthen the English emotions of the Dominions before they died. Loyalty was strong as ever, but the vision of the Homeland had become dim. Every fine old tie was strengthened when the test of patriotism came. The most distant New Zealander believed blindly and passionately in the wickedness of the Emperor and the stupidity of his son. They were caricatured in the Dominion newspapers and given tails and tridents. The raping of Belgian women, the myth of the brutal Hun, and the martyrdom of Edith Cavell; these were no less horrible when news of them reached the Antipodes. The troopships passed from the South to the Northern Hemisphere for destinations unknown. There were no questions or doubts to mar the loyalty and the faith. At first the war had been more romantic than terrible to the new countries, where neither hunger nor actual danger were known. It was not until the hospital ships retraced the way of the troopships that the first stink of war came to the southern countries. Many little white hospitals flowered on the green colonial hills. If there were threats of Socialism and hints of independence in Australia in 1914, they had died in 1918. When the war ended the thoughtful people of the new countries felt almost as Englishmen again.

Perhaps the Prince of Wales sensed this devotion and the great opportunity which it brought to England. Then would have been the moment to talk of Empire Economic Unity—of the great links of trade and commerce. But England was bored by the war, in 1918, and she turned to the old gods of insularity and safety: Instead of worrying about how she could continue to hold, through enterprise, the love her colonial sons had given her during the war, she busied herself about Turkey and Hungary and Greece. The quarrels of her neighbours were more interesting than the devotion of her own children. The new countries were allowed to slip back into their old life, and the stories of the gaucherie of Australian soldiers in London drawing-rooms were told more often than the stories of their valour in the trenches.

There were exceptions in this wave of apathy which came to England in regard to her own Dominions. These exceptions were mostly young men, free from the old burrs of prejudice and insularity; none of them was more zealous and sincere than the Prince of Wales. When the war was over and he went to live in York House, he was still un-settled and anxious. He could not find the repose which was a blessing to the old, who were the custodians of the past. The Prince did not care about the haggling of the European Powers over territory and booty. Bigger issues had been revealed to him since 1914, and it was largely through his own wish that he began the great adventure and duty of visiting all the countries of his father's Empire. As far as he could judge then, their aims were nearer to his own than those of the jealous Powers of Europe. He chose the way of trade and of peace among his own people.

There was nothing unreal or aloof about the good-looking boy who sailed for Canada on August 5, 1919. The cheerful chronicle of H.M.S. *Renown* tells us that "the Prince of

Wales himself" was "all that has ever been said of him—very young-looking, he is nearer seventeen in appearance than his correct age of twenty-five; he is almost crazy about exercise. . . . The Atlantic crossing was quite uneventful, although we did do a little shooting at an iceberg as we were getting near Newfoundland. . . . Every day H.R.H. inspected some part of the ship, and we had some of the officers to lunch or dinner; very enjoyable, informal meals they were, too, without any special ceremony. . . . H.R.H. kept up the old naval custom of proposing the health of ' Sweethearts and Wives.' . . . The Prince and his staff dined in the wardroom, and we had a semi-organised ' rag ' afterwards—quite the leading spirit being H.R.H., who finished the evening about 12.30 a.m. looking very hot and dishevelled, rather dirty about the shirt-sleeves and with something round his neck that might once have been a collar."

On August 15 the Duke of Devonshire welcomed him at St. John's. A little more than two months afterwards he was back in Montreal, having travelled no less than 10,000 miles by railway, car and steamer. He visited fifty towns; he attended hundreds of receptions and made hundreds of speeches. This was the strain put upon a young man who knew no world of experience beyond Osborne, Oxford and the battlefields. He attended Indian pow-wows, cowboy stampedes and dances, and he won the hearts of everybody in Saskatoon when he jumped on a broncho's back and remained there, in fierce conflict, for several minutes. He shook hands with mayors and he inspected Scouts and veterans. At Banff, the last frail remnant of the Indian people came and danced about him. Their chief, Young Thunder, addressed him in a few picturesque phrases and elected him as the white chief, Morning Star. "Accept this Indian suit, the best we have," he said. A headdress of rich and beautiful feathers was placed on the Prince's head. He smiled at them and he shook Young Thunder's hand.

Out in the west the Prince found the new prairie towns

which had sprung up so quickly that they seemed unreal
and unsafe. It was summer time when he went there on
the tremendous train which carried him to the feet of the
Rockies. He paused at Calgary, where, soon afterwards, he
was to own a ranch and therefore become a Canadian. In
the years that followed Calgary became innocently vain
because the nearness of the Prince of Wales's ranch turned
it into a royal town.

"This is the Prince of Wales's town, you know," they
used to say. "His ranch is here, sixty miles out. It's his
retiring-place, you know. He loves riding out over the
rolling Alberta hills. He comes here to rest with us when
you English have worked him to a frazzle. He comes right
out here, and he just crawls under a fence if a photographer
happens to find him, and he makes friends with everyone,
and he just buys his big hats in our stores, and—well—he's
one of us."

In Montreal he addressed the French Canadians: "The
union of the two races in Canada was never a matter of
mere political convenience. . . . The union of England
and Scotland has been in existence for nearly two centuries. . . . Who can doubt that the union in Canada will
produce as great, as powerful and as united a nation as the
British nation itself. . . ."

At Quebec the Prince came upon the supreme test of
his visit to Canada. One likes to view only the sunny side
of the Empire achievement and forget the griefs and antagonisms which had to be buried after war in both Canada
and Africa. To say that those griefs and antagonisms are
completely dead would be absurd, for, especially in Africa,
the enemy of yesterday still groans under the yoke of our
rule. In both countries the groans died away for the
Prince's coming. Even the faint resentment that may have
stirred among the old French patriots in Quebec by the
sight of *Renown*, grey and secure, lying in the river, was
not directed to the Prince. There was only one harmless
note of discord. The *Renown* Magazine tells us: "We

gave one official reception to the people, mostly French, on the Government House list. It was quite successful as shows of that sort go, and provided us, at any rate, with one source of amusement. We did not know, of course, to whom invitations should be sent for the ' At Home,' so the printed cards and envelopes were sent ashore to the Lieutenant-Governor's French aide-de-camp, with a request that he should send them out for us; this he did very readily and efficiently, but subsequently sent us a bill, not only for the postage, but also for an item of five dollars for the clerk who addressed the envelopes."

The Prince made a pilgrimage to the Heights of Abraham and he planted a Union Jack on the battlefield. When the splendid tour of Canada was over his right hand was so sore that he could barely touch anything with it. His left hand was also strained by the shaking it was called on to do. Perhaps the memory of that first unending labour of Canada sprang to him when a stupid man in the East End of London once muttered, " Idle Rich! " as the Prince's car stopped near him. The Prince turned around and snapped out: " Rich, maybe, but not so very idle."

"I feel about my position and the responsibility it entails," he said before he left Toronto. "I can only assure you that I shall always endeavour to live up to that great responsibility and to be worthy of your trust."

Canada was not the end of the Prince's first adventure among the new countries. News of his charm had travelled south, and hundreds of Americans had already crossed the border to see the Prince who reduced people to smiles or tears, as he willed. The fine, transparent hero-worship of the Americans was not to be denied, and he was prevailed upon to visit their country before he returned to England. The King willingly gave his consent. More than half a century had passed since a Prince of Wales had visited the United States. When Prince Albert Edward came back from his American journey in 1860, he showed that he had learned much from his contact with the Americans. The members of his mother's Court had been delighted over the changes in him. He had "grown" and he had become "much more manly." But he had not lost the "youthful simplicity and freshness" which gave his manner "such a charm." The Prince of 1918 came through the fire of America's kindness with similar good results. Americans were not strangers to him. He had stayed with the American Army Headquarters Staff in Coblenz and he had danced with American nurses on the Rhine. He had also stayed with General Pershing at American G.H.Q. Only on Armistice Day had there been such a demonstration in New York as on the morning of the Prince's arrival. They "showered down upon the bewildered, delighted boy a veritable rain of confetti until the streets were a gay carpet beneath his motor-car." He hated few things as much as confetti, but he continued to smile and to woo the spontaneous Americans into friendship. A writer who described the scene added: "And it was not entirely because he was Prince of Wales, but more particularly because we liked him." The tumult was kept up for days. American enthusiasm is an embarrassing and overwhelming experience to a Briton who has been nurtured on repose and restraint. But the great, wild delight of a New York crowd is something of which Roman emperors might have dreamed on the way home from war, and the Prince could not fail to be surprised and happy, no matter how tired he became. There is none of the "pregnant silence" of an English mass when Americans are gay. Their hearts burst and their voices ring in a moment of ecstasy. New York was amazing to the Prince. He became the focus for all their wasted hero-worship and romantic notions. Of his inner sensations we know nothing. One guesses shrewdly at his alarm, when one reads that he "fingered his tie, smoothed his hair and moved about in his chair."

Out of this first visit a great friendliness was born in the Prince. America, with all its unchained enthusiasms and

love of show, was nearer to his sympathies than the preju-
dice-ridden countries of Europe. Anglo-American friendship became one of his enthusiasms after this first taste of
American kindness. "The Atlantic Ocean has grown
noticeably smaller," he said some years afterwards. "The
people of these two great countries are growing ever more
anxious to join hands across it."

At eleven o'clock on Armistice Day the train in which
the Prince was travelling ran through Baltimore. It halted
at the time when the two minutes' silence was being observed in England. It was a happy chance that here, where
the train stopped, there was a group of British soldiers
who were able to join him in the silence. Afterwards, the
Prince went out and shook their hands. He went on to Washington and made his first call at the White House. President Wilson was ill and he could not see him, but, next
day, the Prince went again, and he was received by the
President, who was lying in bed propped up with pillows.
The bed was the same that Lincoln had slept in during his
anxious days at White House, and, Wilson told the Prince,
it was "the very bed" in which his grandfather had slept
when he was in Washington in 1860. He went from the
rarefied atmosphere of the President's bedroom to speak to
the members of the National Press Club. Here, indeed, he
came upon the hard-boiled Americans who were not to be
gulled with the dim appeal of history. His success was
astonishing. He said to them: "You . . . . are very highly
trained critics on public writings and public speech, and
I am not at all your equal in that respect. . . . Your institutions, your ways of life, your aims are as democratic as
ours, and the atmosphere in which I find myself is the same
invigorating and familiar atmosphere I have always noted
in American friends."

"It's the smile of him, the unaffected, modest bearing of
him, the natural fun-loving spirit that twinkles in his blue
eyes," one of them wrote. Some of the pressmen saw deeper
than this, and they realised that he was earnest and intelli-

gent in what he said. The seed of respect was sown as he spoke to them. In the years that followed, thoughtful American writers usually spoke kindly of his achievements, and even in the disastrous months of 1936, when he was the focus for the world's criticism, American journalists tried to comprehend and not merely deride him. They revealed their appreciation of his sympathy when he visited the distressed areas of the North in 1929. A writer in the *American Nation* said: "Condescension was not, we are sure, in the Prince's heart. And what he did no ruler, no statesman, no party leader at present active has ever done. The President of the United States, in the face of the conditions among Pennsylvania miners only a shade better than those in Wales, sat comfortably at home in the White House and did not even make a gesture of sympathy towards those in distress."

The Prince came back to England from the United States, assured that travel had opened his eyes and cleared his brain. He had completed the first important mission as his father's ambassador. He had captured the affection of the Americans, whose friendliness for England was strengthened through his conquest. And he had thanked the Canadians for their service during the war. He revealed the effect of the Canadian visit in a few phrases. He said that he was "filled with admiration for what three or four vigorous and energetic generations" had "achieved in establishing the great Dominion." "I did not feel a stranger when I first landed in Canada," he said. "I have come back with a much clearer idea of what is meant by the British Empire." The last sentence was important because it was deeply true. He added, with suitable modesty: "I am not so foolish as to think that the wonderful welcome given me in Canada and again to-day are mere tributes to myself. I realise that they are given to me as the King's son and as his heir."

The success of the Prince's visit to Canada pleased the authorities in England. Now the old country had a plenipotentiary second to none. No grandiloquent politician or tactful official in Whitehall could ever hope to achieve the special kind of success which was vouchsafed to the Sovereign's heir. He was not allowed to rest now that he had proved his value, and early in the new year he left England again for the Barbadoes, Honolulu, Fiji, New Zealand and Australia.

There was one pleasant ceremony which tied him to England before he sailed. In February the Prince was made a Freeman of Windsor. The royal town put on its most splendid clothes in his honour, and, as part of his pledge as a Freeman, he promised not to "do anything whereby this town or the freedom thereof may be damnified." And he further promised that if he happened to "know of any conspiracy or mischief" against the borough he would "speedily disclose the same to the Mayor." After his picturesque pledge was made he stayed a little longer in London and then he sailed away again across the world.

Chapter Eleven

THE BARBADOES, HONOLULU AND FIJI

But though from court to cottage he depart
His saint is sure of his unspotted heart.

GEORGE PEEL.

Chapter Eleven

THE BARBADOES, HONOLULU AND FIJI

THE first pause in the Prince's journey towards the
Southern Hemisphere was made at the Barbadoes.
One phrase from the record of his visit intensifies
the contrast between the warm and colourful country and
the colder England which was then far behind him. In the
Barbadoes he walked along roads which led through
"pillared aisles of stately sago-palms, past dense groves of
green mahogany and bread-fruit trees or brilliantly red
flowering devil-trees, hibiscus and silk cotton . . . blue sea
and white, surf-swept beach."

Like his grandfather, in whose likeness he grew more
and more, the Prince was more interested in people than
in things. He soon turned from the natural charms to the
social problems of each new country he came to: he soon
opened his battery of questions. In the Barbadoes he was
able to give good news. The people had been disturbed by
a rumour that some of their islands were to be sold to
America. "I need hardly say that the King's subjects are
not for sale to other governments," he said. "Their destiny,
as free men, is in their hands. Your future is for you yourselves to shape." His ship steamed from the Barbadoes to
the Canal. Every pause as he crossed the great spaces of the
ocean brought him in touch with new aspects of life. At
one end of the Canal he was heralded by three aircraft bearing the stripes of the American Air Service, and at the far
end the natives addressed him in wild and glowing phrases.
"In frantic supplication we fling ourselves at the feet of
Almighty God to shower His blessings upon Your Highness . . ." they pleaded. And at the close they said: "If
we be allowed another paragraph, may we then be per-

mitted, in this final gasp, to express our desire that Your Royal Highness will greatly enjoy your visit to this port?" Their wishes were not in vain. He enjoyed everything.

In his book *Down Under with the Prince*, Everard Cotes wrote many fine descriptions of the scenes of the voyage: of the "yellow turtles, as big as footballs," which stuck out their little pointed heads to watch the ship as it passed, of the "schools of glistening porpoises" leaping in the sun, the houses of San Diego, "set among masses of roses, geraniums, hibiscus and purple salt grass in full bloom." Nor was there a lack of humorous notes in the grand progress. At San Diego the Prince was serenaded by the biggest open-air organ in the world. "The organist sat by the roadside, and the pipes of his instrument pointed unprotected to the sky."

In Honolulu the Prince went to the palace of the old Queen of Hawaii, where busy typewriters and all the paraphernalia of the American administration had supplanted the dreamy state of the closing years of Liliuokalani's reign. There was an official ball for him at night. He wandered on, from one startling scene to another, like a bewildered character in a pantomime, and when the ball was ended he crossed the island to see a *hookupu* gathering. The flood of Japanese and Chinese and American intruders was forgotten for a little hour. The old, fading dream was shaken into life again, and the Hawaiian soldiers passed before him in their yellow robes. An unseen choir sang somewhere so that their voices filtered through the branches of the banyan trees, to the accompaniment of music from gourd lutes. There were dancers, gorgeously decorated with feathers, and, in a hole dug into the well-kept lawn, the carcases of four pigs, quantities of chickens, fish, and sweet potatoes wrapped in green leaves, were roasted by the Hawaiian cooks.

Another day he saw an ingenuous tribute to the work of the English missionaries. The new-fledged Christians threw their native idols to the ground before him as proof

The Prince of Wales leaving for Australia and New Zealand.

of their conversion. "There was a tense moment when the first image had to be flung upon the ground, for superstition dies hard . . . but the image was flung and went into fifty pieces at the feet of civilisation."

H.M.S. *Renown* moved into the sultry waters of the tropics. Neptune came on board, and he demanded the royal victim with glee. The good fellowship of Osborne was called on now: the British capacity to grin through five minutes of discomfort. The Prince was docile while the courtiers of the Equatorial king sang:

> Shave him and bash him,
> Duck him and splash him,
> Torture and smash him
> And don't let him go.

The orders were carried out with brutal precision.

Once across the Equator, the Prince of Wales was in the Southern Hemisphere for the first time. The first port in the new world was Suva, in Fiji. These lovely islands, whose clock was once the sun and whose currency was the shells of the seashore, before the white men came, have lost a little of their charm in becoming outposts of the British Empire. The vigour has gone out of the dark-skinned Fijians, who were once bold eaters of the missionaries and traders who invaded their shores. The Fijian now plays a gramophone and he eats tinned salmon. He has to drown much that is noble and picturesque in exchange for the right to sing "Rule, Britannia!" But there was enough of the old beauty left to please the Prince of Wales while he stayed in Suva. He steamed into the harbour, past the island upon which the natives dance upon red stones, in deference to old and more fierce gods than ours. For a day or two he lived among the Fijians, to their immense delight, and then he sailed on, towards New Zealand.

Chapter Twelve

NEW ZEALAND

He has proved his royalty to be something better than a birthright.—LOS ANGELES TIMES.

Chapter Twelve

NEW ZEALAND

NEW ZEALAND is young in English history, but, through the legends of the Maoris, its story can be traced back to about the time of William the Conqueror. While the Norman was planning his conquest across the Channel, another adventurer stood on the shore of Tahiti and dreamed of unfound islands in the southern oceans of the world. This Tahitian made his brave journey in a canoe, and he landed on the wild shore of New Zealand, killed a bird twice as tall as himself, ate his fill and sailed away again. Two hundred years afterwards his descendants crossed the ocean, and those who survived the horrible journey became the first Maoris of New Zealand.

Seven hundred years passed before the first European colonists made their settlements in the harbours of the new country. That was in the 'forties of the last century. Less than a hundred more years had passed when the Prince of Wales arrived in Auckland in April of 1920. In this time the straggling settlements had grown into the strength of a Dominion. More than a million sturdy New Zealanders waited to greet their King's son. Their character had not been disturbed by the menace of vast spaces or the influence of strange climates. They had made another England in the south. Ninety-eight per cent. of their trade was done with the old country, and when they spoke of England they still called it *Home*. Their emotions were not likely to be confused when they saw the silvery-grey hull of *Renown* moving into the sanctuary of Auckland Harbour.

The Prince came on a glowing, sunny day. Hundreds of quick white yachts sped out over the blue water to meet him, and aeroplanes, juggling with the sunlight, swooped down over the cruiser as she moved in towards the wharves. The street through which he drove, now a buzzing thoroughfare, flanked by tall stone buildings, had been the bed of a dribbling creek not more than eighty years before. It was a dark and mighty river of people as he moved on in his car at the beginning of his conquest. Near to the wharf upon which he landed there had been a little group of Labour agitators, gloomy with discontent. When one of them saw him, a radiant, smiling boy standing in his car, he said: "Well, I am no bloody royalist, but he looks such a decent sort we must give him a cheer."

The Prince's progress was slow, for his eyes were busy. He paused when there was an old soldier, his breast gay with medals, or a child clutching a bunch of flowers. These gestures were simple enough to warm the coldest heart. In the afternoon he moved among thousands of children in the domain, and the people surrounding the ground went mad with delight. Hundreds of them were sitting on top of a galvanised iron fence, and they kicked its corrugations out of shape when they saw the Prince, actually standing in his car, but apparently moving over the heads of the mass of children.

Those who were older realised his nervousness; the incessant clutching at his tie and the continuity of cigarettes. But if within himself he was anxious and bewildered, he did not give in to his own feelings. Day after day he faced the crowds. There was no cessation. As the days passed he went from town to town, and in each of them the people came very near him. Girls patted his pillow when they were shown through the royal train, and little boys stole the toothpicks from his table, as souvenirs. Farmers stopped their ploughs and waved as the train passed between the isolated country towns. Some brought flags with them into the fields so that they could greet him, and women ran out on to the verandahs of their small wooden houses to wave their bed sheets.

The great spectacle was at Roturua, the strange inland

town where the earth is torn by holes of boiling mud, geysers and boiling streams. It is in this fantastic country that the Maoris still live as near to nature as civilisation will allow. These graceful, valiant natives have succumbed to most of our notions of comfort, but some of them remain in the little houses of their ancestors, carving pipes, sunbaking on their verandahs or cooking their food in the natural ovens of the hot earth. The Maoris are poets and they adore the legends of kings. In the midst of their steaming town they have built a memorial to Queen Victoria, and the stiff, severe monarch holds her sceptre over hissing pools and gurgling mudholes. The Maoris flocked about the Prince like excited children. They understood when he said: "It is Queen Victoria's great-grandson who speaks to you to-day." They watched him in silence as he spoke of his father. The King had seen their bravery and sacrifice; he had bidden the Prince praise them for their "faithfulness and valour." They understood when he said: "I will ever keep before me the pattern of Victoria, the great Queen, whose heart was with the Maori people from the day on which they swore allegiance to her rule." Some of them cried when the day was over, and there were groups of wondering Maoris outside his hotel, staring up at his window long into the night. Next day many of them walked in the streets with postcards of their new hero pinned to their clothes.

Eight thousand Maoris danced for him. Their background was the Lake of Rotorua, shining like polished steel. The brown men sauntered into the arena, wearing their gorgeous feather mats. They carried big jade ornaments, and their heads were decorated with plumes. They beat the earth with their naked feet, and the women lashed the ground with green branches. They danced until they were tired: the dances of peace and the dances of war. Then one old man came forward with a great mat made of a million kiwi feathers. This was placed about the Prince's shoulders.

From Rotorua the Prince travelled south, through the
pasture country and over the great mountains, to Wellington. Here was none of the spaciousness of Canadian life,
the stark differences between East and West; the hardship
and the isolation of the white stretches of the Arctic. New
Zealand seemed to be a prosperous, gracious little country,
sedately British and asking no more of the world than the
opinion that it was " just like England." The Prince found
people who spoke affectionately of the counties from which
their grandparents came: they showed him the few objects
which had been carried across the world in the windjammers of one hundred years ago; the old prints, the clocks
and the pictures, because these were their tangible bonds
with the parent England. In Taranaki he walked where
Charles Armitage Brown landed in the 'forties, carrying
with him the pencil portrait he had made of Keats, who
was his friend. In Wellington he was told the story of
Alfred Domett, Browning's friend, named Waring in his
poem, who went to New Zealand and wrote the first considerable verses owing their inspiration to the Maori
people. At every step the Prince was reminded of the clear
Englishness of New Zealand's story. And he might have
marvelled at the intensity of sentiment which makes these
southern people celebrate their Christmas with hot turkey,
and plum pudding, and cards, with robins and snow and
holly, although Christmas Day with them is usually one of
broiling summer heat. New Zealand did not present any
subtle problems of race for the Prince; there were no alarming undercurrents of political chicanery to disturb him.
His smile, his graciousness and his indefatigable interest
were enough to satisfy all who saw him.

In almost every town some little incident relieved the
monotony of splendour: some incident which allowed the
New Zealanders to discover the anxious heart of the growing man . . . and sometimes the remaining mischief of
the boy. One day he drove the engine of the royal train,
and in Rotorua he rode on a merry-go-round. One evening

he crept downstairs in the hotel in which he was staying
and wrote on a slate: "Call Lord Louis Mountbatten at
five o'clock." When Lord Louis Mountbatten was awakened
at five next morning he was very angry, until the slate was
brought to him and he recognised the writing on it.

The Prince crossed from the north island of New Zealand
to the south, over the water by which a sailing ship had
carried letters to Charlotte Brontë from her friend Mary
Taylour, after she had joined the little colony. The Prince
went among the mining towns of the west coast, and then
he crossed the Alps and came to the country from which
Samuel Butler conjured up the fanciful world of Erewhon.
He passed through Butler's "millions on millions of acres
of the most beautiful grass country in the world," he followed the "broiling stream which descended from the
glaciers," and he came to Christchurch, the most English
city in New Zealand. The cheering went on. There was
never a moment of quiet. Day after day, fresh thousands of
people sang "God Bless the Prince of Wales." Sometimes
he would halt the procession of cars to step down and speak
to some old woman in her bath chair beside the road.
Windows of cottages were wide open so that he could hear
gramophones inside playing "God Save the King" as he
passed. Every simple device was tried to show the happiness of the people. Even the prisoners in gaols were allowed
to sit on top of the high walls and cheer him. Behind all
this marvellous noise of happiness he carried the burden
of days of strain. One incident shows that his natural kindliness was not yet soured within him. In one town his
servant's hand was cut while he was closing the door of the
Prince's motor-car. This was early in the morning. During
the day he met hosts of officials in several towns, and he
spoke to perhaps five different gatherings of people. He
arrived in the last town in the evening, tired and only wishing to rest. But his first question was for the servant. Was
he badly cut? The Prince saw to it that the man's hand
was bandaged before he went to bed.

The Children

Towards the close of the journey through New Zealand those who lived near to the Prince were able to observe the changes which experience was bringing to him. In one sense he was deceived as to the value of his travels. For ever meeting new people, he gathered a superficial, photographic view of human nature. He stored information, and his kindliness guided him to a sympathetic concern for all who came before him. But the knowledge was transient and disconnected. He was like a camera, catching fresh faces and views. The hurry in which he lived made it impossible for him to enjoy the deeper, valuable experience of the portrait painter, who concentrates upon an individual and learns to seek into character and to know men's hearts. He was never still long enough to experience the difficulty of making a friend or of digging beyond the surface. This speed of living was to affect all his life and his judgement of human nature; it was also to contribute to his unhappiness, when the test of his character came, in the winter of 1936.

The fairest field of his influence was among the children. They naturally adored him because he did not disappoint their story-book conception of what a prince should be. More than this, their untroubled instincts guided them to see immediately the quality of his sympathy. He was equally delighted by the thousands of children who threw their hearts to him. When he returned to England he spoke to a company of Londoners at the Guildhall. "I did not see one single child who did not reflect in its healthy, happy little face that spirit of well-being which is the pride of both these countries," he said. He added, of the New Zealanders: "You have here in the city of London a very sound and powerful notion of patriotism, but I can assure you you would have your work cut out to feel it and show it more than they do in New Zealand."

The Prince returned to England from each of his Empire journeys with a fresh store of information. He became more practical, and the newspapers which described him as his father's greatest ambassador soon talked of him as England's best commercial traveller. He became more and more interested in the fresh ideas about Empire Economic Unity, and he used his inherited talent for accumulating information to learn more of his country's trade. " I would wear a different suit for every man I meet if it would help British trade," he said. Older people were almost shocked by his business-like air, and they sometimes hinted that his dignity was risked when he made so many practical efforts to catch business for Britain in the countries which he visited. They might have turned back to a letter which was written by Charles II to the Shogun, who ruled Japan under the Emperor:

> " England affords such great varieties and quantities of woollen clothes and stuff fit for the clothing of all sorts of persons, which not only tends to ye great health and fortifying ye spirits of and delight to them to wear them, especially in such climates as your Empire, but are much more lasting and cheaper than other clothes."

The Prince of Wales was not the first of his line to beat the drum in the name of British trade. In New Zealand, his patronage of a little-known food turned it into a prosperous industry. On the coast of New Zealand there is a shellfish called toheroa, which makes soup more subtle in flavour than oyster soup. He liked it and he asked for more. It became the Prince of Wales's soup overnight. Its fame spread, and now New Zealand has a small but solid industry, for toheroa soup has become fashionable in England. It was a small beginning to the Prince's influence in trade, but greater ways of help were to be opened for him. In March of 1933 the *Express* called him the Prince of Salesmen, when Messrs. Vickers, Ltd., made a contract worth three million pounds with the Central Railway of Brazil. Lord Dudley announced that the order "was due to conversation between the Prince of Wales and Rio de Janeiro authorities." Although the Prince soon became astute in pouncing upon such opportunities in foreign countries, it was trade within the Empire which interested him most. At the time when the Commons smiled at Edward Marjoribanks for talking of Empire Free Trade, the Prince of Wales was already busy prying into every market in which his hopes could be realised.

Chapter Thirteen

AUSTRALIA

The splendours that belong
Unto the fame of earth are but a wind,
That in the same direction lasts not long.
                                        MRS. RAMSAY.

Chapter Thirteen

AUSTRALIA

THE Tasman Sea separates the Australians and the New Zealanders as definitely as the Atlantic divides the English from the Americans. It is astonishing that two countries can be so near, drawing their colonists from the same parent stock, yet growing up so different in aims and character. The New Zealander is still in love with the past, but the Australian, bred more hardly, is inclined to question tradition and to insist upon greater freedom. Mrs. Gaskell wrote of the Yorkshireman what might also be said of the Australian:

> "The affections are strong and their foundations lie deep. . . . Their accost is curt; their accent and tone of speech blunt and harsh. . . . They have a quick perception of character and a keen sense of humour: the dwellers among them must be prepared for certain uncomplimentary, though most likely true, observations, pithily expressed. Their feelings are not easily roused, but their duration is lasting. Hence there is much close friendship and faithful service."

English people still cling to the foolish legends of Botany Bay and they sometimes imagine that the early criminal colony casts a shadow over Australian affairs to-day. You may sail up Sydney Harbour and be told that the prisoners penned on one of the little islands did not dare attempt escape because of the sharks. You may be told that in another place the prisoners were flogged and made to walk into the sea with quicklime burning in their wounds. These pictures, still surviving in foolish English novels, may be terrible and picturesque, but the life faded from them long ago. Australia has its own character, of fortitude, courage and independence, and its loyalty is as lively as that of the other Dominions, in spite of its experiments in Labour government.

The Prince of Wales did not miss the difference between the two countries. When he returned to London he spoke of the "old country character of the people" in New Zealand, but when he talked of the Australians he recalled their "genius for sport and enjoyment," their "courage and self-confidence" and their "happiness."

The Australians were loyal after the war, but, as one of their writers confessed, they had become apathetic about "crowns, thrones and all this monarchy business." The Prince broke down this apathy in a day, and the *Sydney Sun*, a brave and independent newspaper, wrote of him: "Before the Prince landed the popular idea of princes was of something haughty and remote, but this smiling, appealing, youthful man . . . smiled away the difference which Australians believe lay between royalty and the commonalty."

Melbourne's harbour was so deep in fog when *Renown* turned in from the open sea that the Australian destroyers had to steam out to meet the Prince, and one of them, H.M.A.S. *Anzac*, came alongside and took him on board. She carried him into Melbourne at forty knots, against a ten-knot tide. The fog politely lifted before such a splendid performance, and the Prince saw Melbourne suddenly freed of its mist. From that moment Australia accepted him and loved him.

Melbourne repeated New Zealand's welcome: the same crowded streets, the same high buildings with people clinging to every window-sill and cornice; the same multitude of flags and banners, and the vast company of school-children, spelling the word WELCOME in human letters, across a great lawn. The mayors smiled and enjoyed the glitter of their chains in the sun, and the politicians bowed and smiled and handed the crumbs of their success on to their shy, proud wives. When the Prince's carriage passed along the streets the shouting was wild and happy, but the Australians did not forget their homely political differences when the politicians came along in his wake. The amazing Mr. Hughes was chaffed, cheered and damned within the space of a hundred yards. There was also Mr. Storey, described as " red all through." The Prince's chief personal victory was with him. Mr. Storey became his liegeman within half an hour, and never to the day he died did he cease to speak of the royal visitor with affection.

But it was about Mr. Hughes that the vital interests were centred. This picturesque little man, who had begun life in humbleness and poverty, was the most dynamic Australian the Prince could meet. Only Australia could have produced this ruthless, clever politician, with the imagination of a poet and the vitality of a comet. He was a strange guide for the royal visitor, but, through their talks together, the Prince was able to learn much from him. Mr. Hughes revealed the Australian character to him: the difference between the old world and the new. That he was aware of this difference was shown when he said of the Australians, on his return to London: " We must do our utmost to . . . appreciate their point of view and to enter into their dreams."

When the Prince's easy conquest of Melbourne was over he went to the hinterland from which the city draws its prosperity. He walked over the rich earth, with its crops of oats and its thousands of sheep grazing at the feet of the low blue hills. He walked on the edge of the impenetrable forests of eucalyptus, the sad and beautiful tree which fills the valleys and covers the lower slopes of the Australian mountains. The Australian painter has turned to the eucalyptus as Crome did to the oak. The sight of one carefully nursed eucalyptus tree in an English garden can awaken a vision of all Australia to those who have been in the South. There are retired governors and officials who treasure one delicate tree in their English garden, just as jealously and with as much sentiment as an Englishman exiled in a colony tends the oak which he has planted on the edge of the bush.

Slowly, the strange new sights and smells of Australia added to the Prince's understanding of the country. He went to the deserted gold mines of Ballarat, where the fields are scarred by the holes dug by the early prospectors. The girls of Ballarat gave him a suit of yellow silk pyjamas to which each one of them had contributed a stitch. There was imagination in all the tributes. In Bendigo he travelled under an arch of girls who dropped flowers on his car as he passed. There was no rest and he had to face enthusiasm which might have killed him had his will been weaker or his pleasure less intense. As he went from town to town the Australians themselves became anxious. "Human strength is unequal to the tasks which have been set," one of the reporters wrote. Australia showed that there was sensitiveness as well as enthusiasm in its heart by abandoning some of the plans and allowing him a rest. His hands were swollen from greeting so many people and he was very tired, but good rewards came for all that he did. A new arch had been built on the wharf while he was in Melbourne, and as he walked under it to go on board *Renown* again, he looked up and read the words: "Australia is proud of you."

Every day, during the long journeys across new stretches of country, cables were sent to the King and Queen. The stories of their son's success were written into glowing messages from the governors who entertained him. The descriptions were always of his charm, his smile, his popularity. On the surface, King George and Queen Mary had every reason for being proud. But they wondered, many times, over the wisdom of this haphazard travelling, this roaming, suitcase existence, in which nothing was permanent for him. It is said that Queen Mary was most concerned over the effect upon her son, and that she once said that he would lose all power of ever settling down if the restless career went on. But the acclamation was too loud and the superficial signs of success were too convincing for doubt and reason to be of use. The King and Queen were forced to dismiss their own doubts and to accept the reports of the growing epic. They were asked to believe that their son was winning his spurs and to excuse the trouble of his spirit in favour of the popularity of his name.

The Prince left Melbourne in the shadows of evening, and the last sounds which came to him as *Renown* steamed out to sea were of the aeroplanes overhead, flying out so that their farewell would be prolonged as long as possible.

Again the welcome began at sea, near to the great heads of Sydney Harbour. The cruisers and destroyers guided the Prince in to the broad, lovely water upon which five hundred yachts dipped their flags and five hundred launches marked their courses with skirts of foam. Here the landing was more simple, for the Prince stepped ashore upon the beach and he entered Sydney under arches of wool bales and corn sheaves. The most splendid scene was at the dinner in the Town Hall. Seven hundred men sat down to dine on the floor of the hall, but, in the galleries, three thousand women sat. They did no more than whisper and shuffle as they looked down on the feast. They were there on sufferance, they felt, and they could only gape at the stretches of linen, the glittering silver and the heads of the great. But their moment came. The Prince stood up and proposed the toast of " The Ladies." Three thousand flags were suddenly raised, and the heights of the Town Hall shivered with colour and rang with cheers. It was one of the most startling and beautiful scenes of all his journey. As the dinner went on, thousands more people waited outside, a dense mass stretching down the side streets. As the toasts were proposed the words were repeated from within to without and then down each avenue of watchers. It seemed that all the million people in the city of Sydney were dining with the Prince that night.

Politicians had to be tactful as the Prince passed through

their countries. They had to remember the aftermath when every word they had spoken would be danced in front of them again. One can therefore believe that Mr. Hughes was speaking for his country when he said at the Commonwealth dinner: "Times, circumstances and the age-long struggles for freedom by men who held liberty dearer than life have fashioned the constitution under which we live. The monarchy is an integral part of it. If Britain decided to adopt a republic form of government, that would be the end of the Empire as we know it to-day."

The man in the Sydney street may have said, "I am not so keen on kings," but this was perhaps not what he meant in his heart. The Australians' revolt has never been against monarchy, but against decadence and signs of death. It is only because they have so often been the victims of Englishmen who have departed from their country for their country's good that they are sceptical of the value of an old civilisation. The Australian who has not travelled may be excused for imagining the nonsensical fellow who arrives in Australia full of airs to be a true Englishman, and his prejudices are easily understood. The Prince of Wales gave Australia a new light upon royalty, but he also gave many people in the South a new conception of the English aristocracy. They marvelled at his energy, his reasonable interest in industry and, above all, his inability to patronise. This was, perhaps, one of his greatest treasures in character. Upon his example Australia revised its opinion of the ruling classes of England, and the people of the Antipodes saw, through him, that the monarchy stood for the perpetuity of national life and not for the transient phases of its political existence. This impression of the Prince did not fade as the years passed, and it was a reason why Australians expressed their concern in sorrow rather than indignation when King Edward decided to abandon his throne in 1936.

The Australian liked the Prince most of all for the way he behaved after his train was overturned through a

carriage leaping from the rails. He had been to the west
to see the orange and apple country, the sawmills and log-
ging camps, and he was on his way back to Perth. The
carriage in which he was travelling left the rails, and before
the engine-driver could stop the train, the two rear carriages
had turned over, with their wheels in the air. The horror
did not last for very long, but the sensations of the officials
who hurried towards the royal carriage are terrible to
imagine. As they came near to his overturned carriage,
members of the Prince's staff appeared, one by one, crawl-
ing out of the windows. Some were hurt, and one had his
shin badly cut. The Prince was the last to appear. He had
stayed behind, he said, to gather his papers together. His
genius for managing awkward moments was now in full
flower. He thanked the officials for at last arranging something which was not on the official programme and then
went on to Perth by car. He arrived at the luncheon party
which had been arranged for him, apologised for being
late and did not even mention the reason for the delay.
Now he was Australia's friend. The toughest station hand
read the story of the accident and felt that the Prince could
never disappoint him.

The Prince went on and he came to South Australia. In
some places the aborigines walked a hundred miles to see
the royal train crossing the desert. He drove under arches
of fruit and vegetables, and beds were carried out of hospitals on to the pavements so that the patients could see
him pass. He went to the wine country and then he crossed
to Tasmania. One of the most interesting experiences of
the tour was in Queensland, where the Prince was the guest
of a Labour Government. The tune did not change, and
when he left Brisbane, "everybody waved something; if it
were not a handkerchief, a flag or a hat, it was the nearest
thing at hand." Mr. Everard Cotes, who was with the
Prince, wrote: "I saw a vegetable hawker flourishing his
biggest cabbage, a housewife excitedly using a tablecloth
as a signal of affection, a company of railway carriage

cleaners throwing their dusters upon the wind." He went south once more, and when he came to the border between Queensland and New South Wales the Prince travelled "over a carpet woven of yellow wattle flowers."

Then Australia gave him his reward. He was allowed to leave the crowds and the noise and to rest in the country. His father had also rested in this way when he went to Australia as a boy. The Prince crossed the Blue Mountains, and out in the sweet, sunny places beyond he chased emus and kangaroos and he rode over undulating hills. He went into the Australian homesteads and he shared the food of the squatters he found there. He stayed on the Canoubar run, and, losing the tiredness and nerves which had conquered him towards the end of his travelling, he became fit again. Australia gave him back his health and colour, and, as the squatter who rode with him on the last day said, he returned to Sydney "as fresh as a daisy."

There was no end to the imagination of the Australians in their entertainment. Just after *Renown* had sailed from the wharf in Sydney, on the way to Fiji, the Prince's letters arrived from Adelaide, by air. They were letters from England and they could not wait. A fast cruiser, which was already under steam, sped out in the wake of *Renown* and reached her in time to hand over the Prince's letters at the Harbour heads. "I refuse to say good-bye," he said on the last day in Sydney. "I have become so fond of Australia now that she can never be far from my thoughts, wherever I may be."

The Prince steamed away towards the tropics once more. First came Fiji and then Samoa, where the natives presented him with roasted pigs and island beer. The kaleidoscope kept on tumbling new shapes before his eyes. The sleepy and charming Samoans, so recently snatched away from German rule, begged him to ask his father, the King, not to forget "this small branch of the great tree of the Empire." He climbed up the flank of Mount Vaea, upon

1920. *The Prince of Wales in Australia : Perth, June, 1920.*

which Robert Louis Stevenson is buried. From beside the
grave he was able to look down upon the silver-blue
expanse of the Pacific and the nearer white fringe of foam
where the water broke upon the coast. The world called
to the Prince, and he hurried down Vaea, through the
warm, tropical forest and to the shore line. The ship was
waiting to carry him back to Europe. He paused for a
little time in the town, to observe the awkward new
machinery of British government which was trying to spin
a network of law and order for the islanders. He went to
Vailima, whence Stevenson's ghost has long been chased
away by the noise of typewriters and busy official pens.
Then to the sea.

The Prince crossed the Equator once more and he returned to Honolulu, to the hot sands of Waikiki and the
sophistication of American life. He went to Acapulco
Harbour and then through the Panama Canal to Trinidad.
The grey shape of *Renown* steamed on from island to
island, but the dreams became thin, for the Prince was
coming nearer and nearer to England. The West Indians
danced for him and they sang for him. They put in a little
word of protest about the laziness of British traders. The
Americans were so clever and the British were slow, they
said. But their tongues were not sharp when they complained. They sang at the end, and they showered flowers
on him as he drove to the pitch lake and to the plantations
of cocoa and sugar.

British Guiana followed Trinidad and then came
Grenada. As he travelled nearer home his ancestral voices
were heard in place of the new songs of the South. At
Castries he climbed to the fort over which the Duke of
Kent had hoisted the British flag one hundred and twenty
years before. No figure could remind him of duty more
than that of his great-great-grandfather, who loved parades,
punctuality, clocks and efficiency.

Columbus had also sailed this way, and when the Prince
came to Antigua he was able to look out over the water on

which Cromwell's ships had been attacked three hundred years before. Here, too, Nelson had refitted his ships before Trafalgar. The voices of the new countries of the South were drowned for the traveller now. He came nearer to the Old World, and only the Bermudas lay between him and England. The greeting in Bermuda was as picturesque as the landscape. The Prince drove around the island and he passed under an arch which had been specially made for him from blocks of coral rock. Early in October he steamed over the last stretch of sea in his long journey, and on the 11th Portsmouth put on a thick fog and welcomed him home.

Chapter Fourteen

LIFE IN ENGLAND. RETURNED SOLDIERS

And they made sacrifice to the eternal gods and prayed that they might escape from death and the evil of war.—ILIAD, Book II.

Chapter Fourteen

LIFE IN ENGLAND. RETURNED SOLDIERS

Two years had passed during the Prince's journeys to Canada and the Antipodes, and when he returned to London he was almost a stranger. His brothers were creating their own interests, and the friends he had made at Oxford or during the war were caught up in their own affairs. He was already paying the penalty of his unique position, for he was more like a colonial coming home than an Englishman who had just returned from his travels. His interests and his viewpoint were wandering from the English path, and the gap between the Prince and his family was widening in consequence. He made his own way and his own friends, and, as he took up new interests, he became attached to two problems which stirred his sympathy almost to the end. He devoted himself to Empire trade and to the care of the returned soldiers.

The Prince of Wales realised that there was a wide gap between British business men and the trade of the new countries, and just as his father had told his contemporaries at the Guildhall after his world tour that the " old country " must wake up, so the Prince was frank with his warning. " You have to go away from the old country and see it from a distance," he said. He told them of the Dominions "watching with intense anxiety " the ways by which England was facing her " grave social and economic problems." In every speech which he made, no matter for what cause, he hinted at the sleepiness of England and the need for a quickened understanding with the Dominions. When he went to Oxford to " receive the highest honour the University can give," he talked of the " much shorter gown " which he had worn as an undergraduate, of his pride at being an Oxford man and of the happiness which he had found there. But he soon came upon the real field of his knowledge, the countries of the Empire. He suddenly realised that he was "apt to be long-winded" on the topic and he talked again of Oxford. But there was no doubt as to where his anxiety and interests lay.

By this time the Prince had become a good speaker. The halting phrases and shyness had disappeared after he had made five hundred speeches in the Dominions. The Dons who had known him as an undergraduate were especially pleased. Even if he had not become "bookish," he had become vastly interesting as a talker. He had a talent for crowding information and thought into a thousand words, a talent for balancing ideas, humour and sense. His thoroughness helped him. Secretaries gathered facts for him, but it was always his own hand which gave the final form to what he wished to say. His address to the Royal National Lifeboat Association, running into almost four thousand words, can still be read with interest, for it is lively with information. The Prince did not show great imagination, nor did he employ lordly language in these early addresses. He revealed an average, practical mind, and he often made the boast, "We are a people of common sense." His speeches were impressive, even without imagination and fine words to commend them, for he always fired them with his own sincerity and lightened them with touches of simple humour and, most effective of all, his engaging smile.

As he went from one audience to another the Prince's interests naturally grew. His royal gift of zeal and energy illuminated every occasion. He became more at ease with his little jokes and more confident of his thought. He spoke at the farewell dinner to Mr. Davis, the departing American Ambassador, and he opened the new building of the Chamber of Horticulture. He spoke at Cambridge, and he shook his listeners into laughter when he began, in a quiet, rather plaintive voice: "I am an Oxford man." He

stood beside Admiral Sims to receive his degree, and he
was made Chancellor of the University of Wales. There
he turned the tables on Mr. Balfour, who had addressed
him at Cambridge in Latin. The Prince said that it was a
tongue with which he was not as familiar as he should be.
But he retaliated brilliantly by addressing Mr. Balfour in
Welsh. He could not help thinking that Mr. Balfour
" understood considerably less " of his remarks than he did
of what Mr. Balfour had said to him at Cambridge the week
before. But there was no sentimental nonsense or mere
word spinning as the Prince increased the field of his influence. When he spoke to the London Chamber of Commerce he remained loyal to his simple toast. He asked the
guests to drink to " The British Empire and British
Common Sense."

There was another problem which went deeper with the
Prince than his interest in the trade and life of the Empire.
His natural anxiety made him turn, again and again, to the
returned soldiers. To a nature which was appalled by
suffering, the problem of restoring health, security and self-
respect to the men who were broken by the war was so
terrible that the Prince was almost dramatically unhappy.
He was naturally affectionate and gentle, but he was
denied experiences which would have satisfied this side of
his nature. Those who observed him have said that, lacking
a focus for his natural affections, he developed what might
be described as an obsession about those in want. He did
not consider them in relation to other classes, which was
necessary from the point of view of the State. He could not
tread quietly or work cautiously, which was the true and
helpful way with the poor. Sometimes he helped causes less
than he would otherwise have done because of his exuberance and emotion. But he was unique in the way that he
guided public thought from the dangers of pure veneration
of the dead at the expense of the maimed and workless. In
this his practical sense guided him. When he spoke at the
Mansion House he said: " In six days we are celebrating

the second anniversary of Armistice Day, when the whole nation will pay a solemn tribute to the glorious dead. This tribute, however, must not end there. . . . Some 20,000 officers, 20,000 disabled and 250,000 fit men are seeking work. . . . It is up to us."

The Prince threw himself into the cause of the returned men, sometimes to the exclusion of his rest and often at the expense of his brief pleasures. Once when he was away hunting he learned that the ex-Service men's exhibition at the White City was languishing for want of support. Without a moment of hesitation he abandoned his hunting and hurried up to London. He went to the White City and did not rest until he had made the exhibition into a success through his patronage and encouragement. His feelings were simple and strong. "I want all ex-Service men throughout the Empire to look on me as a comrade," he said. The words were not empty, and, as long as he was Prince of Wales, he did not weaken in his promise.

The busy heir to the throne lived a second, rather secret life during the brief spells in London. He was not content to dispense pity and help from his place near to the throne. He became like a young father to many suffering people, and he bestowed his kindliness and sympathy from his own doorstep. One day when he was in France he had come upon a stretcher-bearer who was serving with the Canadians. The Prince had spoken to him as he passed, some little phrase of kindness which the man did not forget. Life had been harsh with the stretcher-bearer, and the sudden smile and good word must have come at the moment when they were needed. The man was shot in the spine during the battle of the Somme in 1916, and for ten years he lay on a bed in London, a living but motionless body in a framework of plaster. Sheet after sheet was placed under his withering body until he was lying in a mass of plaster three feet thick. His great pride during these horrible years was that he had once been spoken to by the Prince of Wales. When he knew that he was dying, the Prince became the focus for the man's tired brain, and he talked of little else but the scene in the trenches. The story reached York House, and in the morning, when he was told, the Prince wrote a message upon his photograph and sent it before he was even dressed, in case it should not arrive in time to please the man before he died.

Chapter Fifteen

KING GEORGE AS A FATHER

*Behold, a king shall reign in righteousness,
and princes shall rule in judgement.*—ISAIAH
XXXII. 1.

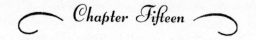

Chapter Fifteen

KING GEORGE AS A FATHER

THE Prince was settling down to the comparative orderliness of his English life, and he was beginning to use his energies of mind and body with fixed purposes. But the Government did not forget the success of his visits to Canada and Australia and New Zealand, and it was suggested that he should be sent across the world once more, this time to attempt the conquest of India. The tragedy of these restless years increases as the story of King Edward is unfolded. It seems to lead on, with growing tempo, to the state of mind in which he signed his abdication in 1936. It is doubtful whether the Government was justified in making this fresh demand upon him so soon after his return to England. Queen Mary had been the first to protest against these dangers, and now that the journey to India was proposed she spoke once more. But Government policy and political usage could not wait upon the subtleties of a growing character. All the fixed principles upon which his nature might have grown were shaken once more. Even Queen Mary's infinite tact and wisdom could not survive these gaps of separation, when her son moved like a comet, beyond her control and beyond the kindly and wise influence which she exercised. For most British people the estrangement of King Edward came suddenly, during the dark month of 1936, but for his mother it began ten years before, when an eager and shortsighted Government exploited her son's charm and talents to the full, sending him hurrying when he should have remained with his parents to grow more and more into the strength of their family example. The theme bears reiteration, for it is like a mournful chorus in a Greek tragedy, warning us of the destruction with which the story ends.

135

The love which might have sustained Prince Edward was constantly interrupted and confused by Government plans, and it must be an added reason for remorse when we realise what the loss of his mother's influence must have meant to him. At Osborne, at Dartmouth and Oxford Prince Edward had not strayed too far from this quiet, wise counsel. One recalls the refreshing scene at Oxford when Queen Mary went through her son's accounts with his servant. Simple domestic questions were not beyond her ken, and when she saw an item for one penny appearing in each day's accounts she asked what it was for. It was, the servant told her, "for His Royal Highness's morning apple."

The Prince of Wales showed more of his mother's qualities as he grew older; above all, her social conscience. Queen Mary has one strength in common with Queen Victoria. She has never attracted people of inferior character about her. She has never suffered the danger which besets so many royal persons of falling prey to the soft voices of sycophants. One of the Queen's ladies-in-waiting once said of her: "It is not only that she attracts people of character. It is more than that. One could not be near to the King or Queen without *developing* character. Nobody could serve them without growing. They give the best that is in them, and, somehow, one finds oneself giving the best that is in oneself. The Queen *makes* character in those who are near her. It is a privilege to serve her and be near her. One realises, slowly, that only the best is good enough for her, and she inspires one to grow in capacity to give the best in return."

At this time and during the years that followed the King and Queen came to represent a new power in English life because of their simplicity and their devotion to duty. Foreign writers no longer belittled the strength of constitutional monarchy, because King George had proved character to be as powerful as prerogative in guiding his Parliament. He had never failed his people, and a genuine

1920. *The Prince of Wales with Queen Alexandra at the christening of
Lady Patricia Ramsay's son.*

affection, in no sense passive, went out to him and to his
Queen wherever they went. Londoners, going home past
Buckingham Palace, would look at the simple stone façade
and feel more safe and contented for the life which went on
inside it. The King was never spectacular, but he had
given England the complete example of what a gentleman
should be; not a gentleman dependent upon class consciousness, but a good man, in the way his grandfather had been.

At a time when no Englishman had a great personal influence in the country, when Mr. Lloyd George's war service and brilliance were forgotten, when Mr. Winston
Churchill was mistrusted in spite of his great talents, when
Mr. Ramsay MacDonald was already a platitudinarian and
Mr. Baldwin seemed to be an honest shade, when we were
so immersed in the second-rate that we had almost forgotten
what a great man looked like, the King became necessary
to our faith in English character. Some time afterwards
an anonymous writer in an American magazine* described
the "paradox" of "the small man" who "filled a great
throne more completely than that throne has been filled in
250 years." The writer familiarly said: "George may not
be criticised, for he is England." And then: "George V is
the most successful of modern British kings because he is
the King for whom the British Constitution has been waiting from its earliest days." The writer was allowed more
liberties than his English contemporaries, and he went on
to discuss King George's life as a parent. He rightly decided
that after the King was married, the "retired naval
officer had become the stern Victorian father whose word
was law. The exemplary commander of the *Thrush* had
become the exemplary Victorian husband with a dislike for
the unfamiliar, a routine as regular as the sun's and a rigid
sense of duty. Children did not speak unless spoken to—
and the parental voice was a voice which could be heard
and obeyed even by an eldest son. . . ."

* *Fortune*, June, 1935. It has been said that the King read this
article and preferred its frankness above any tribute that had been
paid to him in print.

It is true that King George was an exacting parent. His discipline made it difficult for him to comprehend the shaken generation which matured through the war. He had deep respect for those who had been brave and compassion for those who were maimed or in sorrow, but his own insistent self-government did not help him to estimate the psychological distress of the generation which returned to England, only to find that they no longer spoke the same language as the old. The Sovereign's influence therefore lay in his example rather than in sensitive understanding. King George was a critical father, but he never weighed his sons down with the sentimental appeals about parents and children which had been the family stronghold of the Victorians. He disliked humbug and the melancholy habits of Victorian mourning; the bogies of memorials and public grief were anathema to him. His view of life and death was sane and healthy, and he did not allow his sons to suffer from the black-edged devotion to the past which had menaced his peace of mind when he was young. He no doubt felt very keenly the memory of his own boyhood, when he had been obliged to attend memorial services to relatives he had not even known. This view of death went with a sublime, devotional character. His faith was not clogged with theology, neither did it condone weakness. It was the steady star of his example which was the chief strength of his influence over his sons. It was not always easy to live up to his example, but there was never any doubt as to the quality of his standards or the resolve with which he kept them.

One misfortune of sending the heir to the throne on so many expeditions lay in the separation from these two influences in his life. The new countries gained something through fuller comprehension of the English spirit, and the Prince learned much by information and through knowledge of the habits of the men he met. But the knowledge was gathered too quickly and in choking quantities, so that it did not have the opportunity of growing into wisdom.

The wonder of his achievement as Prince of Wales is increased when we remember these circumstances. We still lack the perspective down which we might see him clearly and value his success and his failure. But we are far enough away from the events of 1921 to realise what an enormous task was put upon him when he sailed for India; a task from which the most sophisticated diplomat might have shrunk in alarm.

In 1921 the Prince went to Brighton and dedicated a memorial to Indian soldiers who had been killed in the "fire and stress of Flanders." He spoke of the wounded Indian soldiers who had been brought to England. "India never forgets kindness and sympathy," he said, "and from this chateri a wave of goodwill will pass to India." Then he expressed his hope that the memorial, which was "instinct with compassion and mutual regard," should "strengthen the ties between India and our country."

Early in October the Prince went to India to test the ties of which he had spoken at Brighton some months before. He had crossed the Atlantic and the Pacific; he had gone by the ways of Columbus and Tasman and Cook. Now he went in the wake of Marco Polo. Canada and Australia and New Zealand had been new and shining countries with no history of civilisation beyond what French and British people had given them. Now the Prince travelled over water and to lands with stories older than Christendom. He was to travel forty-one thousand miles, by ship, by train, by motor-car and by elephant.

He went by the oldest way in the world, but the fashion of his going belonged to the twentieth century. The story was still of soldiers in khaki, clicking their heels on the parade grounds of Egypt, of grey cruisers dipping their flags and of dignitaries reading their addresses of welcome.

Gibraltar came first. More than a hundred years before the Prince's great-great-grandfather had walked up the slopes of Gibraltar and had come upon a gipsy fortune-teller, who asked him to cross his palm with silver. She had told him that he would marry and that his daughter would become queen of a great country.

Moors and Spaniards, sailors, nuns and priests joined with the English in making the day in Gibraltar gay for the Prince. Their houses were covered with banners of red and white and blue . . . the sky between the narrow, bustling streets was hidden by the flags they had stretched between their houses. They sang and cheered until ten o'clock at night, when *Renown* steamed into the Mediterranean. Hundreds of men stood upon the harbour walls, swinging red, white and blue lights upon the water's edge, giving the dark, lofty rock a hem of jewels.

The next place was Malta, where the Prince walked towards the Palace to the sound of clapping instead of cheering. The widows of Maltese soldiers, wearing huge black hoods, smiled sadly at him. He opened the first Maltese Parliament, and he went to the gymkhana, where he " had first to run in a sack for twenty yards, then ride one hundred yards on a bareback mule, then be carried fifty yards on a stretcher, mount a pony and ride fifty yards, be wheeled in a barrow another twenty yards and then be driven for a final one hundred yards in a native vehicle known as a *carosse*." He did not win the race, but his triumph with the Maltese was now complete. That he had opened Parliament did not matter very much after such a gallant performance. Their best memory of him was of a rather untidy figure being rushed along the ground in a wheelbarrow pushed, a little uncertainly, by Lord Louis Mountbatten.

H.M.S. *Renown* steamed into the mouth of the Canal at Port Said in the evening just as the jumbled, noisy streets of the town were darkening. The Prince went ashore: he rode along the waterfront, and then he returned to *Renown* to entertain the great men of Egypt at dinner. At dawn the ship moved into the Canal; in some places the rusting barbed wire of the Turkish defences still lay in twisted heaps in the sand. The Egyptians came to the water's edge;

little, black-dressed women with their babies in their arms, and their thin, sharp-eyed men, who shouted to the white Prince as he passed. Hundreds of soldiers lined up on the edge of the Canal in their smart khaki shorts to cheer. The Prince came to Ismailia, where he had stayed during the war. *Renown* moved on slowly through the narrow waterway to Suez. She passed through the Red Sea, within sight of the gaunt, brown-gold peak of Sinai, piercing the hot sky, and on November 12 the Prince went ashore at Aden. The gaunt, flowerless little town greeted him splendidly, and over the wharf on which he landed was spread a banner asking him to " Tell daddy we are all happy under British rule." White men jostled brown men on the kerbstone. The exalted of Aden came to swear their allegiance to him; they wore gold brocade and they carried jewelled swords. The old Sultan of Lahej, heavy with his hundred years and almost blind, also came, dressed in rich purple. Another Arab wore green silk and his feet were dyed with henna. The Prince was leaving the Northern Hemisphere, and the glory of the East had begun.

Chapter Sixteen

INDIA

You have lived and are living true to the letter and spirit of the classic motto of your royal rank . . . "I serve."—From the Address of Welcome to the Prince by the University of Bombay.

Chapter Sixteen

INDIA

H.M.S. *Renown* moved into the Indian Ocean. The vultures and swallows of Egypt no longer flew over the ship. Porpoises gleamed in the undulations of warm, blue water. The Prince came nearer and nearer to the most difficult and subtle problem of his travels. There was a stain upon the face of India's loyalty, for, as the Prince travelled on, Gandhi was perfecting his plans to boycott him wherever he went. On November 17 the Prince stood before the Gateway of India. In front of him were the people of Bombay, certain of their own loyalty, but afraid of the menaces that waited for him in the hinterland. He wore a white uniform and the broad blue ribbon of the Star of India. He walked towards the people over a crimson carpet, and beside him were the Indian Princes, shining with embroidery and jewels. Gorgeous as peacocks, they had moved over the carpet to meet him. The white men cheered and the brown men clapped their hands. His first words were a simple approach to the problems and dangers which were before him. "I want you to know me and I want to know you," he said. "I want to grasp your difficulties and to understand your aspirations. . . . I feel some awe at the difficulty which I may experience in getting to know India."

The scene before the white gates of India was beautiful, secure and happy, but in another part of Bombay Gandhi was celebrating the day by a public burning of foreign clothes. The clever little man had done his best to cast a shadow over the Prince's arrival. He had spread posters over the city and he had told the people to stay within their houses and give the city an air of gloom. Even if loyalty

145

was not strong, love of splendour and ordinary human curiosity spoiled Gandhi's plan. "From the earliest dawn," wrote a journalist in the *Statesman*, "despite the thousands of placards displayed in every nook and corner of the city appealing in the name of Mr. Gandhi for a boycott of the Prince's visit, people of every class and community began to flock towards their chosen points of vantage along the route . . . providing a fitting answer to the appeals of the placards, contemptible in their discourtesy, vain in their effects."

The placards may have been contemptible, but they were powerful, and it was too much to expect that the Prince's charm and simplicity could work a miracle. But it is true that wherever he went there were converts. He was so unlike the officials of the British Raj. Here was no striding or high-minded talk of Britain's responsibility towards the dark races. The Prince had said, "I want you to know me and I want to know you," and this naïve wish coloured almost every scene of his visit. The great event in Bombay was the military display, when twenty-five thousand people crowded into the stadium. The Prince did not add to the theme of militarism. He appeared in a light fawn suit. When the display ended "the Prince's car moved slowly round the whole arena . . . . he stood up in the car during the veritable triumphant progress, and his khaki topi never returned to his head until he passed out of the gates, and then the crowd poured forth once more to take a last glimpse and give a final cheer to the object of its ovations." The writer of this paragraph in the *Pioneer* added a personal note for his editor: "This is no exaggeration, it is the literal truth. The cheers were real cheers, and they came as heartily from the humble classes of Indians, from the clerks, as from the soldiers and sailors. . . ."

The instincts of people ruled by princes die very slowly, and even if Gandhi's voice had been wise and just it would not have stemmed the natural enthusiasm of the mass of the people. The glamour of a great occasion was more delightful to them than the cold light of Gandhi's reason, and on the last night in Bombay there was a scene so extraordinary that one is incredulous as one reads the account in Katherine Mayo's *Mother India*. The Prince's car began the three- or four-mile drive from Government House to the railway station, unguarded "save for the pilot police car that went before." When it came to the city—

> "a cordon of police lined the streets on both sides. And behind that cordon pressed the people—the common poor people of the countryside in their uncountable thousands; pressed and pushed until, with the railway station yet half a mile away, the police line bent and broke beneath the strain.
>
> "Instantly the crowd surged in, closing round the car, shouting, fighting each to work nearer—nearer still. What would they do? What was their temper?
>
> ". . . The police tried vainly to form again around the car. Moving at a crawl, quite unprotected now, through an almost solid mass of shouting humanity, it won through to the railway station at last."

Miss Mayo describes the scene within the railway station, the royal train waiting, the dignitaries waiting to make their formal farewells, and the Prince listening anxiously. He turned to his aide-de-camp and asked: "How much time left?" "Three minutes, sir," he was told. The Prince answered: "Then drop those barriers and let the people in."

The barriers went down, and "like the sweep of a river in flood the interminable multitudes rolled in and shouted and adored and laughed and wept, and, when the train started, ran alongside the royal carriage till they could run no more."

Miss Mayo's book is rich in words, and, while we may accept her facts, we must guard ourselves against her ecstasy. But there is another document to which we may turn for a record of the effect of the Prince's stay in Bombay.

During his tour a number of confidential reports were made by the Political Secretaries in the various centres, and these were afterwards forwarded to the Political Secretary to the Government of India. They were not written for publication, and their value is certain. Mr. A. F. Kindersley wrote, in June of 1922, when the first excitement had passed:

> "In Bombay perhaps the principal political result of the visit has been indirectly to strengthen the traditional loyalty of the Parsee community. . . . The general effect has been that the great bulk of the Parsee community and all their responsible leaders have definitely recognised that their interest as a community lies in opposition to the forces of disorder and of non-co-operation. . . ."

After Bombay came Baroda, the first of the girdle of cities stretching from Bombay to Calcutta. Again the Political Secretary received a comforting report from the Resident, who telegraphed:

> "Reception accorded was considered exceptionally enthusiastic by people of long Baroda experience. Large number of Gandhi caps was only sign of dissatisfaction, but at times people so clad could be seen cheering wildly. . . . Gaekwar . . . expressed to me his extreme delight at complete success of visit and his warm appreciation of unfailing charm and sincerity of manner of His Royal Highness. . . . Politically, both in respect of State and general situation, visit has been triumphal success, of which His Royal Highness's personality has been outstanding feature and main cause."

The people of Baroda and their Gaekwar gilded themselves and all that they touched in honour of the Prince's visit. The elephants were painted with gold, the carriages were made of silver and the Prince was housed in the delicate white Laxmi Vilas Palace, with its fifty domes and towers. The bouquet which was given to him was sprinkled with attar of roses. The nobles who salaamed before him moved over a golden carpet; they wore apple green dappled with gold, and their robes were laden with jewels and orders. In the afternoon the Princes and the people moved, like fabulous butterflies, over the lawns and marble terraces and in and out of the six miniature theatres. In these were acrobats in pink tights, little parrots riding bicycles and firing guns, and nautch girls dancing and singing. There were fireworks at night, and next day there was a cheetah hunt for black buck. The trained cheetahs were brought up in wooden carts, to which they were fastened with red and yellow cords.

The royal train travelled north towards Udaipur, the town of palaces, upon the shores of the lakes. Donald Maxwell has described the scene in his book: the waters from which the lazy turtles came out in lazy companies to rest on marble steps, the trees with green parrots and glades with peacocks, and a boat with rowers in turbans of pale turquoise blue. The Prince crossed the lake. "Wall upon wall, gate upon gate, and palace upon palace was lit by little lamps with floating wicks." He was "carried up to the banqueting hall in a golden chair lighted by torchbearers."

The voice of Gandhi did not sound as far as this. The tales of old India were still told among the palaces, and the aged Maharana, a gorgeous and frightening figure, still held his people with the old cords of power. No train came within three miles of his immense marble palace, and Gandhi's name was not even whispered in the bazaars of Udaipur. The Maharana was too ill to walk out and greet the Prince, but before the banquet he appeared for a moment, "a tall, straight figure in silver grey." He did not eat with his English guest, but afterwards he came to the banqueting hall once more and sat beside him. The princes and nobles of Udaipur watched them as they talked: the noble old Maharana, descendant of the sun, and the shy young Briton who was heir to half the world. The Princes of Udaipur were pleased when they noted the deference with which the young man answered his host. "I am sure Your Royal Highness's popularity will exercise a soothing and healing effect on the present situation in India," said the Maharana. "My pleasure knows no bounds. . . . The British Government has always entertained the greatest possible regard to maintain the dignity and privileges of my State." Then the Maharana told the Prince of the words inscribed on the coins of his State, "Dost-i-London," which mean "Friendship with London."

The Prince answered: "I am on the soil where the flower of chivalry sprang to life. In sight of the hall in which we are now banqueting lies the island where, in the days of the Mutiny, the Maharana of Udaipur kept a number of my fellow-countrymen in safety and preserved them from imminent death."

The scenes in Udaipur were heavy with beauty and they moved in slow dignity, but the undergraduate of Magdalen was still alive within the gracious traveller. Mr. Donald Maxwell allows us to escape from the splendour in the story of a night when the Prince returned from shooting, very tired and asking for sleep. He went to his room, and orders were given that no noise should disturb him. "Imagine, therefore, the horror of the Prince's attendants to hear loud singing just outside his room. Equerries rushed hither and thither, but the serenader could not be located. Finally, it was discovered that the Prince himself, completely pleased with life in general and Udaipur in particular, was the bold performer."

Mr. Maxwell told the story to two or three people. They told others and it reached the palace. A Secretary of State called upon him and asked to hear the story. Then the Prime Minister came and he had to tell the tale again. Then the Maharana's son came and this time, wrote Mr. Maxwell, he was compelled, "out of sheer necessity, to make the story a bit longer." At last the Maharana himself sent for Mr. Maxwell. He wished to hear the wonderful story first hand. With "great kindness and courtesy" Mr. Maxwell was summoned to the palace. He arrived "in great pomp on an elephant." "I kept more or less to the original story, with a few artistic, but imaginary, details thrown in," Mr. Maxwell has written. "A murmur of approval ran around the Court. . . . The Maharana congratulated me, expressed his warmest thanks and presented me with a magnificent ruby."

The Prince went from city to city. He crossed the desert, guarded by camel patrols. There was danger behind the old beauty, and as the train moved on toward Bikaner he was able to look out of the window of the carriage and see the men upon their camels, perhaps two hundred yards apart, with their backs towards him. They did not turn to look at him as he passed.

Bikaner is the desert State of the north; the home of the famous Camel Corps which served in Egypt and Palestine. The Maharajah recalled their service in his greeting. "My troops . . . they will always remember with delight that Your Royal Highness rode on Bikaner camels with some of them on several occasions during their four and a half years' active campaigning in Egypt and Palestine." The glorious story of Udaipur was repeated in Bikaner; again the robes and the coaches were of glittering richness. But the Prince's conscience was not silenced by the splendour. When he was able to escape from the pageant, his enquiries were the old enquiries. Were the returned soldiers being cared for? He did not fail to comment upon a fault when he found one. Some of the returned men at Bikaner paraded without their medals. "Why?" he asked.

"They have not arrived yet," he was told.

There were reprimands and telegrams and the medals were delivered in Bikaner within a few days.

The Maharajah of Bharatpur took up the story of richness and colour. He rode to the polo ground in a silver carriage harnessed to eight elephants. At night, standing upon a new mountain which had been built for the occasion, the Prince watched the soldiers, the golden elephants, the camels, the scarlet infantry and the cavalry.

The fabulous tale of the Native States ended and the Prince returned to British India. He crossed the Ganges and came to Lucknow. Once more Gandhi's malicious plans had to be reckoned with. Sir Harcourt Butler was too old in the tricks of government to be thwarted by the refusal of the Indians to join in the University Sports. He enrolled the Anglo-Indians, who shared the prizes and saved the day from disaster. But Gandhi had laid his plans far beyond the University. The Indian shops were shut and the gharri drivers refused to work. Even the loyal Indians had no way of travelling into Lucknow from the outlying country. British humour and sense eased the situation. The army lorries paraded the city bearing notices, " Come and see the Prince and have a free ride." The cumbersome lorries were soon crowded, for the Indians did not relish being shut in their darkened shops all day, alone with their frigid principles. The Prince went on smiling. His courage was tremendous. Most of the time he was travelling in danger and the guards which surrounded him were necessary. In the columns of the Indian newspapers one does not find stories of an anxious traveller, looking this way and that as he wrestled with the hartals which Gandhi had prepared for him. The stories are mostly of fun when the day of duty was over.

" He never fails to add to the delights of the functions he attends by some distinguished act of courtesy," somebody wrote in the *Times of India*. "The Prince . . . . feels intensely the fascination of modern dance music. . . . He assists on occasions in its production. . . . Yesterday evening he performed *coram populo*, as it were, at the dance given by the Governor at Government House. . . . The Prince worked his shoulders as he smote the cymbals, his feet shuffled in time to the music and his head nodded rhythmically." During the day a gymkhana had been arranged and he had ridden in four races "with overwhelming success." Only those whose blood ran bitter against England could withstand his charm and simplicity.

Before the Prince left Lucknow he presented new colours to the 3rd Battalion the Worcestershire Regiment. The regimental slow march which the band played for him had been composed by his great-great-grandmother, the Duchess of Kent, who had been so fond of playing upon her pianoforte during the winter evenings at Frogmore.

Mr. Gandhi's greatest success was in Allahabad. It was here that Lord Canning had read Queen Victoria's proclamation in 1858. It was a background against which the Prince might have appeared at his best. He was the first English Prince who had ever paused here, for Allahabad had been passed, by both his father and his grandfather. Only a few people came out to greet him and the shops were closed. Within the houses the discontented Indians obeyed Gandhi's orders and hid their faces. The few people who addressed the Prince apologised for the shut doors and the empty streets. But, as evening came, human curiosity conquered: many of the little doors opened and a few of the Indians shed their theories and went to the station to see the Prince leaving for Benares.

The city beside the Ganges was divided in its love. The Prince went out upon the river in the afternoon, past the temples and the hordes of pilgrims and, upon the Benares side of the river, he passed animated hordes whose cheers rang out across the water. But the lively menace of Gandhi had conquered many thousands of people in Benares, although the chief agitators had been arrested before he arrived. The Chief Secretary wrote:

> "They had thrown down an open and flagrant challenge in defiance of Government and there was no option but to arrest them. . . . It is noteworthy that where the ringleaders were arrested before His Royal Highness' arrival—*i.e.*, in all provinces except Bombay and Madras—there was no rioting. . . . The visit to

Lucknow was an unqualified success except with regard to the attitude of the students. . . . In considering the effect of His Royal Highness' visit, allowance must be made for the political conditions of the time. Certain facts, however, stand out. First, wherever His Royal Highness spent more than a day, the non-co-operation movement broke down. Secondly, the countryside is eloquent of His Royal Highness' interest in and kindness to the pensioners and all those who suffered in the war, while men on leave tell the same story. Thirdly, all those who came in contact with His Royal Highness succumbed to the magnetism of his charm, and the fact that he had sufficiently mastered the language to be able to talk simply to the people has impressed itself on all. Fourthly, the remarkable energy of His Royal Highness in carrying through his programme, his punctuality, and his earnest desire to learn and to exchange views with all conditions of people gave great pleasure to, and excited the admiration of, all concerned. The effect of his example will, it is hoped, remain long after the particular incidents of the tour have receded in point of time, and has already produced some diminution in the acerbity of the relations of those who before his visit were extremely hostile to each other."

From Benares the Prince went to shoot big game on the Nepal border. No reporters disturbed him for seven days and he returned to his duties " bronzed and perfectly fit " and with several trophies, including a ten-foot king cobra which he shot on foot.

The struggle against Gandhi went on. At Patna the vehicles were all laid up, so that the Indians had to tramp in from their country towns if they wished to see him. The officials who knew India well began to wonder more and more at the Prince's tact and good humour. Then came Calcutta, one of the most bitter tests of the illustrious journey. The loyal newspapers described his entry as "a triumph without a discordant note." This was true, but there were many thousands of people who stayed in their houses in obedience to Gandhi's wish. The cries in the streets were mixed. "I saw him, I saw him," cried a little Indian girl, but her older neighbour called, "Gandhi ka jai." The Chief Secretary to the Government of Bengal waited three months before he wrote his report of the Prince's visit.

> "The vernacular papers, both Hindu and Muhammadan," he wrote, "expressed the view that the reception accorded to H.R.H. fell far short of the standard set at similar royal visits. The visit in its detail received very meagre treatment in these papers. . . . . It was, however, generally admitted by these papers that the crowds at the functions were increasingly Indian . . . . the visit must be regarded as very successful . . . . the enthusiasm towards His Royal Highness' person continued to grow throughout the visit. . . . Since His Royal Highness' departure there has been a marked improvement in the political situation."

The plans to boycott the Prince had simmered in Burma long before he arrived there, but when the nine most ardent leaders had been spirited away to prison, the people of Rangoon put on their rich gold and fine linen and they smiled and sang as they wished. To quote the official report, "the people . . . . poured into the streets. From that moment the visit was a political and social success." Ten weeks after the Prince had left Rangoon the Chief Secretary wrote that the "seditious movement" had not yet recovered "the prestige that it lost" during his visit.

The Burmese know the sweet pleasures of idleness. They laugh and they dress in gay colours; they smile at the morning sun and they smile at it again when it sets. The Prince

could not have stayed with these charming people without
complete success. He went to the races, where thousands
of Burmese girls peeped at him from beneath big, gay
paper umbrellas. He went to Mandalay, where the people
came in from the hills and gave him a Shan entertainment.
Dragons thirty feet long, birds which were twice as tall as
men, and fabulous bulls, elephants, tigers, peacocks and
llamas danced madly for him; a vastly amusing Noah's Ark,
let loose in the fiery night, dancing to music from instruments so heavy that three men were needed to lift one of
them.

The Prince returned to Rangoon, and the Commissioner
of Police reported that "the political atmosphere" had
"never been quieter" since he arrived there. The Chief
Secretary wrote to Sir John Wood, in London, "The visit
was a splendid success; socially because it brought so many
in close contact with their future Emperor, and politically
because it showed decisively that Burma had not strayed
far from the path of loyalty." One of the Divisional Commissioners wrote: "At Pyu all were greatly impressed by
the Prince walking the whole length of the station platform
to go and see the school children and the persons who were
at a distance from the officials meeting the Prince, and who
were not able therefore to see him at close quarters. But
here too it was the personal element that came into play.
The East likes personal government, and it was from the
Prince's personality that sprang the effects I have tried to
describe above."

India had been crossed. Now the Prince was to travel
north, from Madras to Karachi. There are newspapers and
reports from officials in which the scenes are painted, but
the identity of the Prince himself seems to be lost in the
splendour. He saw too much and he did too much: the
demands made upon him were inhuman. Yet he did not
complain. One of the few records there are of any personal
comment is in Lord Rawlinson's *Life*. Lord Rawlinson
saw him at Delhi and the Prince confessed to him that he

went to bed "dog-tired every night." The Prince entered the harbour of Madras. His grandfather had laid the foundation stone of the harbour in 1875, and there was a stone to commemorate the landing of his father in 1906. Mr. Gandhi chose impudent and foolish ways of demonstrating the anger of his followers. They did not emerge into the happy streets until the Prince's carriage had arrived at Government House. Then they tore down the palms and decorations and smashed the flower pots in the road. They removed pictures of the Prince from a near-by theatre and stamped on them. Then they fired a cinema, but this was the end of their display of temper, for the Leinsters cleared the streets at the point of the bayonet and armoured cars were placed at the corners. While these excitements were being brought into control, the majority of the people in Madras were surrounding the Prince with happiness and affection. His willingness did not abate, and some who travelled with him marvelled more than ever. His courage wore down the demonstrations, and even if he could not turn malcontents into loyalists he at least assuaged their spite. At the races he walked down from the stand and strolled into the public enclosure. This was a daring thing to do and the mass of people were amazed. They parted to make way for him. For a moment they could not believe that he was among them; then the air rang with cheers.

In Mysore the Prince and the Maharajah sat upon gold thrones, they passed under an arch decorated with peacocks and doves, and when the Prince drove into the country the farmers left their work in the fields and ran to the roadside to salaam and to kneel in the dust as he passed. Here was peace as well as beauty, for Mysore is within the Native States, and Indian Princes are not as patient as the British Government with Gandhi's insurgents. The Prince drove out to Karapur to shoot elephant, bison and tiger in the jungle. From a platform within a stockade, he saw twenty-eight wild elephant captured and herded, fighting, screaming, charging the beaters and tearing trees up by their roots. He moved on to Hyderabad, where the Nizam's subjects held their little babies in the air so that they might grow up with the blessing of having seen him. For one brief day Nagpur salaamed and clapped hands. Gandhi had tried to start his hartal here, but, in the official report, one is told that "All the functions were most successful and not a single untoward incident marred the pleasure of the visit." At Indore the Maharajah of Dhar had placed his eleven-year-old daughter astride a horse, and thus she led the Light Horse past the saluting base. The Prince hung garlands about the necks of eighteen Princes, and then he left by the royal train to be the guest of the Begum of Bhopal.

This little old lady, living behind a veil, but making no mystery of her power and charm, came to the railway station to meet him. One remembers the Begum in London, sitting in her hotel, looking a little incongruous in her English setting. In her own State she sat upon a silver throne and her head was ornamented with diamonds. Painted elephant saluted her with uplifted trunks; their mahouts were dressed in gold. The Begum made her speech in English, and she chose the day of the Prince's arrival to announce to her subjects "the formal concession . . . to participate in the moulding of its destinies." Then she said, "I will bring my imagination down from the giddy heights of politics to the pleasanter ground of the forests." She wished her guest good sport and pleasure during the three days he was to shoot in her jungles.

Bhopal's neighbour is Gwalior, and here the Prince travelled to the palace at the head of a procession of jewelled elephant; the one upon which he rode was a hundred years old, and when it moved its colossal gold legs a hundred silver bells tinkled on its crimson mantle. When the Maharajah appeared he wore a belt of pearls over a mauve robe, and when the great men of Gwalior came to the Prince they carried trays of precious stones, and the table upon which the banquet was served was a stream of silver and gold. The people tore down the decorations after he had gone and kept them as talismans; they gazed at the chair on which he had sat and sought blessings by touching the earth upon which he had walked.

The greatest occasions of the tour were no doubt those of the welcome in Delhi, which the Prince entered "amidst a hurricane of cheers." A few days before, he had been at Agra, where the sign "No Welcome to the Prince" was painted across the doors of the closed shops. Here Gandhi's white caps had succeeded, but they had little power in Delhi. There is a frank comment on the reception in Delhi in Lord Rawlinson's journal. He viewed the visit to Calcutta as "a fiasco," but of Delhi he wrote:

> "The Prince's visit has gone off splendidly, which
> . . . . is a tremendous relief. He has worked very hard.
> . . . . His winning smile and extraordinarily attractive
> manner won the hearts of all. He had another great
> success with a speech in Hindustani, which he learned
> by heart, to the 11th and 16th Rajputs, to whom he
> presented colours. The men were delighted and
> cheered him to the echo."

The adjectives of the journalists were spent when the Prince arrived in Delhi. When they looked upon the grandest scene of all, the Durbar, with the Prince, Lord Reading and fifty ruling Princes on the dais, one of them described it as a "flashing effulgence." The laurels for speaking went to the Maharajah of Nawanagar, who said:

> "In my happy and, I trust, not unfruitful earlier
> days in England, I was once vastly astonished to find
> myself described in cold print as a conjurer. . . . I
> surely need, and sadly lack, some magic power in order
> . . . . to attempt a tribute of welcome to Your Royal
> Highness. . . . You come . . . . bearing on your shield,
> fostering in your heart, realising in your work and

actions, the noblest and most princely of all mottoes, *I serve.* . . . You come to us as our friend and bene-factor, willing to help us bear our burden, willing to know and love us as we would know and love you."

The most dramatic occasion during the visit to Delhi came as the Prince was driving away after laying the foundation stone of the Kitchener College. He came to the camp in which twenty-five thousand Untouchables were waiting to see him. Their spokesman walked towards him humbly, and begged for the Prince's intervention on their behalf. The twenty-five thousand were amazed and they cried with joy when the Prince stood up before them. They were so used to persecution that they could not believe their eyes as they looked at him. The effect of this one gesture was extraordinary. In his notes upon the Prince's visit, the Chief Commissioner of Delhi wrote: "I am informed by non-official workers among these depressed classes that this recognition has had a most remarkable effect in stimulating their self-respect and in strengthening their determination to lift themselves out of the thraldom which custom and caste regulations have hitherto assigned to their lot."

The Prince moved on. He played polo, he went pig sticking and he danced at Patiala. He was no doubt pleased to find that the Maharajah had not dressed up his programme with quite as much formality as his neighbours. He went on to Jullunder and then he faced the long, splendid programme at Lahore. Half a million people were packed into the streets to welcome him. On the surface Lahore was gay and pleased, but Gandhi's attempts at a hartal were not easy to break. Three thousand troops guarded the way, three aircraft flew low over the city, five motor-lorries filled with armed infantry, three tanks and three armoured cars warned the Mahatma's followers. The precautions were necessary and the vigilance of the troops was not relaxed for a second. A writer in the *Statesman* said that "Sentries, with fixed bayonets, constantly patrolled

1924. *The Prince of Wales and Lord Baden-Powell at Wembley.*

the edge of the footways behind the cordon of infantry, even during the passage of the royal barouche." Nowhere else, except in Bombay, was there "such a dense pack of humanity."

Once more the Prince's fearlessness won the day. When he went to the big native gathering he rode slowly through a crowd of thousands of Punjabis and made "many of the pessimistic observers of his tour stare with amazement." He insisted upon the most simple appearance, and even when he was greeted by Sirdars in gold coats he wore ordinary riding kit. The twenty thousand Indians who watched him were surprised. When King George went to them he had been urged to wear robes and crown wherever possible, and they did not understand that the heir to a throne could move among them so simply and with so little show. He must have been right in this decision, for when he left Lahore in the evening, darkness "loosened the tongues of the Indian crowds." The platform was a seething mass of excited and gesticulating humanity . . . . the white saloon slowly moved out. . . . It was a triumph.

He moved north to Jammu, nearer and nearer to the frontier. He met the caravans which had come over the mountains, camels laden with shawls and carpets and silver; and he met the Thibetan monks who had left their monastery five months before, in donkey carts, so that they could travel four hundred miles to dance for him. He turned west again and came to Peshawar. The frontier was tranquil then, but he was able to see the ways over which the ceaseless watch is kept. He was able to look out over the plains of Afghanistan, the earth of invasion and war. Gandhi had caught the imagination of the townspeople, but he had failed with the tribesmen who came in from the hills. They found, when they arrived in Peshawar, that the malcontents had closed their shops, so they begged the Chief Commissioner to allow them to take the law into their hands. They suggested that five thousand of them could easily reopen the shops, for all time, by removing their roofs. The gallant gesture was forbidden, but when some-body interrupted the Prince's speech by crying, "Gandhi ki jai," the tribesmen were so incensed over the blot upon their hospitality that the police who were protecting the Prince had to abandon him and guard Gandhi's followers from attack.

Again one is able to find a calm record of the visit in the report of the Chief Commissioner, who wrote: "Effect of visit on trans-border population has been to rekindle personal interest in the Royal House. The gathering of the clans both in the Khyber and the Malakand was a spon-taneous and striking demonstration of loyalty and good-will. . . . Summing up, we must put the city hartal and the hooliganism on the debit side."

The Prince turned east again. His journey was almost ended. He accepted the salute of ten thousand troops at Rawalpindi; he went on to Dehra Dun, the hill station on which the Gurkhas are trained; and he went to Hardwar, where his hosts threw thousands of flowers into the air so that they rained upon him as he walked. He crossed the Empire once more, and, too tired to contemplate the size of his own success, he boarded *Renown* at Karachi and steamed south towards Ceylon.

The morass of India's political issues has no place in this story. To keep the Prince of Wales as the central figure one must turn from the glory of the Indian Princes and the beauty of the welcome which they prepared for him: turn also from the rights and wrongs of British rule in India, and search into the story of the effect upon the Prince him-self. The reports of the Commissioners, written in the cool afterglow of the Prince's visit, provide the best answer to the challenge which Mr. Gandhi had prepared for him.

The newspapers used grand phrases to describe the final result of the tour. The *Englishman* described the Prince as "the greatest ambassador of his time," and added that "he did more to establish the relations between the masses of India and the Crown on a solid basis of personal contact

in four months than edicts could have done in a generation." If this is true it was because of his good nature and
because of his democratic manner that the Prince succeeded. His easy address, which would have been impossible in a permanent official or in a Viceroy, was engaging
in an illustrious visitor who passed quickly by. King
Edward VII had referred to the British people as his
subjects and King George spoke of his *people*. King
Edward VIII stepped down still further and usually
addressed his *fellow-men*. This freedom of manner, which
sometimes alarmed conventional governors as much as it
delighted the mass of people, soon brought him popularity.
Men of a philosophic turn of mind might have commented
on this; they might have said that popularity is a fleeting
sensation and that it has nothing to do with respect and
stableness. But it was not until the end of King Edward
VIII's life in England that this truth showed itself. While
King George slowly amassed a great bulwark of respect
about him, because of his character, his son gathered the
gayer rewards of popularity which were to sustain him
while he was heir to the throne, although they were not
enough to sustain him when he became King.

It has been said that the Prince was sometimes deceived
as to the value of his success; that he mistook the gay accident of popularity for calm esteem and that his self-confidence flourished accordingly. If this is true he cannot be
blamed, for the tumult in which he was forced to live was
beyond human endurance, and an old, cynical philosopher
could not have passed through similar experiences without
over-valuing his own talents and success.

There were no frowns for the Prince of Wales in Ceylon.
He needed no guarding upon the lovely island, as he stood
in the burning sun to greet a thousand old soldiers, or as
he walked out at night into streets which were rivers of
light. He travelled to Kandy by train, and out of every little
hut, cooled beneath palms, there came smiling women and
children. The peasants in the rice fields ran towards him

and waved, and when he came to the mountain stronghold
of the old Kandyan kings he went into the temple where
Buddha's tooth is guarded within seven gold caskets.
Silent monks in saffron cassocks moved across the floor of
the temple to receive him, and a priest took him into the
tiny sanctuary which is built into a cage of steel. The
golden reliquary was opened. The priest lifted out a
casket of gold. Within this was another casket, and within
this a third, a fourth, a fifth and a sixth. In the last box,
which burned with the little flames of jewels, was the sacred
relic. The priest moved the oil lamp until its light shone
down upon the lid. Then he opened it and the Prince
saw the tooth of Buddha inside.

The Prince went down to the sea again and he steamed
on to Malaya, where the friendly people tore blossoms from
the trees to throw at him, and then to Japan. The Prince
taught the Japanese to behave like a London crowd. They
threw away their old prejudice against cheering as he drove
from Yokohama to Tokio between nineteen miles of eager
people. Special theatres were built for him, and at the
Opera he sat with six Imperial Princesses in a theatre so
brilliant that even the Japanese nobles blinked before the
splendour. Two thousand school children sang "God Save
the King" for him in English, and the Japanese Government threw away convention to the extent of allowing an
armed guard to come ashore from *Renown* to take part
in the unveiling of the Allied War Memorial.

Sir Percival Phillips records a scene at the garden-party
where the Prince met Admiral Togo, standing "apart from
the other guests, a silent, shy little man in naval uniform,
his eyes fixed meekly on the ground." The stiff woodcuts
of Japanese life to which we are accustomed in the West
came to life during the gay journey to the cities of temples
and shrines. Through them all the slim English figure
moved, sometimes sitting upon the floor to eat Japanese
dishes with chopsticks, sometimes watching the fishing with
cormorant at Gifu, sometimes moving over the water of

the inland sea, while thousands of Japanese formed an animated shore line, waving little flags in the daytime and, at night, setting thousands of tiny lanterns afloat upon the lake so that they drifted towards his boat "like coloured flowers."

There was no political chicanery to harass the Prince in Japan. He lived through a month of beauty, and when he returned to England in June he had added still another conquest to his story. He had scattered many fears in India and he had shown regard for an old friendship by shaking hands with Japan.

Chapter Seventeen

SOUTH AFRICA

The people of South Africa admire and respect the Prince very much. They love his simplicity, his human ways, his sincerity. . . . He has lived a life of duty from his earliest days.—GENERAL SMUTS.

SOUTH AFRICA

THE Prince was not allowed to stay in England very long. The interlude of London life soon ended and he was once more on a battle-cruiser, which he described as his "second home," bound for South Africa. He was to travel 35,000 miles on this journey, to add South Africa and South America to his store of knowledge. The people he was to meet numbered thousands.

This time the Prince travelled in *Repulse*; there was one splendid hour on the way to the Cape when she met the Atlantic Fleet of thirty-eight vessels coming home. The Prince steamed down the avenue of cruisers, battleships and flotillas; twenty-one guns saluted him and a whaler came alongside for his letters. The fleet moved on towards the colder north and the Prince steamed on towards the Gold Coast. He went ashore at Gambia, "whence baboon skins were carried off to Carthage by Hanno and his explorers" twenty-five centuries before. The chiefs drew white gloves over their fingers before they dared to touch his hand, and some stroked his sleeve when they overcame their shyness. At Sierra Leone the dark aristocrats were carried to him in hammocks, borne on the heads of their nimble little bearers; savage men from the hinterland whipped themselves with snakes before him until their arms and legs were bleeding. The pageant of strange countries and customs had begun once more; the speech-making, the long hours of travelling and the cruel demands upon the Prince's temper and strength.

At Takoradi he left the sea and his train travelled into the gorgeous forest of "teak and camwood and ebony, tall rubber trees and mahogany giants," and when he slept at night, during his journey across Ashanti, the darkness was

lively with the piercing alarms of the crickets. The Ashanti
chiefs placed a cloth upon the ground for him and on it was
embroidered the word "Okoasa," which means "No more
war." The company turned towards the coast, and at Accra
the Prince saw *Repulse* again. She lay, grey and formidable, in the sea below the high town. A few fifteen-inch
guns were fired into the water, so that the people of Accra
could know the amazing strength of British order. But the
natives did not mind these shows of power. They liked
King Piccin, as they called him, and at night, when he slept
in Christianborg Castle, they dozed over their refreshments
and recalled the days when their grandfathers were once
herded in the castle to be sold as slaves. Their thanks for
the freedom which they enjoyed were to King Piccin rather
than to the booming guns. Also, through a fortunate accident, they discovered that he shared their sense of humour.
To the childlike nature of the Gold Coast natives, laughter
is a sweeter tie than any palaver of power and dull government. When so many of them climbed a tree that it broke
and scattered them on the ground, the natives laughed and
the Prince smiled with them. They saw him laughing and
from that moment their friendship was secure. All that
they felt was written into an ode by the Gold Coast Court
poet and sung to him:

> Best gratitudes to the King,
> And to your mother, the Queen,
> Gratitudes to House of Lords,
> To Governor of Best sorts,
>   Who all good provided
>   That the Prince here guided.
>
> He is the real Prince of Wales,
> Born in the diamond Palace,
> Dear son of King George the Fifth,
> But he oft the palace leaves,
>   Wanders in dominions,
>   To know himself Nations.

The dusky loyalists were required to sing their ode to
the melody of Sankey's "Jesu, Lover of my soul." From the
Gold Coast the Prince went to Nigeria for the great Durbar

on the Kano Plain. Twenty thousand horsemen rode before him, mile upon mile, in the greatest display of horsemanship ever held in the world. There were chieftains, their calm, dark faces shaded beneath gay umbrellas, with dancers and jesters prancing at their heels. Their approach was heralded by trumpets twelve feet long. The horsemen, stretching from horizon to horizon, had come from the farthest corners of the land to herald the son of the English King.

When the wild beauty of the Nigerian welcome was ended, *Repulse* steamed south, and after a few days at sea the Prince stepped ashore in Capetown.

A stroke of good fortune had already sent the Earl of Athlone and Princess Alice to South Africa. The new Governor-General had brought a refreshed conception of English life and ideas to the South African people. When he went there, with Princess Alice, many South Africans had come to look upon the appointment of a Governor-General as an expensive survival of old and threadbare customs. The sense of duty, the charm and the example of family life which Lord Athlone and Princess Alice gave to South Africa had already stimulated a new belief in English standards, and when the Prince of Wales arrived at the Cape, in 1925, he benefited from the friendliness which his cousins had inspired.

Capetown had copied Melbourne and was hidden modestly behind a fog as the Prince approached the harbour. Table Mountain was so heavily veiled that searchlights were thrown upon it to penetrate and reveal its broad crest. The Cape is a melting place of human races, and the chattering, jostling crowd which waited for him in the streets was not single-minded with delight. There were critics as well as friends climbing the boughs of the trees to see him pass. He faced his duty with grim energy and shook hands with two thousand people in one day. Some who travelled with him thought that his smile was less spontaneous than in Australia and New Zealand, as if he were conscious of the old hates and suspicions which still disturb the peace of South Africa's daily life. If he doubted his own powers, these doubts must have been quickly and pleasantly scattered when, during the first day, he was kidnapped by the students from the University. Here, at the southernmost gate to their country, they swept down upon him at Government House in a vast voor-trekker's wagon. They were dressed in crazy clothes, some in lion skins and plumes. Behind the wagon, hundreds of girl and boy students formed a mad tail, holding each other and running in his wake up the hill to the University. Again the player of the bagpipes in the cloisters of Magdalen came to life. He was surrounded by affection and young nonsense, and even the burden of the past three years had not withered his power to throw himself wholeheartedly into their fun.

When the Prince met the old, serious leaders at dinner in the evening, he had to talk with Dutchmen who had once fought against England. He had to listen to clever men who were still inclined towards secession and who had already woven the design for their own separate South African flag. His speech won their first applause. He did not speak grandly, nor with phrases cunningly written to catch their favour. "I come to you as the King's eldest son," he said, "as heir to a throne under which the members of that Commonwealth are free to develop each on its own lines but all to work together as one. . . . My travels have taught me this, that the throne is regarded as standing for a heritage of common ends and ideals." It was the sincerity and the smile which went with these conventional words that warmed his audience. At the end he ventured into Afrikaans. "I am very pleased to meet you to-night, and thank you again for your warm welcome." When the dinner was over the old Dutchmen gathered about him, and one, we are told, pressed his hand and said that it would be very nice if he could remain in Africa and be their first President.

A Commando

The problems of the new countries are not all the same, nor has their history of struggles and chicanery been alike. The protest of the Maoris was faint when the white men went to New Zealand, and when the windjammers of the 'forties sailed into the harbours of Australia the aboriginals scattered like animals into the Bush. The Indians of Canada were a finer race to conquer, but they soon allowed their old brave arrows to rust in their quivers. Africa was the only country whose natives were mighty in their fight against European civilisation. Their hordes had measured millions, and they still measured millions when the Prince of Wales went to see them in 1925.

The Maoris and the aboriginals and the Indians are subdued for ever, and even their old habits and their rude culture have withered away because of the new and exciting life which the white man has taught them. But the lithe black boy who walks down the street of Johannesburg, with his wonderful European boots slung over his shoulders, to save their precious soles, is still untamed. He is making his way towards a cinema and he likes his European clothes, but he is one of the horde of black people who are a nation still. Nor is this the end of the Briton's problems in South Africa. The dour Boer has not forgotten Mafeking and Ladysmith, for all his apparent peacefulness. His strength has also to be reckoned with, and he does not always feel at peace with the world when he sees the Union Jack fluttering upon his horizon.

In South Africa the Prince's duty was different from that in any other country in which he travelled. He was certain of the welcome of the British colonist. But the Dutchman is a Dutchman still, nor have the Kaffirs and the Zulus been scratched very deep by the pin of British culture. One town in the Cape Province soon showed how willing the Dutchmen were to succumb to the Prince's friendliness. The long white train drew into the station, which is two miles away from Oudtshoorn. A commando of Dutch farmers had ridden out to meet him; heavy, strong men, used to adversity. In the town, two miles away, twenty-five thousand people were waiting on the recreation ground for the Prince and the commando. The horsemen had brought a spare stallion with them, and when the Prince saw it he rejected the car which had been sent for him and he rode into the town at the head of the astonished farmers. The guest arrived at Oudtshoorn at the gallop, with the commando in the dust cloud behind him. When the Prince went to Stellenbosch, where the students have had time to spin theories about freedom and the leisure in which to make dreams of ideal republics, it was a young Dutchman who stood up and said, "We cheered because we know a man when we see one. Our presence here is intended as a tribute to your manliness which the most persistent attempts of the whole world have not been able to spoil." It was, perhaps, the most frank and sympathetic tribute which had ever been paid to him in a public address.

By this time the Prince of Wales was almost sadly used to speeches. The harmless vanity of mayors was not to be denied and he had listened to many thousands of sincere but weary tributes to his excellence. His manner of dealing with mayors became more and more clever as he travelled on, and there were many occasions on which he gently imposed his own will. In one South African town where he had to listen to a long speech, he rolled up his reply, handed it to the mayor, and told him he could read it afterwards. One enjoys the story of his visit to the mayor of a town in Canada where His Worship had mixed the pages of his speech. He fumbled with the confused sheets of paper. He had read as far as "Not only do we welcome Your Royal Highness as the representative of His Majesty the King, but we . . ." and there the mayor paused, for the next page was missing. The Prince knew the formula well by then and he was able to whisper, "we welcome you for *yourself*." The Prince's white coach threaded its way through the fertile valleys of the Cape Province. He paused in towns beside the sea; he ate oysters and he talked to the fishermen; he turned inland and nodded to the drivers of the great wagons that passed him, drawn by teams of eighteen oxen. Little brown children came to the roadside and threw ferns and flowers on to the parched dust so that his coach should run over them. When he came to the mountains he passed a place where his great-uncle, the Duke of Edinburgh, had hunted elephant, almost sixty years before. Sometimes he stayed to shake hands with soldiers who had fought in the Matabele War, and in one place two old men held their still older father in the air, a man who had passed his hundredth year, so that Prince and centenarian could wave to each other as he passed. Sometimes the fields were rich with orchards, with peaches and oranges which lent their colour to the green. Ostriches strutted across the open country, and in one town the Prince danced in a hall which was almost covered by feathers: canopies of gold and yellow and blue plumes trembling from the agitation of the dance. As he travelled he gathered more and more information. While people cheered and smiled he asked questions and he made notes. He wished to know the costs of production and the methods of manufacturing. Like his mother, he seemed to have an inexhaustible appetite for facts, and what he was told he usually remembered.

Sometimes the white coach paused and the Prince stepped down and went out over the veld to shoot springbok and guinea fowl. The richness of the land through which he was passing was proved in arches of produce which had been built across the roads. On the way to Port Elizabeth the train stopped while a group of eager Kaffir minstrels played and sang to him. One of the songs he knew. Again the boy of Magdalen stirred: he jumped down from the train and joined them with his ukelele.

Port Elizabeth is the Melbourne of South Africa. Here are the descendants of the 1820 settlers to whom England is "home." Their welcome was glorious, particularly when the Prince went out to the crusaders' ground, upon which seven thousand white children and seven thousand brown children joined in singing his anthem. As they sang, silver aircraft pierced the clouds or dipped down to salute the son of "the great White King over the seas." Hordes of natives came over the hills, dressed in skins, and they called him

> The beloved of the young children,
> He who can be stern as the mountain,
> Yet dances as the young wind.

He was wise in his replies to these dreamy phrases. When he spoke to the ten thousand Bantus who danced before him at King William's Town, until the dust at their feet was muddy with their sweat, he said: "I would caution you against tendencies to mistrust those in authority, or to turn to those whose smooth promises have yet to be translated into performance. To fight these dangers you should learn to manage your own affairs."

In *Southward Ho!* Mr. Ralph Deakin gives many good pictures of the Prince's journey through Africa. In a sentence, one catches the scene of the luncheon in the Valley of Perpetual Spring, where "Baboons chattered among the aloes on the opposite bank and a few natives were silhouetted in all their blackness above the topmost crags." Then the scene with the chiefs in the Transkeian territory, where twenty thousand natives came with their shields, their elephant tusks and chests of stinkwood, their assegais and corn to place at his feet. The Prince had brought imposing silver-topped walking sticks as presents for the chiefs, and when they advanced towards him they were "trembling so violently with emotion that they could scarcely trust themselves in mounting the steps. Two of them had to be assisted across the dais." One old Basuto chieftain who knelt before him paused when he stood up. Then he came closer and stared deep into the Prince's eyes. The Prince accepted the startling examination without moving.

The tour of Cape Province ended and the Prince moved on. Even in the train he seldom rested. His pen was busy, or he would sit at the window of the carriage, hour after hour, waving to the little clusters of natives who had gathered beside the shining rails to wait for him. He came to the Free State Province. He sang hymns in the church at Jagersfontein in Dutch as well as English; at Bloemfontein a commando of two thousand horsemen came out to meet him, and as the Prince rode in beside the leader, a man who had fought as a rebel under de Wet, they talked in Afrikaans. The overflow of their conversation was heard by the horsemen behind them. " He is talking in Afrikaans," they whispered. The wonder was whispered by one to the other of all the two thousand, and if any of them had come unwillingly, their unwillingness died before the gesture he had made. He had bothered, as he had bothered in India, to learn the language of his hosts, so that he could speak with them in their own tongue. On the borders of Natal and the Free State he was thanked for this thoughtfulness. An English child and a Dutch child were waiting for him on the frontier, holding a chain of flowers across the track as the train hurried on.

The most splendid meeting of the Basuto natives was on May 29, when more than one hundred thousand of them gathered into a great basin of earth. They came, still panting and sweating from the long and terrible journeys which had brought them there. Fifty thousand of them were mounted. The others came on foot. They crowded into the great valley, legions of them, pressing in towards the place where *he* was to appear. The outer fringe of the multitude watched from the rock hills; stiff, hefty dark figures, mounted on their horses. The Prince often disappointed the natives by wearing dull clothes. This time, he dressed grandly: when he approached them he was wearing the blue ribbon of the Garter, the symbol of Edward III's Order of Chivalry, across his scarlet tunic. A murmur of worshipful approval sounded in the hot valley. A hundred thousand dark heads craned forward to watch the old chief, the "one about to die," who spoke for them. "I rejoice," croaked the old voice, "as old Simeon of the Holy Scriptures rejoiced when he was privileged to set eyes upon the Lord Jesus." The Prince's answer was gentle, but its note was of common sense. "To-day you live in peace and prosperity under British rule. The King continues to watch over you with fatherly care. You will show yourselves worthy of his protection by listening to the words of the officers appointed to guide and instruct you. They will educate you to bring up your children, to make best use of your land, to free your cattle from disease and to restrict their number so as not to tire out the land."

From the Basutos the Prince went to the leper colony. He walked down among the withered victims and he talked with them. And then to Durban, to be there in time to celebrate his father's birthday. It was in Durban that Gandhi had first raised his voice in the cause of secession, but the twenty-three thousand Indians in Durban do not seem to remember what the Mahatma told them. There was a Natal Indian Congress which tried to create a hartal, but their efforts were niggardly and their success negligible. The mass of Indians ignored the agitators. They placed garlands about the Prince's neck, and when he offered to speak to them in Hindustani they begged him, instead, to speak in English, because this was now their tongue. At Maritzburg the Zulus shouted before him, "Thou whose loveliness surpasses the loveliness of butterflies . . . we bow down to our adorned ankles before thee in homage."

Then came Zululand, where the great dark men rode in to greet "the Lord of the Great Ones." A chief who was a hundred years old had ridden eighty miles on a donkey to see the Prince. Legions of big, proud Zulus danced and yelled in front of him, their cow-hide shields waved in the air and the fountains of ostrich plumes on their heads moved wildly as they jumped upon the earth. "There is only one House," they shouted, "and that is the King's

House." One young warrior stepped out from the vast company and danced alone. His body was decorated with feathers and beads. He danced like a great flame, a flame that leapt until it was subdued by its own strength and fell at the Prince's feet. Through all this primitive ecstasy the Prince moved quietly, advising them to educate themselves, to work and to bury their old lazy dreams.

The royal train passed from the coast to the Transvaal between miles of immense bonfires. Again the commandos rode out to meet him; again the chiefs led their black followers up to salute him as he passed on to the goldfields, without which the Transvaal would be a poor and desolate place.

Chapter Eighteen

THE TRANSVAAL

We thought that we were conquered, that we were crushed and finished, but we have lived to learn that it is not the British way. Having experienced the mildness of British rule, we rejoice the more because it subdued us.—The Zulu chiefs speaking to the Prince on behalf of the Zulu people.

Chapter Eighteen

THE TRANSVAAL

PRETORIA and Johannesburg are not more than thirty miles apart, but the thirty miles might be the Atlantic for the difference one finds in the people of the two cities. Johannesburg is rich and noisy and it is the home of millionaires. In Pretoria there are touches of Cheltenham; there are old ladies who make needlework covers for their chairs, who read the *Cornhill* and smile over English jokes. If there is this difference between Babylon, the city of gold, and Cheltenham, the town of culture, their voices were one in greeting the Prince of Wales when he came to them from the little towns and the open country, heralded by artillery and droning aircraft. Three hundred people, each more than sixty-five years old, lunched with him; thirteen thousand children sang to him and twenty thousand natives performed their frenzied dance before him.

The most interesting hours during this part of his journey were those which he spent with Mr. Hofmeyer, the Administrator. Mr. Hofmeyer's Dutch blood was cooled in an English university. He seems to be free of old prejudices, unvain, humorous and simple. He lives a domestic life which is so unpretentious that it is not easy to believe in his importance during the first moments in his house. When he spoke to the Prince he said, "You have shown that you understand us; you have spoken to our people in their own tongue, thus giving recognition to their language. In doing so you have touched a cord in our hearts which will continue to vibrate. We recognise in you, sir, if I may say so, a certain kinship of character with our own people. Ours is a simple people, big-hearted and frank. .... In you, sir, we recognise that the keynote of character is sincerity." The Prince replied in Afrikaans, and next day he placed a wreath of white carnations on Kruger's grave. Then he went on to Johannesburg.

At night the Prince of Wales climbed on to the roof of the Rand Club, the powerful core of the goldmining interests of the Transvaal. He saw rockets and fireworks, a stream of dancing light, stretching for thirty miles along the lofty reef which gives the world half its gold. When it was almost twelve o'clock he was dancing with the young and fair of Johannesburg. Suddenly the electric lights failed, and he was left to dance with his partner while the others hurried forward with candles. They made a way for him, moving with him so that he was always waltzing in a pool of candle light. As the clock struck twelve somebody near to him said, "Many happy returns of the day." It was his thirty-first birthday.

Johannesburg was jubilant and kind. The Chamber of Commerce gave him a casket to which every mine of the Witwatersrand had contributed an ounce of gold. They brought him bars of gold and silver boxes, travelling rugs of fox fur, lion skins, dogs, flowers and fruit. One old lady sent him a cheque for two thousand pounds and begged him to buy a horse for himself. He pleased everybody, especially the old man of one hundred and three years who brought his sons, aged eighty-five, and apologised for the absence of his grandson who had been driven to his bed by the weakness of age. The Prince pleased them all more than ever when the mayor had said, "This hall has very bad acoustic properties." "Well, in that case," said the Prince, "why have any speeches?"

Although Johannesburg is six thousand feet above the sea, some of its mines go down to the level of the coast. The Prince descended into one of these, travelling through the labyrinth of tunnels and asking questions of the miners whom he saw at work. When Johannesburg was spent by its own pleasure the Prince left for Rhodesia.

The flowery streets of Bulawayo were roofed with flags and banners. The story was the old story lived again. Natives came out in their thousands. "Royal Bird, come out and let us see thee," they cried, heaping karosses and shields and treasure at his feet. But his common sense was not shaken. "The loyalty of the mouth is not equal to the loyalty of the spear," he said. He climbed the Matapos, the roof of the world, where Rhodes is buried. When he drove through the streets of Salisbury, half-hidden girls threw violets down upon him from high windows. But it was not all picturesque and gay. He spent long busy hours enquiring into the lives of the tobacco growers. He heard the old Rhodesians thank him for the stimulus that Wembley had given their trade, and in the evening, after dinner at the Governor's house was over, he invested Sir John Chancellor and others with honours from the King. The natives brought more leopard skins and so many pairs of elephant tusks from which gongs could be made that one shudders at their number. He went out to the citrus orchards and then, as a unique gesture, he went to Gatooma and laid the foundation stone of a Masonic temple.

The Prince left Southern Rhodesia behind him. At Livingstone he danced in the open air. Just as he was going in to supper he saw a company of natives walk on to the dance floor. They carried mealie sacks and ropes, which they placed on the floor. Each sack was weighted down by a black boy and then the older men dragged them over the floor to polish it for the dancers. Again the bagpipes were playing at Magdalen. The Prince formed the natives, their sacks and their black boys into a line and offered a prize if they would sprint-race around the dancing floor. The Prince was starter and the Governor acted as judge. They whirled about madly, round and round the dancing floor, so madly that they crashed into the Governor and brought him to earth.

When the dance was over the Prince went on to the Zambesi in a long boat, and next day he saw the Victoria Falls. He walked through the rain forest, where a million pearls of water fell about him; he held out his hands so that they played with the little rainbows. Hundreds of white moths flew about his head. He climbed up to a high place where he saw the whole magnificence of the falls. Then he went up the river beyond the thunder of the water. Crocodiles blinked at him, natives tapped drums in the forest, and in the afternoon, far up the Zambesi, he met the great Yeta, chief of all the Barotse. Yeta had come three hundred miles downstream. For a week his company of canoes had threaded their way through the jungles, through the rapids. Yeta travelled with great ceremony: his ambassadors came in a flotilla of dugouts, his retinue were about him in long, slim barges, each with a white awning under which the chiefs of the Barotse sat. Forty oarsmen, lively with coloured feathers, brought Yeta's barge in to the bank of the river. Yeta himself came ashore, elegant in a uniform of black and gold. Drums crashed. Still the Anglo-Saxon common sense did not miss an opportunity. "The Governor has told me how you, Chief Yeta, and your counsellors recently agreed to give up one of your old customs, that of making your people work for the chiefs without payment. I am glad to hear it. You have adopted two of the great principles of civilisation—that a man is free to give his labour where he will, and that the labourer is worthy of his hire."

The Prince came to the northernmost place in his tour. Here, at Broken Hill, the diligent Governor of the Katanga had travelled many miles to greet him. The last company of natives danced in front of him. Some of them had walked four hundred miles through the forest. His last meal at this northern point was an odd luxury to find in such a setting. More than forty miles from the nearest white man's house, with deep brown valleys and immense blue mountains rising and falling between him and the horizon, he sat down to a meal of caviare, iced consommé, chicken, partridge, and strawberries. The luncheon was served in a pavilion of thatch and grass and flowers. Mr. Deakin, who describes so many of these occasions in *Southward Ho!* says that in the midst of all this sophistication the Prince sat down and ate nothing but an apple and a piece of toast.

Chapter Nineteen

ST. HELENA, THE ARGENTINE AND CHILE

I have called the New World into existence to redress the balance of the Old.—GEORGE CANNING.

ST. HELENA, THE ARGENTINE AND CHILE

FROM the Cape of Good Hope *Repulse* steamed north-west towards St. Helena. The little island, of which one cannot think without recalling the exile of Napoleon, was proud and hospitable, but the Prince was allowed a respite from the usual speeches and busy hours. For a moment he was able to forget the present and to contemplate the past. As a boy at Windsor he had spent many hours over his history books. When these were closed he was able to play in the park which held the story of a thousand years within its glades and shadows. He had been used to the sight of a tree which was grown from the willow beneath which Napoleon sat when he was at St. Helena. There are many trees and memorials at Windsor; some are oaks which grew there in Elizabeth's day—one stands in the place where Herne's oak once grew—and there is a cedar, under which Queen Victoria's dog used to wait for her holding her gloves in its mouth. But none of the great company of trees awakens a more vivid and melancholy picture than Napoleon's willow which the Prince knew as a child.

He went to the glen where Napoleon was buried; he planted an olive tree beside the empty grave and he drank from the stream beside which the exile used to sit in the summer evenings. When he returned from his graceful pilgrimage he was shown the records of the island for the year 1821, and he read the brief sentence, "Saturday the 5th, died General Napoleon Buonaparte."

From St. Helena *Repulse* changed her course south-west, and on August 4 she came to Montevideo. Uruguay gave the first sign of the depth of its pleasure when the President stepped forward and welcomed the Prince by extending both hands.

The first hours after the arrival were dignified and beautiful, and the Prince, wearing his scarlet tunic and his bearskin, set the fashion for grandeur and pomp. But pleasure soon conquered the day and there was a programme of receptions, dinners, dances and opera. This visit to South America was important to the Prince, for he was to make many secure and profitable friendships with South American leaders during the years that followed. He chose the country as a fresh field for his campaign for British trade, and he planted the first good seed of his cause when he said to the President of Uruguay, "If we penetrate outward forms and appearances we find, in the essential trend of thought and policy, nothing inconsistent in the larger aims which animate the peoples of Uruguay and Great Britain."

When Montevideo had cheered itself hoarse the Prince travelled to Buenos Aires, which is as beautiful as its name. The cry was the same in every country, even if it was in continually changing tongues. "Viva el Principe de Gales!" the two million people of Buenos Aires cried with immediate delight. In place of the sober sincerity of the Dutchmen who had ridden with him in South Africa, the Prince found careless, noisy, Latin fun. The black horses which drew his landau through the streets were harnessed in gold, and as he passed he bowed beneath a rain of roses, daffodils and lilies. The country which owed much of its security to British capital and enterprise overwhelmed its guest with kindness.

Once more the Prince showed that he had been a busy student, and he surprised those who were used to his versatility by introducing phrases of Spanish into his speeches. The note which he played upon persistently was of friendship between Argentine and Britain, but he avoided high-sounding phrases and moralising in favour of statistics and facts; he talked also of democracy and of "equal oppor-

tunity." Mr. Ralph Deakin wrote in *Southward Ho!* that
the "Argentine treatment of the Prince of Wales stood
quite alone." He described the arrival at the Naval Dock-
yard: "It was not the mere welcome of a single city; it was
an extraordinary tribute that came spontaneously from the
citizens and seamen of half a hundred different lands, including Germans, who were here in full force. It is
doubtful, indeed, whether anybody has ever listened to such
a volume of sound as they combined to make. It was a
nerve-racking experience; one wanted to escape, yet wanted
to stay and witness the almost barbaric effect of it all."

The Prince turned from the acclamations whenever he
could. He demanded time for his journeys of enquiry,
and one day he went to one of the vast freezing works. "He
saw experts fell the animals at a blow, without a sound and
with never a second blow. From butcher to butcher each
carcass glided on the overhead cable until it hung in sides
of beef, wiped and cleaned by hands provided with damped
and sterilised hot cloths. One of the floors of the establishment is 330 feet long and has a capacity for 25,000 carcasses.
There and on the sheep-killing floor, where 4,000 are dealt
with at once, he asked questions by the dozen while standing over the smock-frocked dressers, each doing his allotted
task, and examined the methods of sorting the all-important
by-products. He took keen interest in the cooking and canning departments and spent some time in the hides de-
partment, in which some 60,000 skins are stored." Every
chapter of Mr. Deakin's interesting record of this tour gives
us such side lights on the Prince, pursuing knowledge with
his now famous earnestness. When he was driving back to
Buenos Aires from the freezing plant he looked up and saw
thousands of pigeon which had been released flying over
him. Their wings had been dyed red, white and blue in
celebration of his presence.

Buenos Aires almost killed the Prince with kindness,
but there were simple scenes wedged in between the
pageants. One evening he was expected at a Toc H gather-

ing. He was late, and while the members were waiting for him they gathered about a pianoforte and sang songs. During the day somebody had told the Prince of an old Englishwoman, sick and bedridden, who was unhappy because she could not see him. He had gone to her on his way to the Toc H party and he had stayed beside her bed for half an hour. When he arrived at the Toc H building he could not find the main door. He entered the hall alone and found himself at the end where the group of men were standing about the pianoforte. He joined them, unnoticed. One by one the singers turned, discovered the Prince, and fell away. The singing thus became fainter and fainter until the pianist turned and said, "Why the hell don't you sing?" He saw that he was alone with only the Prince leaning over his shoulder, trying to follow the music.

One of the most delightful incidents of the Prince's stay in Buenos Aires was when a young Argentine Britisher, named Sammy, was chosen to present the Prince with a rawhide whip on behalf of the members of Toc H. Sammy was elected because he was the youngest member. He spent many days in preparing his speech, and when the great hour came, he had to face a hall crowded with people and, at the far end, the Prince himself, upon a dais. Sammy was to walk the length of the hall to make his speech, but he could not move. He fumbled with his tie and his pockets, and he seemed almost to be parodying the Prince's early shyness on great occasions. The Prince saved the moment gallantly. He walked down from the dais, advanced towards Sammy and led him back to the other end of the hall. "I can quite understand," he whispered. "It is exactly how I used to feel when I had to make a speech."

Early in September the Prince crossed the Andes into Chile. He might have taken advantage of the journey into the mountains to rest and read, but he rose in company with the sun every morning to sit at the window of his carriage, for ever searching the landscape or asking questions. He might have pitied himself for the long months of duty

which lay behind him, but his zeal seemed to grow stronger.
Whenever the train rested he would jump down into the
snow, sometimes to tramp away from the track, sometimes
to make snowballs which he threw at his equerries. If the
engines were changed he would run along the track and
watch the men at their work. At Uspallata, twelve thousand
feet above the ocean, he saw the big bronze figure of the
Redeemer rising from the white slope of the mountain as
a signal of peace between the two republics. He passed on
to the ancient town of Santiago and, as the welcome of the
Argentine faded behind him, the welcome of Chile began.
The grand moment during his stay in Santiago was when
he laid the foundation-stone of the Canning monument in
front of the British Legation. One hundred years had
passed since George Canning "raised his voice to tell a
continent that its political and economic recovery was to
be obtained . . . . by consolidating the ideals of independence." There had been days of rain before the ceremony
and, sitting in his room, the Prince had improved the hour
by learning more Spanish. When he spoke of Canning, "the
Saviour of Chile," he was able to recall his achievement to
the Chileans in their own tongue. His Spanish was now so
good that he could talk to the officials with ease. On September 12, the Prince was near to Valparaiso. The outward
journey was now ended and the noise of the great, free
breakers of the Pacific induced him to sleep. Ralph Deakin
writes that the Prince's stay in Valparaiso was "as a sailor
among sailors." He steamed out to the Chilean fleet, at
anchor, and he boarded *Latorre*, which had fought as
a British ship at Jutland. The President of the Republic
chose the occasion for an imaginative and charming speech.
He raised his glass towards the Prince and spoke of the
"great honour and satisfaction" it was for the Chilean Navy
to receive its guest on a vessel which had been built in an
English shipyard and which had once flown "the flag of
the British Empire." There were rocks of action behind
these clouds of compliment, and while the Prince was on

board *Latorre* he talked of the plan, then afoot, to attach British officers to the Chilean Navy "to advise on matters of organisation, training, gunnery, submarines and aviation." Before the Prince left Chile the scheme was placed on the tables of the War Office in London.

On September 19 the royal train passed over the crest of the Andes once more, this time through a terrible storm. Less than a month afterwards *Repulse* was back in English waters. The journey of thirty-five thousand miles was over and a new phase of the Prince's life was to begin.

Chapter Twenty

WORK AMONG THE POOR

I have done the State some service, and they know it.—OTHELLO.

Chapter Twenty

WORK AMONG THE POOR

THE Prince ceased roaming the earth when he returned from South America, but, more than ever, he was a stranger to England and it was not easy for him to change the tempo of his life. It was observed by those who travelled with him that there were hours of contemplation, touching upon moroseness, when he was not facing a cheering crowd. The manacles of his father's Court were unwelcome to him after years of freedom and hurry. The gap between father and son had widened, for they thought in different worlds. It is said that the Prince was distressed by his return to London and that he wrote a letter to his father asking for greater independence. The letter is believed to have travelled ahead of *Repulse* to warn King George of the changes which had come over his son. Rumour said that the Prince's wish for freedom and the right to choose his own staff was so fierce that he wrote of his decision to renounce his rights and settle in one of the Dominions if he was not allowed to follow his own way. The tragedy of his isolation had already begun. His stubbornness was alleviated by his great charm, his sympathy and his desire to do what was right. But he discounted his powers by turning from advice and, whenever possible, playing a lone hand. His scattered experience of men had not taught him the value of quiet conference, and his restlessness and superficial view of human nature still debarred him from realising the difference between popularity and respect.

Despite these private misfortunes, which were naturally hidden from the public view, the Prince learned to make a unique place for himself in the public life of England.

He could say that the world was his oyster with more conviction than any heir before him. He had gone, with his good heart and his keen, enquiring mind, into the farthest corners of the earth, and his lively memory held the scenes and the experiences through which he had passed. They did not fade. As London interests increased their hold on him, with pleasure and duty hand in hand, he did not become a Little Englander and forget. The field of his interests widened along every way. The Prince's diary of engagements shows us how in one day in January of 1926, he received a deputation from the Society of Apothecaries, visited the Sargent Exhibition and received the Japanese Ambassador. Each of these duties called for informed conversation. In one morning, General Hertzog called on him to talk of South Africa, the Maharajah of Burdwan climbed the stairs of York House after Mr. Hertzog to talk of India, and, soon afterwards, Mr. Coates sat with him for thirty minutes to talk about New Zealand. Within half an hour on a morning in 1927, the Prince received the Portuguese Ambassador, the Bulgarian Minister and Sir Thomas Cook. But his visitors were not all plenipotentiaries and representatives of foreign Courts. Men of business and artists claimed his time. In one morning he received Mr. J. H. Thomas, Mr. Gordon Selfridge, Mr. Henry Ford and Sir William Orpen. The Prince's manner became more assured as his thoughts matured, although his nervousness and dislike of advice persisted. He was not capricious in his devotion to duty, and when the great strike came, in May of 1926, he found what was to become the focus for his deepest anxiety—the discontented unemployed. From this time the Prince of Wales identified himself with the mass of the people in a way no monarch or heir to a throne had ever done. He became the prince of the people. In the years that followed the General Strike, the poor and the distressed learned to turn to him for encouragement rather than to their own leaders. His cry on behalf of the unemployed was so persistent that he broke down every barrier

1927.   *The Prince of Wales's visit to the East End :   The Prince at Pell Street Club, Cable Street, E. 1.*

and turned hard-bitten old agitators like Mr. J. H. Thomas
and Mr. Cook into friends. The American newspapers,
always willing to suspect the merit of princes, told of his
growing friendliness with the Labour leaders, and one of
them admitted that "the age of miracles" had "not passed."
The first real sympathy between the Prince and the people
of the distressed areas was stirred. The story begins in 1923,
when he went to a provincial town in which there were
awful poverty and suffering. He had been used to scenes of
prosperity during his journeys into the great countries of the
south. France had shown him one way of horrible human
suffering, but in 1923 the misery of England's poor was not
tangible to him. When he came to the town in the provinces he was taken to a soup kitchen and there he stood
back in the shadows, watching the hungry men being fed.
He was silent for some minutes. Before him he saw a
hundred men who lived in shadows he had never known
before. The first time he spoke, in the surprised way he
did when he was shocked, he pointed to a young man of
perhaps twenty years and said, "That man has no shirt
under his coat." He went from the dismal soup kitchen to
a Toc H party, but his depression stayed with him. In the
little adjoining room he walked up and down, pressing his
hands together and saying, "What can I do? What can be
done?" His social conscience was awakened and the most
powerful theme of his early life had begun.

The Prince returned to London, complaining that sympathy was not enough. From this time all other interests
took second place for him. He hammered on every door for
help, and, as patron of the Lord Mayor's fund for distressed
miners, he asked that he might be allowed to go to the
mining areas so that he could see for himself how the
money was being used. The Prince had appealed for money
for the miners on Christmas night, and the story of the
effect of this plea made over the wireless is best told in a
speech which was made by Mr. Cook, who had led the
strike in 1926. "You, sir," said Mr. Cook, "have done a

marvellous thing. Never was I so impressed as by your speech on Christmas night." The Labour leader who had once cried "Revolutions will come" and who had been described by his colleague, Lord Snowden, as a "raving wrecker," went on, addressing the Prince: "I was with two Communist friends, and when your name was announced to speak on behalf of the Miners' Fund they undoubtedly scoffed. But they listened to what you had to say, and when you finished, with tears in their eyes, they put their hands in their pockets and gave what money they had on them to the fund."

In case one's English pride should lead one into a narrow view of the Prince's service in going to the mining areas, it might be well to turn to the columns of an American newspaper for an account of the strange pilgrimage of March, 1929. Mr. G. Patrick Thompson wrote in the *New York Tribune*:

"Curtis Bennett,* a big man with a direct way about him . . . . went across to St. James's Palace and knocked on the dark polished door under the low arches. Behind that door are the quarters of Sir Godfrey Thomas . . . . private secretary to the Prince of Wales. Curtis Bennett and Godfrey Thomas had a talk. The result of that talk was that the Prince decided to go North and see conditions for himself. He would go informally, with Godfrey Thomas and Curtis Bennett. No receptions. No dinners with county magnates. No mayors' addresses of welcome. No organised plan. No equerry and no police escorts.

"This latter provision upset the chief constables of selected districts. They couldn't see how the Prince could get along without police protection, and one or two rather thought there ought to be troops around. Otherwise they would have to wash their hands of all responsibility.

* Now Sir Noel Curtis Bennett.

"Off went the trio. They put up at a station hotel in a northern city. Curtis Bennett had the name of an elderly miner in the first village to be visited. The miner shook his head. He had a death in the house. His wife had died that morning. Curtis Bennett went back, despondent, to tell the Prince what had happened and to explain that he scarcely knew what to suggest next.

"'I'd like to go in,' said the Prince quietly. He went in. The miner's daughter was inside, a nice girl, employed as a domestic servant in a good family. The Prince caught her arm and gave it a comforting little shake.

"'I understand.'

"That broke the ice. It also emboldened the girl to ask, with the simplicity of a child of the people, 'Would you come up to see my mother, sir?'

"The Prince nodded. They went upstairs.

". . . It chanced that in the early afternoon, in another village, they came to a row of terrible little houses. They picked out one by chance and knocked. Could he come in, the Prince asked the miner who opened the door. The man recognised him, but stood dubiously in the doorway. Then he said, 'Ay, ye can, sir. But my wife's sick, if ye understand.'

"The Prince didn't understand until he got inside. And then he did. In that dreadful little bare room the miner's wife lay in the pangs of childbirth. For a moment the Prince stood looking at that twitching figure under the rough bedding.

"'If ye wouldn't mind holding her hand just for a minute, she'd never forget it.' The Prince stepped up, put down his hand and the mother's sought it and clutched it."

The Prince tramped through the mud and cold for four days. Mr. Patrick Thompson reminded American readers that " King Edward, for all his shrewd tact and diplomacy, never entered the workshop, never toured the industrial areas, never associated himself with the people as his son and grandson have done." The Prince's search into the life of the miners was penetrating. He asked for their pay sheets and he asked the cost of their food. And as he passed from one house to the other he was the object of a tribute which was unique in his life. The photographers and press-men who usually gathered at his heels left him almost alone. They waited in the towns nearby to gather the facts for their stories; he had asked them not to follow him and they obeyed. It is said that not one of the miners in his long pilgrimage complained to him. They answered his questions, but they did not grumble.

When the fourth day ended the Prince's companions were very tired. They were motoring from Newcastle to Darlington, hungry and exhausted, and Sir Noel Curtis Bennett could contemplate nothing but the pleasures of sleep. On the outskirts of Darlington they came upon a cluster of tall chimneys. Fearing the worst, Sir Noel Curtis Bennett diverted the Prince's attention to the opposite landscape, but he failed. " What are those chimneys?" asked the Prince.

" They are part of the railway wagon works," he was told.

" Then we'll get out and see them," was the answer.

The Prince found a small boy who took him to the foreman. He asked the man many questions and then hurried back to his car. Just as he left the factory he told somebody to telephone to the Mayor of Darlington and ask him to be at the railway station. When the hurried talk with the mayor was over the Prince went to his own compartment, and Sir Godfrey Thomas and Sir Noel Curtis Bennett at last fell back in their seats and courted sleep. Ten minutes passed and the door of their compartment was opened. The Prince needed their help with a crossword puzzle. So they had to shake themselves out of their doze and wrestle with rivers in Brazil, Australian birds in three letters and obscure Greek gods. He left them when the puzzle was finished and they turned once more to their sleep. Again the door of the compartment was flung open, and the Prince reappeared, carrying his portable typewriter. He was writing a long letter to the Prime Minister and he wished to know the names of all the villages he had visited during the four days.

Seven months after the Prince's visit to the mining areas Sir Noel Curtis Bennett went over the ground once more, and in a letter* which he wrote on August 28, 1929, he said: "I was in Northumberland and Durham again last week, and it was very interesting to find that all these people put the improvement in the coal trade entirely down to the Prince's visit—and, indeed, nothing would or could persuade them otherwise. Also, almost all the public houses in the 'red' villages have now hung a picture of H.R.H."

* To the author.

Chapter Twenty-one

LIFE IN ENGLAND: AVIATION

IT would be wrong to present the ex-King as a unique character. His position made the closing tragedy of his reign more terrible than if any other man had been the victim, but it is to be remembered that the confusion he suffered was shared by thousands of young men at the end of the war: men who found that the problem of living for their country was more terrifying than the threat of dying for it. When the Prince of Wales returned from his long journeys, many of the returned soldiers had already shaken off their melancholia and they were fitting into the scheme of English life once more.

In the darkness of December, 1936, when King Edward signed his abdication, we did not pause to realise that the King belonged to the generation which took a violent view of its problems, perhaps because they had lived in violence of mind and action from 1914 to 1918. Psychologists and faddists may swell simple facts into imposing theories, but there is no doubt that the Prince never gained the repose of mind which was taken from him during the war and in the years of his travels. He was doubly punished for belonging to his generation, and the effort he made, from 1927 until the year before his father's jubilee, is therefore all the more wonderful and to be remembered in his favour. He must be understood in this time before he can be understood at the end.

King George's calm sense of duty and his cult for orderliness still prevented him from understanding his son's perplexity. It was his sense of duty which urged him, perhaps too often, to criticise the Prince, sometimes quoting the opinions of other, older men in support of his argument.

an appeal for pictorial posters, in 1923, he said: "I do not believe for one moment that industrialism and artistic development are necessarily antagonistic, and that because a man has keen business vision he is artistically blind. . . . A nation's art is the mirror of its inner mind; the quality of the one is the true reflection of the other."

In all the activities which he created, the Prince's tendency was towards the practical. He was already playing an active part in the management of the Duchy of Cornwall estates, and he showed himself to be a careful and even parsimonious master. His house was as modest as the London house of any well-to-do bachelor, for he disliked grandness and was apparently not pleased by lavish entertainment. His economies and experience in connection with Duchy of Cornwall affairs affected his policy in public speeches, and he was usually able to speak to business men in their own language. He never clung to aery notions, and he consoled the members of the London Chamber of Commerce by saying, "Commercial education is essential in a commercial nation." He said also, "Commerce is no longer a haphazard affair, but calls for a cultured intellect and a great power of mental concentration." Two years afterwards he spoke at the British Industries Fair dinner at the Mansion House. "Time and trade wait for no man . . . . a trade opportunity missed is gone for ever," he said. He sponsored all the modern devices. "Films are a real aid to the development of imperial trade," he said in November of 1923, and in the same year he told a company of pressmen that "modern science working hand in hand with modern journalism" had "put a girdle round the earth." He talked of the "science and art" of advertising and of the psychology of salesmanship. The Prince realised also that his own power was increased by what was written about him in the newspapers. He admitted that he had come to look upon the Press as his "publicity agents" when he spoke to the Company of Stationers and Newspaper Makers in February of 1932. By this time the business men of the country had

self with a succession of personal enthusiasms rather than face the experience of deep-rooted friendship. These facts must be realised, not in criticism, but as indicating gaps in his kind yet uncertain nature. Kings are usually afraid to give their confidence to their friends. Queen Victoria said, when she was married, that it was a new thing for her " to *dare* to be unguarded in conversing with anybody." Perhaps this fear mixed with the Prince's natural friendliness and made it difficult for him to create the relationships which would have strengthened him. He seemed to need affection and to be willing to give it, but the muddled experience of his life had prevented him from learning how this could be done.

The Prince had no great desire to read and he was restless with conversation when it lacked a practical purpose. He was in no sense highbrow, and he once said that he did not like Russian plays "where they spend three hours talking about life without bothering to live it." This comment is a key to his thoughts about art. He was impatient with the abstract. If he met an author he would become interested in his work. When he went to see Thomas Hardy, in Dorset, he returned to London and read one of his novels. When he met George Moore he was so charmed by the talk of the celebrated writer that he read a book of his reminiscences. His approach to books was therefore more human than literary. It was natural that a man who lived so busily should have time-tables at his elbow rather than thoughtful literature.

His travels prevented the Prince from becoming interested in inanimate objects such as pictures, furniture and decoration until he came to rest in York House. In later years, when he went to live at Fort Belvedere, the joy of possession stimulated his interest in his home and he soon became house-proud.

But any development of taste in the Prince did not shake his conviction that art should be harnessed to the practical issues of life. When he spoke at the Royal Academy, making an appeal for pictorial posters, in 1923, he said: "I do not believe for one moment that industrialism and artistic development are necessarily antagonistic, and that because a man has keen business vision he is artistically blind. . . . A nation's art is the mirror of its inner mind; the quality of the one is the true reflection of the other."

In all the activities which he created, the Prince's tendency was towards the practical. He was already playing an active part in the management of the Duchy of Cornwall estates, and he showed himself to be a careful and even parsimonious master. His house was as modest as the London house of any well-to-do bachelor, for he disliked grandness and was apparently not pleased by lavish entertainment. His economies and experience in connection with Duchy of Cornwall affairs affected his policy in public speeches, and he was usually able to speak to business men in their own language. He never clung to aery notions, and he consoled the members of the London Chamber of Commerce by saying, "Commercial education is essential in a commercial nation." He said also, "Commerce is no longer a haphazard affair, but calls for a cultured intellect and a great power of mental concentration." Two years afterwards he spoke at the British Industries Fair dinner at the Mansion House. "Time and trade wait for no man . . . . a trade opportunity missed is gone for ever," he said. He sponsored all the modern devices. "Films are a real aid to the development of imperial trade," he said in November of 1923, and in the same year he told a company of pressmen that "modern science working hand in hand with modern journalism" had "put a girdle round the earth." He talked of the "science and art" of advertising and of the psychology of salesmanship. The Prince realised also that his own power was increased by what was written about him in the newspapers. He admitted that he had come to look upon the Press as his "publicity agents" when he spoke to the Company of Stationers and Newspaper Makers in February of 1932. By this time the business men of the country had

Chapter Twenty-one

LIFE IN ENGLAND: AVIATION

IT would be wrong to present the ex-King as a unique character. His position made the closing tragedy of his reign more terrible than if any other man had been the victim, but it is to be remembered that the confusion he suffered was shared by thousands of young men at the end of the war: men who found that the problem of living for their country was more terrifying than the threat of dying for it. When the Prince of Wales returned from his long journeys, many of the returned soldiers had already shaken off their melancholia and they were fitting into the scheme of English life once more.

In the darkness of December, 1936, when King Edward signed his abdication, we did not pause to realise that the King belonged to the generation which took a violent view of its problems, perhaps because they had lived in violence of mind and action from 1914 to 1918. Psychologists and faddists may swell simple facts into imposing theories, but there is no doubt that the Prince never gained the repose of mind which was taken from him during the war and in the years of his travels. He was doubly punished for belonging to his generation, and the effort he made, from 1927 until the year before his father's jubilee, is therefore all the more wonderful and to be remembered in his favour. He must be understood in this time before he can be understood at the end.

King George's calm sense of duty and his cult for orderliness still prevented him from understanding his son's perplexity. It was his sense of duty which urged him, perhaps too often, to criticise the Prince, sometimes quoting the opinions of other, older men in support of his argument.

The name of a prelate or of a statesman would be brought in to support the King's opinion. Perhaps King George did not comprehend the care with which his own father had avoided the same error. He might have recalled a day when Lady Augusta Stanley congratulated King Edward upon the good behaviour of his sons, when the King answered, "*We* were perhaps a little too much spoken to and at; at least, we thought we could never do anything right, anyhow." King George's son no doubt suffered similar confusion as to what was right and what was wrong.

Frequent chastening made the Prince of Wales secretive, stubborn and more self-willed than ever. Still in tune with his generation, he came to look upon his father, the Archbishop and some of the older Ministers as a critical and unsympathetic company, designed to frustrate his natural eagerness. He therefore made his own life as he wished. It took him into three worlds. One was in the circle of friends which he gathered about him, often to the distress of his father, who suspected their influence.

The second world was that of his father's Court, in which he was not at ease. The third world was that of his good deeds and his popularity. Here he let all the charming aspects of his character flourish at ease. He enjoyed his popularity and he allowed his self-confidence to prosper upon it. But if he enjoyed the privileges of his position, he often showed impatience with formality, and he liked to be hail-fellow-well-met with people, providing that he still withheld the right to cut off his familiarity when he chose. It is said that he once allowed a golfer to call him by his Christian name. When the friend carelessly called him David before a crowd of people, he abandoned the game and, it is said, the friendship closed. On another occasion he retired from a golf club because the officials remonstrated when he invited the professional into the club house for tea. These inconsistencies always had a foundation of good intention, but the foundation sometimes wavered and his judgement of people was affected. He therefore satisfied him-

realised that their cause was the Prince's cause and that he was their most illustrious champion. Commercial organisations clamoured for his help. In the early years it was perhaps because of his name that industrialists sought his patronage. But this compliment was no longer necessary when he proved that it was no empty boast which was written beneath his shield. He gave meaning to his motto, *Ich Dien*. Once, in a speech to a gathering of business men, he pressed both his hands upon the table, leaned over, and said, "I shall always pull my weight." The serious promise rings a little sadly after six years have passed, but he was sincere when he made it. Freedom from humbug, frankness and energy soon gave the Prince a position in British industry which had never belonged to another royalty in our history.

The Prince was inconsistent in his treatment of sycophants, sometimes enjoying their manner and sometimes snubbing them. All kinds of men were admitted to York House to describe their schemes, but he was seldom deceived if their plans were mixed with self-advancement or their arguments tainted by humbug. He was quick to reprimand. He was slowly bringing a new meaning to the royal office which he held. Mr. H. G. Wells has said, "Nowadays . . . the stuffing is out of princes." Perhaps he saw only Europe and forgot the country at his feet. The Romanoffs were annihilated and the head of the Hohenzollerns was an exile at Doorn. The Bourbons were near their end and the Habsburgs lived upon hope. The House of Savoy was hidden under the shadow of a dictator. While these fierce changes shook the peace of Europe, almost more violently than the war which preceded them, England turned more and more to its Royal Family for consolation. It moved towards Buckingham Palace as towards its own conscience, for there lay its example in citizenship and its font of moral courage. The people learned also, as the years passed, to expect a certain kind of leadership from the heir to the throne. He spoke for the young and he urged the cause of the practical. Mr. H. G. Wells was lonely in his pronouncement. Great minds do not always think alike, and it was possible to turn to another writer of the time and find Mr. G. K. Chesterton announcing that "the most popular institution left is monarchy."

The popularity was not without reason. It seemed that in Britain alone life was secure and self-respect a possible aim for man. While the Prince led us in action, we drew our inner refreshments from a different kind of example. This was the example of the King, his father. While the Prince sounded the bugles of the young, the Sovereign spoke more gently, with the voice of the old. "With the ancient is wisdom: and in length of days understanding."

Foreigners sometimes smiled at the complacency of English life, and the newspapers of Europe often warned us that we were living upon a volcano. Perhaps the volcano which was shattering their security in these years had no influence upon the English earth. The life of the stolid Briton went on. One turns to a day in 1934 to understand the difference between our balanced life and the disasters which unsettled Europe. On one Saturday, early in December, there was revolution in Spain and a raid on the Italians on the Abyssinian border. Signor Mussolini was alarmed over the state of the lira, the Hungarians were being expelled from Jugo-Slavia and, in Russia, Stalin's friend, Serge Kirov, had been assassinated. England's news of the week was not melodramatic enough to deserve the front pages of its own newspapers. The first air mail had left for Australia and among the one hundred thousand letters was one for the King's son, the Duke of Gloucester, who was spending Christmas in New Zealand. Within a few days of this event the Duke of Kent was married in Westminster Abbey. While monarchs and dictators in other countries walked, like Cromwell, with a coat of mail beneath their clothes, in fear of their lives, the King, the Queen and the Prince of Wales drove through the streets of London, at one with their people.

In November of 1928 King George suffered his great illness, and from this time, the duties of his son were increased so that pleasures were lessened for him. During the ten years since the end of the war, British people had learned to take their King for granted. It was part of his example of security and calm that he should always be with them. He became the symbol of the continuity of English life. The sudden alarms at the time when it was feared he might die were therefore terrible. The people's anthem became their prayer. Seventy years before, the Prince Consort had lived in Buckingham Palace, slowly destroying himself with the flame of his own sense of duty. It had been said many times that King George was his grandfather's counterpart. He also remained at his desk when others rested. He was also working in the early morning, when the London labourers were on their way to work. He was used to the sight of them from the window of the room in which he sat before his papers. The fear which gripped the country can be comprehended only by those who lived through that dark winter, when rich and poor pressed against the railings of Buckingham Palace all through the night, wondering if the heart of England would stop beating. The King emerged from the shadows, and he lived long enough to complete the twenty-five years of his reign. But in the time left to him, his son was obliged to accept greater responsibilities and to learn more of the secrets of government.

The Prince of Wales was on safari in Tanganyika when he learned that the King was ill. During the first anxious days, while Londoners waited in the rain at the palace gates for the news bulletins, the Prince left his hunting camp and hurried towards the sea. He travelled on *Enterprise*, at thirty knots, and as he passed through the Red Sea, merchantmen of every nation, bound for the East, sent him their messages of hope. The worst time had passed when the Prince arrived in London, and his father was half-conscious as he tiptoed into the bedroom at Buckingham

Palace. We are told that the King turned upon his pillow and whispered, "Did you get a lion, David?"

There were to be no more months of shooting in Africa. Even hunting seemed no longer possible and the Prince gave up his delight in

> A gleam of November sun,
> The far-spread English counties,
> And a stout red fox to run.

When he was younger, the Prince had always enjoyed both hunting and point-to-point races. He had a lust for exercise and he loved his horses. Part of the sacrifice he made after the King's illness was to sell his stables and turn to less hazardous and exacting ways of satisfying his energy. Miss Sanders, in her book on the Prince, writes of "a very well-known rider to hounds" who said, "Having hunted all my life I have naturally been following the Prince of Wales's fortune in the hunting-field with great interest. Many are the tales told in clubs of the fences he had jumped and his fearless riding." Then he went on to describe a special occasion: "The field was small—not more than sixty people —so there was every opportunity of observing the Prince. . . . I can vouch for it that the Prince rode about as straight a line as a man could take. . . . The hunting-field is one of the most democratic institutions in the world, and it is no wonder the Prince has made himself loved in it. He takes his place quietly, unostentatiously and on his merits. . . . When hounds run he takes his own line and requires no preferential treatment at gaps."

Riding had given the Prince a release from the duties of York House, and it was not a light decision for him to forsake his pleasure. He had won his first point-to-point race in 1921. From then on he had appeared at many meetings, and there were times when the members of his father's Government were worried by his recklessness. Even the venerable old Maharajah of Udaipur had protested with him in India. He had said, "I have seen in the English papers Your Royal Highness's pictures in different games

The Prince of Wales riding at the Beaufort Point-to-Point.

of horsemanship. Sometimes I found them dangerous and risky. Hence I request Your Royal Highness not to take such risks in future, for the safety of exalted personages like Your Royal Highness is most important."

The Prince did not heed the Maharajah's picturesque appeal. When he returned to England he still rode, often dangerously. But the seed of duty was virile, and in 1928 he obeyed the frightening warning of the King's illness and turned, perhaps sadly, to milder games such as squash rackets and golf. The same zest hurried him on. If he was to play golf, he was to play it well. It was exercise but not a relaxation for him, and he learned the game as if it were to be his career. The Prince was Captain of the Royal and Ancient Golf Club, in the wake of his grandfather. King Edward had performed his duties by deputy. "Not so the Prince of Wales," wrote a correspondent in *Country Life*. He "gallantly drove himself into office in the traditional manner, and later in the day played his medal round despite the too loyal crowds that surged out on to the links to see him do it." The journalist could not help adding that "to drive off at a breakfastless hour, with a crowd of caddies waiting to field the ball, sometimes at insultingly close range, and with the prospect of a gun going off with a formidable bang immediately afterwards, is no mean test of early morning courage."

The adult subjects of his Empire were able to console themselves with theories and knowledge of the vagaries of human nature when King Edward abdicated. Their disappointment was of a different order from the bewilderment of the millions of children who had always accepted him without question. The Prince always had a special talent with the young. There was great understanding between them, and through the years of his travels he built up a bulwark of child love and loyalty which was tremendous. In time they would have been his responsible subjects and they would never have forsaken him. When he spoke in Bombay the Prince said, "In my journeys about the

Empire it has been my special desire to meet and mingle with the youth of each country. I want to understand what is passing in their minds, I want to know to what they are looking forward." He never seemed to talk down to the young or to patronise them in his mind. A hundred sentimental and engaging scenes leap to recollection upon this theme; none more pleasant than the day in Canada when, after he had spoken to some children, the teacher said that she would give them a holiday. "Please don't grant it to-day," he said, "for it's half gone. They want a whole day."

These touches of genius with children brought the Prince success wherever he went. In later years, when he disciplined this interest into educational schemes, he became a vital force in shaping the thoughts and lives of the rising generation. The Prince's sensitiveness and frankness were at their best in the young world. One traces the wide field of this interest from the thousands of schools which he saw in the Dominions to the day in 1921 when ninety thousand school children cheered him in Manchester. When he spoke at the opening of a Barnardo school at Goldings he pleaded for discipline, but not unkindly. He urged the advantages of education upon every possible occasion and expressed conventional views on the progress and training of the young. "Give us more and more education," he said to the teachers of nine foreign countries who had gathered in London for the Vacation Course. Had he remained as Sovereign there is little doubt that he would have turned more and more to this problem. As he grew older, his interests naturally sorted themselves, but his devotion to youth never faltered, and it must be one of the saddest aspects of his abdication that the hundreds of promises he made to children have been broken and that the millions of young hearts which he captured with his charm have been subjected to bitter disappointment.

When he was a boy at Windsor the Prince of Wales had seen aircraft flying over the castle, and when he was a little older he saw model aeroplanes included among his brothers'

1933. *The Prince of Wales, with Princess Elizabeth, returning from Crathie Church during a visit to Balmoral in September, 1933.*

toys. But it was not unil 1913 that he was reminded of their military importance, when he saw them drawn up on the snow at Stuttgart. He talked with Count Zeppelin and he flew over Thuringia, whence his grandfather came. These brief views of aeroplanes tantalised him, and he returned to England eager with questions. During the war he flew several times, and those who saw him after his escapade over the Austrian lines said that he showed no signs of fear. One recalls that he was present at Mons on Armistice Day, when the aircraft flew back after firing the last shots of the war. When the war ended and when aircraft had proved themselves to be the new ships of peace as well as of war, the Prince shared the excitement of his generation. A new world had been discovered; an aloof, different world of which soldiers and sailors had never dreamed. At the close of the war the growth of flying came as a blessing to the young. What the sea had meant to restless adolescents in the days of the windjammer, the air meant to them in 1919. The Royal Air Force was created out of the material and experience of the war, and Prince Edward was identified with its growth from the beginning. He wished to know about new designs, and he was seen reading aeronautical journals when he travelled in trains; he sought the companionship of pilots and he entertained them at his house. When Hinkler flew the Atlantic the Prince was one of the first hosts to receive him on his return to London. They dined together at York House, where the Prince had dined with Kitchener in 1914. Hinkler was coaxed out of his modesty and made to talk. Sir Harry Brittain reports in *By Air* that "the Prince asked Hinkler to let him see his maps used on the flight, Hinkler blushed and stammered out the fact that he had not carried any maps at all."

Although the present King was official royal patron of flying and a qualified pilot, it was his elder brother who cared most for aviation; he was the only member of his family who became "air-minded." The time came when the Prince could restrain his enthusiasm no longer, and he begged his father to allow him to fly, if only as a passenger. He used the impressive argument that he could save time and do more work. The King relented, unwillingly. King George was not only apathetic about flying; he actively disliked and distrusted aircraft, and it was always understood, when he appeared at a review or in a public place where there were machines in the air, that they should give the royal dais a wide berth.

The Prince therefore began his flying in an atmosphere of frustration. It was about this time that he was being forced to give up riding to hounds and in steeplechases. In 1924 there had been a protest in the House of Commons when a Member expressed "grave concern at the repeated risks run by the Heir to the Throne." A horse had recently fallen on him in an Army point-to-point and many people were anxious because of his rashness. Now that he contemplated flying there was equal anxiety, but he had his own way in the end and towards the close of 1927 he began to fly as a passenger. Early in 1928 Sir Hugh Trenchard chose a pilot, Flight-Lieutenant D. S. Don,* to fly the Prince to his far-scattered public engagements. His real life in the air began at this time. He was given a pilot's flying log book upon which was written, *Name*, H.R.H. Prince of Wales; *Rank*, Group-Captain R.A.F. Within was written the record of the many flights which followed. On April 27 he made a local flight over Northolt for thirty minutes, and next day he kept his first public appointment by air. He was flown back from Scarborough, where he had been to meet Marshal Foch, in time to keep an appointment in London. He flew over Sandringham House on the way, and the fact was noted in his diary. His reaction, after the first excitement of flying was passed, was not romantic. He liked the speed, the punctuality and the opportunity of avoiding crowds. But he was impatient on long journeys and would keep up a busy conversation with the pilot by telephone. In these days he flew in an open Bristol Fighter; it was not for some time that

* Now Squadron-Leader D. S. Don, M.V.O.

The Prince of Wales ready for a flight.

he indulged in a closed and comfortable machine of his own. Squadron Leader Don was an enthusiast for his service. He explained the science of navigation and he induced the Prince to read his maps. On the ground also, he acted as instructor, explaining the principles of aviation and analysing modern flying instruction. He flew him over the Leicester hunting country, and he took him for a tour of Cornwall, landing in fields and covering the multitude of Duchy interests as no Duke had done before. The speed and efficiency fascinated the Prince. He would insist upon punctuality, to the point of ordering a cruising speed rather than arrive too early. He was now so delighted over flying that, in 1929, he changed over to a Wapiti aeroplane with a Jupiter 6 engine, with a higher cruising speed and longer range, for Continental tours. He went to play golf at Le Touquet by air; he flew to Windsor and to Scotland. The time came when he wished to learn to pilot his own machine, but King George was still adamant. The Prince was forced to subterfuge. He bought a De Havilland aircraft and registered it in Squadron Leader Don's name. He prejudiced the success of his trick by having the machine painted in the colours of the Household Brigade. But his secret was apparently safe and his adventure began. There were murmurs against the risks which the Prince was running and the Air Ministry was naturally perturbed by its responsibility. It was unthinkable that he should ever be allowed to fly alone.

The Prince used his stubbornness well. He persisted until Squadron Leader Don was at last inveigled into a plot. If the Squadron Leader took out the rudder and stick in the front seat, if he had no controls and promised not to speak a word, then surely they could fly together and count it as a solo for the Prince. The plot was laid for Northolt, which the Prince knew well, and one day, when the aerodrome was deserted, they took off, in the machine with which the Prince was familiar, and flew to one thousand feet. It was a brilliant, silver-blue day, and the Prince made three perfect landings. Squadron Leader Don kept his promise and did not speak once while they were in the air. He hoped that the Prince would now be satisfied. The secret remained safe. Neither the King, the Air Ministry nor the eager newspaper reporters ever heard of the escapade.

But the Prince was not satisfied. He wished to fly absolutely alone and, with good-humoured threats of what he would do if Squadron Leader Don would not be his accomplice, a further plot was made. Again they went to Northolt when the aerodrome was deserted. Only one mechanic stood by and he was sworn to secrecy. The Prince flew to eight hundred or a thousand feet alone. He made one good landing and then took off again. This time the landing was not so good and Squadron Leader Don thankfully saw the end of his half-hour of anxiety. He has said that the Prince was like a schoolboy who has just won a race. All the shy delight with which he once started a merry-go-round beside a road in New Zealand came back again. "He was as excited as a Cranwell cadet after his first solo flight," Squadron Leader Don has said.

About this time a newspaper coined the phrase "Flying Prince." It became one of his new labels. He went to golf at Sandwich by air and to the Grand National at Aintree. When the Prince went to Denmark in the summer of 1932 he travelled by an Imperial Airways machine. Sir Harry Brittain has described the scene of the arrival at Kastrup aerodrome when "tremendous scenes of enthusiasm greeted them." "Just as the sun was setting, a flight of twenty-seven aeroplanes appeared against the crimson sky. First came the giant air liner *Hercules*, carrying the Prince, with all her lights on. Behind her, in perfect formation, came sixteen machines of the Danish Air Force and eleven other planes. As the air liner came to ground she parted from the escort, which circled overhead. The Prince was greeted by the Danish Crown Prince and subsequently driven to the Palace." Sir Harry Brittain adds: "In Denmark the Prince experienced flying in Danish naval seaplanes. While in

Sweden he flew from Stockholm to Gefle and back in a Junker flying-boat, accompanied by the Crown Prince of Sweden." These flights were good for the reputation of flying. Within England he made many a tardy corporation air-minded by announcing that he would arrive at a function by air. Landing grounds were hastily made to receive him and the towns were thus placed on the air map of the country. One of the most interesting flights King Edward ever made was with his younger brother as pilot. This was at Croydon, when King Edward, while still Prince of Wales, suddenly asked the present King to fly him over the aerodrome, to the consternation of the officials, who realised that they were in part responsible for the lives of two heirs to the throne.

The Prince was never loyal for long in his enthusiasms, and once he had satisfied his wish to fly solo his interest in flying became more practical. By 1932 he looked upon it as a convenient and hasty way of travel and the element of adventure faded. But he used the air more and more, and in one month he flew on eighteen days. In 1931 he made his commercial tour of the Argentine by air, with Flight Lieutenant Fielden* as his pilot. He began his short, unhappy reign by flying from Sandringham with the present King so that he could interview his Minister in London for the first time, and one of the most important duties of his term as Sovereign was the inspection of the stations of the Royal Air Force, made by air.

King Edward VIII was not wholly to blame if his eagerness over flying died some years ago. He had made every step in aviation against opposition. His father, his father's Ministers and his advisers were alarmed by his wish to fly, and the Air Ministry welcomed the transfer of responsibility to Flight Lieutenant Fielden when he assumed control of the Prince's aviation in 1929. When he had wished to be a soldier during the war the Prince had been discouraged and frustrated, just as he had been disappointed by the in-

* Now Wing Commander E. H. Fielden, A.F.C.

terruption of his career as a sailor. When he wished to ride, his recklessness was responsible for protests in Parliament. Every time he manifested an enthusiasm there were obstacles; voices to remind him that his life was more precious than his neighbour's. The Prince disliked empty titles and honorary commissions. It was his wish to earn his wings —the wings which he already wore by virtue of his honorary rank. He disliked them for their unreality and many times he told his pilots how dearly he wished to qualify for them. This was not allowed. In flying, as in soldiering and hunting, he was met with a chorus of warning, and he turned away in disappointment. It was in 1932 that the Prince showed the first signs of moping and secretiveness which so sadly tortured him in the end. Perhaps it was that the refusal to allow him to enjoy aviation to the full completed the long theme of frustration. He seldom referred to his disappointment, but when he did so it was with extreme bitterness. A sad end to the story of his flying in this country came in December of 1936, when King Edward was waiting at Fort Belvedere to complete the miserable formalities for his abdication. His aircraft was ready if the weather had been good enough for him to leave the country by air. As it was, time was the essence of the close of the tragedy, and every hour he stayed in England was an injustice to his brother's assumption of the responsibilities of the crown. So he did not fly from his country, as he had flown down from Sandringham almost a year before to take his father's place. He turned to his first love, the sea, as the way to his exile.

Royal persons usually live in strange isolation from the rest of the world. However much they wish to encourage confidence, a wall of deference is raised between them and most people whom they meet. Because of this, they sometimes act as if there are but two classes in the world—their own and the rest of humanity. This isolation from the broad stretches of society sometimes confuses the judgement of princes, and they often imagine qualities into

persons who break down the barriers of reserve by affecting familiarity. These are usually second-rate flatterers,
but their manner doubtless comes as a relief in lives made
tedious by formality and impersonal relationships. King
George's long experience in the Navy taught him to appreciate the differences in men, and Queen Mary, who was
brought up with no hint of her future eminence, has never
been bewildered in discriminating between the wheat and
the chaff. For some sad reason their eldest son was not
equipped with this power to judge, and early in his life he
was inclined to gather about him those people whose
familiar manner made it easy to talk with them, rather than
those whose loyalty and respect made their manner seem
reserved. This incongruity first showed itself during his
American and Dominion tours. He did not seem to know
"the halfway house between jest and earnest," and when
his official duties were ended he often sought his pleasure
in society which was unsuited to the needs of the heir to the
throne. It was as if the burden was so heavy for him that
when he needed relaxation he ran to the extreme of gay
and casual people whose objects in life were different from
his own.

It is not possible for princes to lead double lives, if the
second life interferes with the dignity and grace of their royal
responsibilities. With all his free and easy social pleasures,
King Edward VII seldom neglected his high station in
pleasure's name. He worked while he worked and played
when he played, and, during his long term as Prince of
Wales, he was never accused of being casual over his duties.
His grandson seemed unable to uphold this wise division
in his life, perhaps because of the hustled state in which he
lived and perhaps because of some sad fault in his judgement. While he travelled over the face of the world on
waves of compliment and praise; while the English newspapers coined fine names for him and increased the record
of his dutifulness and his chivalry, there was a growing
undercurrent of discontent. It left a shadow wherever he

went. Everybody loved him, for it was his nature to attract devotion even from those whom he hurt in passing. But his talent for making friends among superficial and unimportant people persisted and grew. It might be forgotten now if it were not the spring of a river which finally engulfed him. The story is all the more pitiful because of the innocence of its beginning. While travelling in Australia, Canada and India, he would often step on the toes of his hosts by ignoring official parties and dancing with some shy girl who pleased him. While in Africa he chose a partner, already engaged, and danced with her continuously. His official hostess was ignored, and he did not pause to realise that his overwhelming favour might be embarrassing to a girl who had to settle back into obscurity after he had gone. This seems to be but a trivial complaint, but, once upon the bridge, a captain must observe the science of navigation or renounce his place to one who will. The rule is hard, but it is essential in the twentieth-century machine of State.

It was easy at the time for newspapers to rejoice over the Prince's democratic habits. When he ignored his hostesses and chose to dance with some modest girl, who almost died upon the suddenness of her fame, it made an engaging story. All contributed to the theme of popularity. But popularity was not enough, and even in America, where life is more free and class consciousness allegedly grown thin, there was criticism of his habits when he went there once more in 1924. The signs on his arrival were of popularity, but not of respect. He received the reporters and was obliged to listen to their questions: "Have you learned to play poker?" "Are you engaged?" and "Are you going to marry an American?" Although he performed his duties, the stories which were hurried across the Atlantic were of his winnings at the races at Belmont Park and of his dancing until six o'clock in the morning. American newspapers did not appreciate the prevailing theme of frivolity, and when the Prince decided to stay longer than planned, thus inter-

1933.   *The Prince of Wales at an Unemployed Camp near Sutton Courtney, Berks.*

fering with public thoughts over the Presidential Election, the *New York World* criticised him calmly but with decision.

"He managed, by his choice of friends and diversions, to provoke an exhibition of social climbing on the part of a few Americans which has added nothing to his prestige nor to the prestige of royalty in general. In fact, he managed to demonstrate to Americans, grown tolerant of the business of royalty, that it is, whatever his personal democracy may be, in fact a pyramid of snobbery.

A good deal of hot fuel is added to the fires of the old-fashioned republican conviction that civilisation would survive if the King business were wound up."

On this second visit to America the Prince began to unravel the good reputation he had made when he went there after the war. American people were delighted because he learned to tap dance and to play the ukelele; because he was deliberately scornful of formality. But the delight was of a different kind from the first victory of five years before, when they were able to view his charm and his royal purpose as one.

From the time of the Prince's return to England, in 1924, the murmurs against him grew louder. They were always drowned, in the end, by the wealth of his public success. He was the hero of the masses and he was perhaps the most celebrated figure in the world. But serious people watched him with alarm. Tales of his casual social life leaked out and depressed those who were too genuinely fond of him to quicken the harm of gossip. Serious and conscientious men, who saw him day by day, hoped that his good gifts would guide him in the end and that the taste for unsuitable people would pass as a phase. But the error went on, and when, in 1925, he returned from his tour of South America, stories of his late hours travelled ahead of him. He lived in pitiless limelight and there was no escape. That thousands of his contemporaries were equally restless did not matter to the gossips. More was expected of him than of any other man of his age, and the affection which most people felt for him was tinged with disappointment. There was one hint, in an English journal, that he might mend his ways. With care and understanding, the *Spectator* suggested that the Prince would "rightly interpret the wishes of the nation if he made it impossible for people to have any excuse for saying that he is unduly restless or that he exhausts himself in giving to amusements time which might be spent in preparation for work that is always and necessarily exacting and tiring."

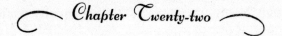

Chapter Twenty-two

KING GEORGE'S JUBILEE. THE PRINCE'S FRIENDS

King George has left the monarchy in England at a higher standard of respectability and popularity than ever before.

The unquestionable sincerity with which the late King spoke, the humility of the man—in fact, his whole attitude—was such that it made us all say, "A man, God bless him."—GEORGE BERNARD SHAW.

Chapter Twenty-two

KING GEORGE'S JUBILEE. THE PRINCE'S FRIENDS

*D*URING the year before King George's Jubilee, the usual celebrations of loyalty were not enough for the British people. They were on the threshold of a great year in their history, a year in which the anniversary of their Sovereign's accession reminded them of the comparative calm in which they lived and made them grateful. When Mr. G. K. Chesterton broadcast in December he talked of the "vast buried inarticulate England" which was "deeply and dangerously discontented." It was then that he added, "I should guess the most popular institution left is the monarchy." There may have been deep and dangerous discontent among the inarticulate English, but it was not focussed upon the King.

Mr. Chesterton might have chosen a better word than *popularity* in paying his tribute to the monarchy. King George was not loved because of any wild sentimentality in the public heart, but because, on the eve of his Jubilee, people realised the significance of the slow, steady flame of his character, which had burned for twenty-five years; they realised that neither the theories of scholars, the cynicism of twentieth-century prophets nor the casual habits of the younger generation could obscure the simple fact that the King was a good man, a father to his people and an example to all who place character above cleverness and duty above popularity. British people realised, during this year, that they belonged to the only considerable European Power which was not governed by fear.

King George had never possessed the popular gifts, nor had he ever been a grand king, if grandness lies in manner and outward show. One of the few men who saw his merit when he was young was his father. King Edward always said that his son possessed character superior to his own, and he alone prophesied the strength of his reign. From the beginning King George was a humble man, and when the Empire placed its heart at his feet during this year he was surprised. When he had been young he had not seemed to be a very interesting person. Some months before the Jubilee a remarkable article on King George, already quoted in this book,* appeared in the American magazine *Fortune*. The writer described King George as "the most successful king in the last 250 years of English history." And then, "he prefers whisky and soda to vintage wines, musical comedy to more ambitious theatre, British boiled dinners and sweet puddings to more sophisticated food, Jules Verne and Captain Marryat to more arduous reading, and almost anything on earth to a picture gallery . . . . he lives by the clock like his father and his grandmother before him . . . . his greatest passion next to punctuality is radio . . . . his gramophone records are Gilbert and Sullivan or *La Bohème* and never jazz." Then one reads of the mottoes on the walls of the study at Sandringham, especially of the one, *Teach me to be obedient to the rules of the game*. The writer made deductions from these simple pieces of evidence and said, "That a man of George's limitations—an almost Pickwickian personification of the average—should have made such a monarch is curious enough. But that such a man should have made such a monarch in such a time is all but incredible." Perhaps the writer did not understand that our standard of character is what he conceives to be the average. In a country which knows neither the dark state of peasantry nor the rule of a rich and idle aristocracy, the average, or the normal, is the usual standard. In a middle-class country, devoted to security, suspicious of the unusual and distrustful of intellectual theories, it was inevitable that King George should ultimately come to be looked upon as the father of his people. The months passed,

* Page 137.

1923.   *The Prince of Wales in Canada, riding on the Bar U Range Ranch.*

and towards May of 1935 the show of affection grew. People
who knew the King intimately in Norfolk had always realised this fatherly aspect and to them he was a squire rather
than a Sovereign. A man from near Sandringham once said
to a friend in the trenches—no doubt when the nip of
November was in the air—"Gawd help you if you was a
pheasant coming high over the covers at Sandringham when
the *old gentleman* was out with the guns."

In 1935 the old gentleman came into his own. The wide
and well-deserved popularity of the Prince of Wales was
bright and transitory as a rocket compared with the emotions which his father stirred. "Bless the old man," cried
somebody in the crowd at Leeds as the King passed by.
All the quiet laws of character were represented in him;
all the laws which are mentioned shyly nowadays, or not at
all. The old-fashioned virtues of sincerity, devotion to duty,
fidelity to promises: all the king-becoming graces flowered
in him and impressed themselves upon a troubled, cynical
world. The impression made by King George in the closing
year of his life must be described if one is to understand
the eclipse which it brought to the popularity of the Prince
of Wales. The Prince's own changed character was in part
to blame for the rift which grew between him and his
father's people. But there was another reason, and it lay in
the fact that the post-war period was tired of the standards
which it had invented for itself. When the people realised
that there was one man ruling a country who upheld the
graces of "justice, verity, temperance, stableness, bounty,
perseverance, mercy, lowliness, devotion, patience, courage,
fortitude," they thought him good to behold.

Two tributes to King George from foreign newspapers
allow us to realise how far the story of his achievement had
travelled. The *New York Times* wrote of him: "The King
has always shown himself a good friend of America. Feeling
that the United States and Britain ought to co-operate for
common ends and world purposes is perhaps stronger here
to-day than at any time since the war. As the King is known

to share this belief, it is not improper or immodest for America to claim a right to take part in his Jubilee."

A writer in *Le Jour* said: "He is loved as a father of his people. Everything is dignity, honour, almost a patriarchal comprehension of life in the glass prison of his palace. He is a ruler who consults, questions and listens with prudence and discernment. This crowned bourgeois who has lived without pomp, fulfilling all his duties, must undoubtedly win over to the idea of parliamentary monarchy many of those who think that people, like families, cannot do without a father above political parties to bring them up and love them wisely according to the laws of God and men."

During the month before the Jubilee, King George was sublimely calm. His repose in agitated times had been revealed in the previous year when a Socialist member interrupted the King during his speech at the opening of Parliament. The intrusion was clumsy and the House gasped before such impudence. There was one calm man, one voice, continuing. It was not until he was disrobing that the King made a comment on the incident. He muttered, in his gruff, abrupt way, "Apparently somebody else wanted to make a speech, too." His life was still in keeping with the motto which he had learned as a sailor and which he so often repeated, "Keep your hair on." He still appeared at his desk early in the morning. He still opened his own letters and telephoned his sister every day, as he had done for twenty years. The habits of his life did not change while the wide streets of the city were being festooned, the gardens trimmed, the window-boxes in the slums planted with geraniums and the farthest cottage in his Empire bedecked with flags as tangible proofs of the good feeling of his people.

When the idea of celebrating the Jubilee was first formed, neither the courtiers nor the members of the Government anticipated more than a graceful acknowledgement of the twenty-five years of the King's reign. In the first meetings for those who were to arrange the day, it was thought that a State drive to St. Paul's and a thanksgiving service would be all. The final thunder of excitement and thankfulness, which embraced half the world, was never expected; certainly never imagined by the King himself. It was when every little village wove its own scheme for celebration, when every Dominion made plans for thanksgiving, that the authorities suddenly realised that their small ideas were inadequate; that they were out of all proportion to the wishes of the people. No Sovereign in our history received his tribute more clearly from the mass of his subjects. The wave of feeling did not go out from Buckingham Palace to them; it began in the remote villages, in the tenements, in the crofts of Scotland, the shanties on the edge of the Australian bush and the log cabins of northern Canada. It grew and it surged towards the King, and it was because of this, not because of his wish or the plan of his advisers, that the Jubilee became such a great occasion. It was on the day of the celebrations that the King revealed his surprise and thankfulness. The acclamation was splendid, from the hour when he drove out of Buckingham Palace to the moment when the curtains moved, in the night, for him to walk out on to the balcony. There had been the deep, softened thunder of the prayer in St. Paul's, the sunny drive through the city, the mad dancing in the streets when evening came. The noises of Cockney good cheer penetrated into the most sedate retreats of the West End, and no story of this gay invasion was more pleasing than that of the father who brought his son from the Mile End Road to Park Lane to see the decorations. A big painted portrait of King George caught the youngster's eye and he asked, "Who's that?" The father answered, "That's the King, and if I ever 'ear you say a word against him I'll knock your bloody block off."

It was the moment when the King's tired, friendly voice spoke over the radio, using the phrase *My very dear people*, that his subjects turned to silence and to awe. And then, the dark figure on the balcony, emerging through the window before which Queen Victoria had sat for her Jubilee almost forty years before; this moment, and the one in which he turned while Queen Mary extended her arms towards the huge tide of people below. They had cried up to the window for a long time, "We want King George." Cynicism and theory withered before such emotion. It was towards the end of the evening, when the vast old trees of the surrounding park were unnaturally silver from the floodlights and it seemed that all London was pressing against the railings of the Palace, that the second cry went up, "We want the Prince." He was not there to stand by his father, so the cry died and the people sang *God Save the King* again and again until the Sovereign drew to the inner scene, leaving them alone.

With all the tumult and affection which King George enjoyed during the last year of his life, private grief made him an unhappy and disappointed man. He had seen his people coming nearer to him in comprehension, but, in grim contrast, he had seen his eldest son retreating into a wilderness in which he could not help him. Before beginning on the end of King Edward's story, the theme of his isolation must be revived in extenuation. He was without friends, because he had lost, or never seemed to have, the capacity for making solid friendships. He was therefore thrown back on a succession of amusing acquaintances who neither strengthened his character nor elevated his spirit. This lack of friends was sadly felt when he came to the throne in 1936. Both his grandfather and his father had succeeded with a circle of tried friends from whom they had been able to form their Courts. King Edward VIII had no such company when his turn came, and even his old staff had been almost depleted. It was before King George's Jubilee that his son began to pay the supreme price for the errors in his training, the hurrying from one place to another, the ever-changing procession of faces and the loss of home life during the years when his special character needed its influence so much. Uncertain of values in living, confused over the strength and weakness of human nature and bitterly resentful of all interference and even affectionate advice, the Prince became a law unto himself. He built up the usual defences of a lonely man who is not certain of his own strength. He became increasingly stubborn and conceited over his popularity. Every incident of fifteen years of his life had contributed to the weakness of self-centredness, and his fantastic vanity over his own capacity was a matter for disappointment rather than blame. His natural graces, his charm, his kindliness, the serious and compassionate note which used to come to his voice when he spoke to suffering people and the promises he had made, all seemed to turn sour within him.

Some people have said that if King George had died two years earlier his son would have come to the throne prepared to make the sacrifices asked of him. Perhaps it is true that his apprenticeship had gone on too long and that his weaknesses had become stereotyped.

One of the first signs of the change in the Prince's character was in his treatment of servants. Kindness and consideration for those who serve them have always been characteristics of members of the Royal Family. Like many old ladies of her day, indulgence for servants became an obsession with Queen Victoria, and she was always willing to blame a lady or gentleman for a fault rather than one of the employees. This extravagance was typical of Victorian times. King Edward was less extremist in his treatment of his servants, but he was consistent and kind. King George and Queen Mary always ruled their great houses with consideration for the least of their servants; indeed, this might be described as one of the strongest bonds which held their household together. From childhood King Edward VIII had shown the same goodness of heart in dealing with those who served him. One of the strongest themes in his early story is of his anxiety lest people should be discomforted through his presence. In 1928, when he travelled in an ordinary passenger steamer, the directors juggled with the cabins so that he was able to occupy a suite of rooms. He wrote, from the ship, to the chairman of directors: "If I can make any criticism it is that you've been over-generous as regards cabin accommodation which may have caused some inconvenience to the other passengers. . . . I mention it only because of my great desire when travelling unofficially not to take advantage of privileges and special arrangements that may be made to the discomfort of others."

The Prince was similarly thoughtful with those who served him in his private life. One recalls his anxiety when he travelled to Germany with Herr Fiedler, his German tutor. Herr Fiedler was an older man, and nothing would induce the Prince to sleep in the more comfortable bed which had been prepared for him. Although his compassion often ran dangerously near to emotion, it always guided him to kindness, and when some future historian comes to reckon with his virtues and his faults, this gentleness and consideration must emerge as the noblest aspect of his early life. It was terrible, therefore, to find this instinct withering, so that he broke down the affection of his household by his lack of consideration. His entire nature seemed to change, not in the great field of which tragedies are made, but with a pettiness which had always been foreign to his heart.

The Prince's troubled spirit found its focus some time before his father's Jubilee, when he was introduced to an American lady, married to a business man who had made his home in England. Up to this time the Prince had never seemed to find fulfilment in the people who had engaged his affection. The bond which holds people in love is their own, and neither prose nor poetry can define it. The Prince found that his American friend, already happily married, gave him the contentment which he had never known before. Her history is important for its contribution to the moral indignation which was part of

1935. *The Prince of Wales at Ascot Races.*

England's protest against their union. She had been born in Baltimore and had been married, when she was twenty, to a lieutenant in the United States Navy. She obtained a divorce from her first husband in 1925 on the grounds of incompatibility, which is accepted in America as sufficient reason for closing the contract of marriage. They had been husband and wife for eight years. Two years afterwards, she met a shipbroker, Mr. Ernest Simpson, and some time afterwards, when the marriage which then engaged him was ended, they were married in London. This union continued, and Mrs. Simpson's talents eventually brought her into society in which she met the Prince of Wales. Mrs. Simpson always appeared in public with her husband, and there was no indication of want of happiness in their relationship. The friendship between the Prince and herself nevertheless developed, and during the August of 1934 he met her at Biarritz, afterwards upon the Duke of Westminster's yacht at Cannes, and later in the year at Kitzbuhl, the charming little Austrian village which was made famous through the Prince's patronage. When Mr. Simpson was not present, an aunt of Mrs. Simpson was usually in attendance. Mr. C. A. Lyon wrote of Mrs. Simpson in the *Daily Express* at the time of King Edward's abdication:

"What was it that appealed to the King? . . . . What, in short, charmed him? Mrs. Simpson, first, is a good hostess. She prefers the drawing-room to the night club. . . . She ranks among the few hostesses in London, perhaps fewer than a dozen, who have a real and deserved reputation for good cooking.

What of her personal appearance?

When her face is in repose few people would consider it a particularly beautiful face. But it has character, and its most notable feature is the fine high forehead. . . . Her hands are competent and strong, but her fingers are short and usually she wears no rings. . . . She is exceedingly tidy, and has probably

never been seen by anyone looking otherwise than
that. . . . Her voice is American with a strong Baltimore accent. It would never pass as an English voice.
She is good-tempered and with a sense of justice, but
can be determined, not to say pig-headed, on occasions.
She has the American woman's tendency to reform
men in small ways."

Royal behaviour is particularly subject to gossip, and
the friendship between the Prince and Mrs. Simpson soon
became the talk of the scandal-loving section of society.
Neither the mass of people nor the newspapers took up the
story, and for many months only a few knew of the Prince's
infatuation. It was an instance when English journalism
showed at its best, voluntarily keeping a barrier of silence
between the Prince's private life and their readers.

The Prince of Wales was already drawing his own society
about him at Fort Belvedere. This small country house, on
the fringe of the Great Park at Windsor, had become the
Prince's retreat. The garden, the arrangements of the house
and the society which moved in it were all his own creation.
Gardening caught his transient fancy and held it for a long
time, and it seems that he found much happiness and release from his duties while he was there. It was in this
setting, free of royal pretensions, that the Prince entertained Mr. and Mrs. Simpson for week-ends up to the time
of King George's death.

Chapter Twenty-three

DEATH OF KING GEORGE V

And when Jacob had made an end of commanding his sons, he gathered up his feet into the bed, and yielded up the ghost, and was gathered unto his people.—GENESIS xlix. 33.

Chapter Twenty-three

DEATH OF KING GEORGE V

KING GEORGE died, as he had lived, with his mind upon his duty. There was no drama in his going; he passed slowly, on a crisp, January morning. His last duty had been performed during the day; a scene which the Archbishop of Canterbury described some days afterwards in the House of Lords. "He was propped up in his chair, looking so grave and thin." The Order constituting the Council of State was placed before him. "He gave in his old clear tone the command, 'Approved.' Then he made deliberate and repeated efforts, that were most pathetic, to sign the last State paper with his own hand.

"Then, when the effort was too great, he turned with a kindly and kingly smile to his Council. It was a scene that those of us who beheld it will never forget . . . . in his last conscious hours his thoughts were for the claims of duty."

In the seven months of life since the Jubilee, King George had enjoyed a new kind of happiness. His son's friendship with Mrs. Simpson was a perpetual grief to him, and the Prince's presence in his father's house brought little peace. But the unsuspected devotion which was shown to the King during the Jubilee seemed to be a compensation: it had seemed to unlock a new door in him and release a wistful gaiety which showed itself in simple ways. He had never cared much for the theatre, but he went, several times, and once he proposed himself for a matinée. These closing months provided a great experience for sensitive people. There was an air of veneration in place of the old expressions of ordinary loyalty. "The King must be a fine old man," a West Australian said to an English visitor in Perth. Queen

Mary was associated with her husband in the new, calm devotion which the Jubilee had inspired. She was described in an American journal as " one of the few altogether admirable figures of our time." This was the closing theme of their story together. They shared distress and disappointment over their son, but they were consoled in knowing that their married life together had taught the world a lesson—a lesson which spread out to the farthest edges of civilisation. People turned from the exciting figure of the Prince of Wales, especially when the story of his unfortunate attachment was told in the American newspapers. The English Press was still silent, but enough alarming extracts from New York journals found their way into England for the secret to begin to assume the proportions of a scandal. This was the only menace to the King's peace during the last days at Sandringham.

On the morning of Tuesday, January 21, all the world was stunned by the news of King George's death. Grief swept over the lands in which his Jubilee had been celebrated only seven months ago. Thirty-five years before, when Queen Victoria died, people had thought it proof of the width of her Empire when a chief in Zululand said, " Then I shall see another star in the sky." The limit of reverence for King George was not territorial. The Speaker of the House of Delegates in Virginia spoke of him as *The King*, as if he belonged to them also. Jews prayed for his rest, at the Wailing Wall in Jerusalem, and when the news of his death was received by wireless in an Imperial Airways aircraft, flying at six thousand feet from Calcutta to Akyab, the machine dipped in salute and then flew on.

So the new Sovereign came to his great opportunity, and the grief of the people was mixed with anxiety. King Edward's private life was now the prey of inventive gossips. The long, exacting apprenticeship was over; the long wandering through experience and doubt and melancholy; the frustration and the striving. The power in his hands was terrible to measure, and the Government and those who

knew him well were keenly afraid. The mass of people were
ignorant of his growing tragedy, and to them his accession
meant that he would fulfil the many promises he had made.
On the morning of his father's death, King Edward flew
down from Sandringham to London, with his brother, to
see the Prime Minister. No king in the history of the world
had ever flown into his capital to announce his accession.

Two days afterwards, King Edward followed his father's
coffin from Sandringham to Westminster Hall for the lying
in state. A sunny morning followed a cold night, on
January 23, and the lawns of Sandringham were sparkling
with frost. The coffin was carried between the banks of
rhododendrons to Wolferton station, whence it was taken
to London. At ten o'clock, King Edward and his brothers
ended a walk of five miles—a slow, agonising march during
which thousands of people watched the new Sovereign's
unhappy face. It was grey and drawn by emotion and
anxiety, and the pity of the people changed to marvelling
over his fortitude. Wherever he walked in the days that
followed and when he stood in the shadows of Westminster
Hall, near to his father's coffin, his face was grey and grimly
set. A reporter who saw him in Westminster Hall, where
the twelve great candlesticks threw their light on the cata-
falque and up into the intricacy of the carved beams, wrote
of the glow upon his face as he stood there, of it being
"so changed with grief that one turned one's eyes away
from it." His hair gleamed "with the familiar boyish fair-
ness," but his features were "drawn and set." "It was the
look of a man who in the midst of personal grief has taken
the strain of a new and tremendous responsibility on his
shoulders. His pale face looked in that moment as though
he could never smile again."

King Edward's grief must have been bitterly mixed with
personal conflict during these mournful days before King
George was buried. He apparently suffered no self-reproach
in staying away from his mother, at Fort Belvedere, in the
hours when his place was beside her. The misfortunate

friendship was not allowed to suffer in deference to sorrow.
The King's conscience seemed to be able to reconcile the
unusual habits of his new life with his promises to the State.
There was no hesitation in his words when he wrote to the
Commons of his father: "I am well assured that the House
of Commons mourns the death of my beloved father. He
devoted his life to the service of his people and the uphold-
ing of constitutional government. He was ever actuated by
his profound sense of duty."

The King was able to add, with apparent sincerity, "I
am resolved to follow in the way he has set before me."

People hoped and wondered then. Were the words an
empty formality or did the grey face tell of a struggle
towards greatness? Were the winning characteristics of
years before, the natural kindliness and the wish for nobleness, to gather their forces together and exalt him to kingli-
ness? Sometimes in grief, words are chosen for their sound
rather than their sincerity. The language of sorrow and of
hope is dangerously near to rhetoric, and if King Edward
threw a fine promise to us to assuage us, Archbishops and
Ministers were likewise rich in good prophecies. Mr. Baldwin said in the House of Commons on January 23: "King
Edward VIII brings to the altar of public service a personality richly endowed with the experience of public
affairs, with the fruits of travel and universal goodwill. He
has the secret of youth in the prime of age. He has a wider
and more intimate knowledge of all classes of his subjects
not only at home but also throughout the Dominions and
India than any of his predecessors."

Mr. Baldwin, knowing the circumstances of his new
Sovereign's private life and doubtless hoping that courage
would bring order to his troubled mind, was able to say
that he "looked forward with confidence and assurance to
the new reign." "Under God's providence," he added, "he
will establish the Throne more firmly than ever on its surest
and only foundations—the hearts of his people."

Some time before the King's death his son had quoted

two sentences from Disraeli which the Labour papers had reviewed in great comfort. He had said, "Once England was for the very few. Now we have made it a land for the many, and we dream and contrive for the days when it shall be a land for all." A writer in *Forward* recalled the quotation when King George died, and he added, in hope of King Edward's reign, "If this is the spirit in which he intends acting through his reign he will be interpreting the mood of the democracy and be the most popular of kings." The theme of anxiety showed in some of the newspapers, for it was the theme of public feeling allied to grief. "What sort of King will he make?" asked a writer in the *Herald*, without a balanced answer to the question. The Archbishop of Canterbury, who was to play the part of moral judge over his King at the end, spoke with careful choice of words. His new Sovereign had been called to a "position so exalted —a task so difficult," he said. "Yet he comes singularly equipped for the fulfilment of that task. He has acquired a unique knowledge of the life of the people of this country and of our Dominions overseas." There was little hope and no enthusiasm from the venerable prelate who had been King George's friend. Perhaps more than any commoner in the land, Dr. Lang knew the inner story of divergent opinion, scolding and final disappointment which had marred the glory of King George's last year of life. He did not bend his conscience to the occasion for fine phrases, and his reception of the new King was cold and dark with presentiment.

King George was buried in St. George's Chapel on January 28. The bell in the Curfew Tower gave warning of the procession as it began its march up the hill; the hill up which the Norman Conqueror climbed almost nine hundred years before. It was the same bell that Gray heard from the churchyard at Stoke Poges when it tolled "the knell of parting day." Within the chapel, five hundred chosen subjects waited for the body of their dead King. The dim January light came in through the robes of the saints in the high stained-glass windows and sent shafts of rose and green and saffron light on to the stone tracery. How strange it was, as one sat in anxious silence, to remember that kings were buried in St. George's long before Columbus dreamed that the world was round. Every stone should have been worn deep with history, but the vast Gothic arches seemed fresh and young. They spoke also of strength and of to-morrow; of a future as well as a past. In the choir, the gorgeous banners of the Knights of the Garter, spreading towards the altar, reminded one that it was not a great spectacle but the quiet home-coming to Windsor of a knight who had kept his covenant.

The congregation which waited, some in the candlelight of the choir and some in the broader nave, seemed to be more personal than the procession which was following the coffin up the hill. The old, white-haired verger who waited by the west door was a sailor once and he had served in *Bacchante* under the King fifty-nine years before. They used to join in sailor talk whenever the monarch came here. One of the choristers who stood within the sanctuary sang here at the beginning of the century, when they brought Queen Victoria from Osborne on her last journey. There were others who had played their part in the life of the dead King. Near to the west door was the Dean, whose ancestors served the Royal Family in the time of George the Third. There were old ladies, dimly seen behind their veils, who used to dance in the Castle in the gay days before the war. In front of the altar four candle flames moved gently against the golden reredos.

From outside came the growing murmur of the procession. The west window was a vast curtain of stained glass; a company of saints looking down to the great door of the chapel. It is said that choristers stood here in the quiet summer evenings of 1916 and heard the boom of the guns in France.

The form of the coffin darkened the doorway, and one knew that George the Good was being brought into the home of his fathers. The Archbishops, the Dean and Chapter of St. George's, led the procession towards the door of the choir. One hardly dared to look at the group of mourners walking behind the coffin: the young King, his mother and his brothers. As the Bishops and clergy moved before the coffin the voices of the choir were heard singing:

> *I am the resurrection and the life, saith the Lord: he that believeth in me, though he were dead, yet shall he live: and whosoever liveth and believeth in me shall never die.*

The procession moved on, past the memorial to Princess Charlotte, past the memorial to the blind King of Hanover and then into the shadows of the choir. After they passed under the low, carved doorway, the words of the twenty-third Psalm were sung. The coffin passed over the tomb of Charles I and Henry VIII and then it was placed on the purple bier over the royal vault.

As the Bishop of Winchester read the Lesson, "I saw a new heaven and a new earth . . . ." most eyes turned towards King Edward. Many who do not make a habit of prayer must have prayed for him on that day. No man in the world has ever had so much to decide and yet been so alone and beyond help in his perplexity. Along both the ways open to him there lay renunciation. The one way offered loneliness: the loneliness which made Queen Victoria cry, at the beginning of her widowhood, "There is nobody to call me Victoria now." Along this way was the compensation of great honour and the deeper strength of courage, which sustains when love is spent. Along the other way lay the excitement of private happiness, but also the ghost of failure and no vision or goal at the end. Grief over the dead was not the chief emotion for those who thought over the problems of the day. Moses was dead, but it was of young Joshua that they thought and of the Lord's words to him, "Only be thou strong and very courageous."

Some phrases in the Lesson remained in one's memory: "And God shall wipe away all tears from their eyes; and there shall be no more death, neither sorrow nor crying." And, towards the end, "He that overcometh shall inherit all things."

When the lesson was ended the choir sang the hymn best loved by the dead King, *Abide with Me*. For those who knew Windsor well the old hymn must have had special importance. It awakened the memory of early summer evenings when the King used to walk down the hill to the chapel, always with the Queen and sometimes with one of his Ministers.

When the singing of the hymn was ended the Archbishop of Canterbury read the burial sentences. The stillness then was terrible. "Man that is born of a woman hath but a short time to live, and is full of misery. He cometh up, and is cut down, like a flower; he fleeth as it were a shadow, and never continueth in one stay. . . ."

The regalia had been removed from the coffin, and now it bore no ornament but flowers and the King's colours which the young King had placed there. As the Archbishop spoke, "Forasmuch as it hath pleased Almighty God of his great mercy to take unto himself the soul of our dear brother," the coffin and the bier slowly sank into the vault below. There was no movement in the world, it seemed, except the trembling of the flowers on Queen Mary's wreath, sinking into the purple darkness. As the words "Earth to earth, ashes to ashes, dust to dust" were spoken, King Edward took earth from a silver dish and scattered it upon the coffin.

King George had joined the great company of England's monarchs, and, as the eyes of the mourners turned from the dark vault to the new King, standing beside his mother, the Garter King of Arms stepped before the sanctuary and proclaimed the styles of the dead Sovereign. "The late most high, most mighty and most noble" King was with his God, and the Garter King raised his voice to proclaim, "God

Save the King." The choir sang once more and, from the altar, the Archbishop pronounced the Benediction. The Dead March in Saul was played while the Queen and her son remained before the open vault. Then, bowing over the coffin, they walked out of the south door of the chapel. The short spell of sunshine which had come an hour before passed by and the stained-glass windows lost their brilliance. The new King was walking out among his subjects and into the world, his grey face sad and frightening. One remembered Joshua again and murmured, "Only be thou strong and very courageous."

Chapter Twenty-four

THE REIGN OF EDWARD VIII

For Princes *more of* solid Glory *gain*
Who are thought fit, *than who are* born *to*
  Reign.

                    THO. SHADWELL (1689).

Chapter Twenty-four

THE REIGN OF EDWARD VIII

DURING the first weeks of King Edward's short reign it seemed that he was trying to gather up the fragments of his life and to fulfil his early promises. The wide mass of people were still unaware of his association with Mrs. Simpson, and they were encouraged in the illusion of security by the stories of the King's service. The newspapers for this time gave a constructive record of his busy days, of his continued anxiety over the poor and his apparent devotion to duty. The interests of his public life did not change, and there were stories of his kindliness and consideration which made many people hope that his evil spirit was leaving him. When he went to see the great ship *Queen Mary*, and then visited the Glasgow slums, he asked, "How do you reconcile the world that has produced this mighty ship with the slums we have just visited?" This was the young Prince of Wales whom England knew so well. One afternoon he walked in Oxford, recapturing old pictures of his days at Magdalen, and he went to the porter, without fuss, and asked, "May I use the telephone?" There was another story, of the director of a London hospital who telephoned Buckingham Palace and asked, "Who's speaking?"

The answer was, "The King; can I do anything for you?"

The director apologised.

"That's all right," answered King Edward. "Tell me what it's about. I may be able to help you."

Those who loved him recognised his true nature in these incidents, and hope became high again. Britons were impressed also when he announced generous sacrifices in the grants usually made to sovereigns. Working men and old soldiers still had supreme confidence in the King. Mr.

George Lansbury, the once fanatical Labour leader, had said of him, "I take my hat off. We do what we can, but he goes into the houses. We don't." Every pleasant sign was treasured by those who watched him; those who watched him as if he were a patient in fever. When he attended his first Council meeting at St. James's Palace, the Ministers and leaders who were there were comfortably pleased by his dignity and his apparent wish to do what was right. It did not seem possible that he could have his tongue in his cheek as he renewed his promises before them. It was not in his nature to deceive other men, but it was a sad fault in his nature that he was able to deceive himself. He said to the Privy Councillors:

> "When my father stood here twenty-six years ago he declared that one of the objects of his life would be to uphold constitutional government. In this I am determined to follow in my father's footsteps and to work as he did throughout his life for the happiness and welfare of all classes of my subjects.
>
> "I place my reliance upon the loyalty and affection of my people throughout the Empire and upon the wisdom of their Parliaments to support me in this heavy task, and I pray that God will guide me to perform it."

Many people within the circle of the Court and Government had thought that abdication was already in the King's mind. But the words he spoke at the Privy Council rang sincerely. Promise was being heaped upon promise, and it was reasonable to hope, therefore, that he would make the decision which the country required of him. He had always been sincere and ill at ease with guile. Perhaps scandal had run amok! "The tongue is a little thing, but it ruins families and overthrows kingdoms." Human nature leaps quickly to hope, and it welcomes signs of confidence. When Queen Mary wrote of her son, many people were soothed: "I commend to you my dear son as he enters upon his reign, in confident hope that you will give to him the

1936. *King Edward VIII and Queen Mary arriving at the Cenotaph on
Armistice Day, 1936.*

same devotion and loyalty which you gave so abundantly to his father."

Again, in March, King Edward spoke over the air and repeated the good intentions which he had expressed before the members of the Privy Council. "I am better known to you as the Prince of Wales," he said, "as a man who, during the war and since, has had the opportunity of getting to know the people of nearly every country of the world under all conditions and circumstances.

"And although I now speak to you as the King, I am still that same man who has that experience and whose constant effort it will be to continue to promote the well-being of his fellow-men."

Foreign journalists, who had doted upon the scandalous story of his private life, were so encouraged by these earnest promises that they hoped for a change. The *Deutsche Allgemeine Zeitung* said:

"Wherever he can, King Edward expresses his wish to come together with the simple people of the nation. Since his accession, he has fostered, exclusively, the union with them and the union with the Army. Already, as Prince of Wales, he made no secret of his social ideas and, as King, he has not changed his self-willed attitude in this respect in the least. This makes itself evident in the most diverse ways. He arranges his private life just as it suits him and, apart from his official duties, he recognises no social responsibilities of any kind. He entertains whom he will. Also, in regard to other prejudices, he does as he wishes. It would have been unthinkable, during the reign of King George V, that a divorced woman should be received at Court. It is well known that the views of the Church of England are very strong about divorced women. . . . The King is only a few months on the throne, but one has no doubt that it will be an extraordinary reign. . . ."

King Edward still performed those duties which had made him popular with the mass of the people. He sang *Tipperary* with the bluejackets in H.M.S. *Courageous*, and he continued his freedom of manner with people, but with variations. He had never been a liberal spender and, with the acquisition of great lands and houses and fortune, he became curiously parsimonious. Old servants were dismissed from Sandringham, expenses were pared, and new, hard economies were introduced, revealing eccentricity rather than ordinary meanness. There seemed to be a hint of Franz Joseph's iron bed or the Duke of Wellington's habit of sleeping in his service bed when the story of King Edward's occupation of Balmoral was told in the summer. He used one of the rooms ordinarily occupied by a major servant, he reduced the number of canteens from three to one and he travelled with little more than half the usual retinue of servants. He ordered the Highland servants not to line the avenue for his arrival, as they had done in his father's day. If these economies had been necessary they might have assumed the shape of a virtue. But the King did not seem able to cope with the new intricacy of problems and he avoided decisions whenever he could. It seemed that his judgement was no longer calm and, instead of finding peace and grace in his infatuation, he found only a means of bringing distress to his staff and disappointment to the servants who had always found him, in the past, to be a considerate and friendly master. He became a piteous figure as he estranged himself from those who served him and who had respected him. Some who saw him murmured that there was a fault in his reason, and they wondered how far he was bringing his country to peril. The campaigns of scandal in the foreign Press slowly percolated throughout England, and by the end of the summer a sense of insecurity was spreading into the country.

An incident in July brought a sudden check to the growing resentment against the King. He was riding down Constitution Hill after presenting colours to six battalions of the Brigade of Guards. He was passing between two banks of cheering people when a man pushed his way to the front and threw a revolver, loaded in four chambers, into the roadway. The reporter for *The Times* wrote: "Witnesses of the alarming incident state that the King saw what happened, reined in his horse and, after a surprised look in the direction from which the missile had been thrown, calmly proceeded on his way."

The incident was likely to catch the imagination of the world. The King had never failed in courage and, for some days, the Press of all countries spoke of him affectionately. Coincidence gave a romantic twist to the incident. Ninety-six years before, a miscreant standing on almost the same stretch of Constitution Hill, had fired a shot at Queen Victoria. The Prince Consort had described the alarming moment in a letter to his brother: "My first thought was that in her present state* the fright might harm her. I put both arms around her and asked her how she felt, but she only laughed." This story was recalled and used as a background for King Edward's happy behaviour. But the comfort from his courage was shortlived. The end had already been prophesied when, on May 27, the names of Mr. and Mrs. Ernest Simpson appeared in the Court Circular as guests of the King. They had dined at St. James's Palace, and the King had added an incongruous note to his defiance by inviting Mr. and Mrs. Stanley Baldwin and Colonel and Mrs. Lindbergh. Six days before the revolver incident, the name of Mrs. Simpson appeared once more in the Court Circular, this time without her husband. Now the talk reached remote places and, for once, widespread gossip was ahead of the newspapers. With estimable patience the editors still resisted what was to be the greatest journalistic sensation of the century.

It must not be imagined that the King wholly neglected his duties. He was harassed, unreasonable and vain, but he continued to play the rôle of popular monarch.

* The Princess Royal was born five months afterwards.

Afterwards, when people guessed over King Edward's motives, some said that he relied upon this rôle to sustain him, if a crisis came, and that he played upon the theme deliberately. It was even said that he imagined a state of royal dictatorship without a Constitution; a giddy and unreasonable interpretation to put upon his own powers. But it is doubtful if he came so near to the megalomania upon which dictators thrive.

It is reasonable to imagine what might have happened to King Edward had he come to the throne in different times. He inherited his crown when the country was sleepy. Neither the Italian campaign in Abyssinia nor the revolt in Spain had unsettled the true foundations of British complacency, and the people were free enough from national anxiety to spend their feelings in grief over one Sovereign and in high hopes over the promises of another. There was no outside stimulus to King Edward's talents and character at the time of his accession. Had he come to the throne during a war or in a time of fierce constitutional crisis, he might have shaken himself free of the ghosts that haunted him. He might have risen to magnificence with the ordeal of war or the anxiety of domestic strife. But he assumed his crown surrounded by old and comparatively tired men: with a Prime Minister who stood for the safety and apathy which he could neither respect nor endure, and with an Archbishop to whom he was hostile. There were no influential members of his Cabinet of his own age and experience and, once more, he suffered the penalty of belonging to the army that came back from the war. One has insisted upon the unhappy fact that he had no friends; it was also true that there were no contemporaries in the Government of whom he could make both advisers and intimates. He quickly showed that he was to be impatient with the old voices that grumbled against him. The first three acts of his reign—his flight to London from Sandringham, his insistence that the funeral of King George should be seven days earlier than was usual and his decision to walk

in the procession—were convincing portents. It was to be
a young man's reign. King Edward would not realise that
the unconventional ways of a popular Prince of Wales, the
hurry and the spontaneity, did not suit a monarch's stride.
He might have imposed them upon his Government over
a period of years, but as it was, he bustled and he failed.
Had there been a violent national distress to inspire him
the King might have acted differently. It is certain that he
would not have spent so many weeks of his brief reign on
holiday, skirting the Mediterranean and pausing in middle
Europe, not to gather experience which might have helped
him to estimate the voices which were prophesying war at
the time, but to amuse himself in the way his will and fancy
guided him.

One other interest might have helped to divert King
Edward from his selfish way. It will never be denied that
his devotion to the poor was sincere and calculated to be of
great benefit, and it was well known that one of the chief
objects of his reign would have been to lift the unemployed
and the wretched from their darkness. Many members of
the Government resented his campaigns among the poor.
They found his eagerness discomforting since it exposed
the methods of the authorities and proved their work in
the distressed areas to be slow and blighted by caution. As
Prince of Wales, the King had been discouraged in his
charity. It was clear to him that he would be similarly
frustrated now that he was Sovereign. His eager hands
were tied by the red tape of conventional methods. This
lack of encouragement in the one cause which stirred his
heart no doubt contributed to his disappointment and
helped his quick and emotional nature to go its own way.
He was accustomed to frustration, but he had not grown
patient with it through experience.

Early in the summer of 1936 the King chartered Lady
Yule's big and comfortable yacht for a cruise in the
Adriatic. The consoling figure of Mr. Simpson now with-
drew from the picture, and a party of nine embarked upon

a sunny, beautiful holiday. The pity of it all was that the photographs showed a happy King. The newspapers were still discreet, placing the good name of their country and the sober reputation of the Government before their own purposes. But those photographs which were reproduced revealed the King of ten years ago. The boy who smiled from the platforms in Canada, from the wharf in Melbourne and from the edge of Mount Vaea when he was in Samoa, was resurrected. One had known him thus for a long time. He bought skittles from the fishermen, he swam, and always, he was laughing. Even if one plunges into the depths of psychology one cannot explain some of the changes which come suddenly to a man's nature. One knew only that King Edward had involved his Government, his Court, his country and his household in great and painful anxiety and that the reward for all this was the joy which was written in his face. On the way back to England he paused in Vienna. He dined in small restaurants and courted success by his old and charming familiarity. Everywhere Mrs. Simpson was beside him, and if the society which gathered about them was sometimes of the kind that sparkles but does not endure, there was no denying that the King was supremely happy.

Chapter Twenty-five

THE KING AND THE PRIME MINISTER

His will is not his own;
For he himself is subject to his birth,
He may not, as unvalued persons do,
Carve for himself; for on his choice depends
The safety and the health of the whole state.

> "Hamlet," Act I, Scene 3. Quoted by the Prime Minister to the House of Commons when announcing the abdication of the King.

THE KING AND THE PRIME MINISTER

WHEN Mrs. Ernest Simpson's divorce action came before the Judge at Ipswich, the newspapers restrained themselves from a full account of the surprising evidence, in which she complained that her husband was guilty of adultery. The case depended upon the evidence of a number of hotel servants, and at the end Mr. Justice Hawke stated, "Well, I suppose I must come to the conclusion that there was adultery in the case. Very well—decree nisi."

The modesty of the newspaper reports of the divorce action did not save the story of Mrs. Simpson's life from becoming a widespread scandal. The weeks of whispered gossip and rumour were ended. The talk which had never gone far beyond the ruling classes and the knowledge of the journalists now became the subject of after-dinner quips; old limericks were remodelled and puns were invented to suit the occasion. Every ugly device was used to spread the distressing news. But as the days passed, a nobleness in the public mind conquered the cheap aspects of the coming tragedy. While the story piled itself up towards the inevitable end, there was true greatness in the reaction of the mass of people. They were patient and they seemed to respect the King's problem as a war for his own character. They were too disappointed in him to enjoy moral indignation, and their resentment was not against the throne but against his failure to fill it with honour.

The constitutional crisis had begun before the divorce at Ipswich. On October 13 the Prime Minister had asked to be received by the King. Some day Mr. Baldwin may write the story of this first unhappy interview, but for the moment we know only that for some time previous the Prime Minister had been beset by letters revealing the uneasiness of hundreds of people over the King's friendship. Mr. Baldwin was also aware of the impending divorce action, and, in his own words,* he "felt that it was essential that someone should see His Majesty and warn him of the difficult situation that might arise later if occasion was given for a continuation of this kind of gossip and of criticism, and the danger that might come if that gossip and that criticism spread from the other side of the Atlantic to this country." "I felt," he said, "that in the circumstances there was only one man who could speak to him and talk the matter over with him, and that man was the Prime Minister. I felt doubly bound to do it by my duty, as I conceived it, to the country, and my duty to him not only as a counsellor but as a friend. I consulted, I am ashamed to say—and they have forgiven me—none of my colleagues."

Mr. Baldwin did not pass through the crisis and time of abdication without severe criticism. Many Americans still imagine that both the Government and vested interests pressed King Edward into abdication, and this crazy view is still expressed in the United States. In such an imagined plot, Mr. Baldwin naturally appears as a villain. Also he has been criticised for taking so much responsibility upon himself. This criticism of the Prime Minister and the Government remained long after the abdication of King Edward, in the form of smouldering resentment. Public opinion upon the matter was divided. Some viewed Mr. Baldwin's independent conduct as being inevitable and wise. Others considered that the Government had approved of the newspaper campaign against the King and that they had encouraged it, while expressing a different view, through the Prime Minister. It was felt, also, that such a mighty problem should have been placed before the House of Commons; that the broad will of the people should have

---

* In his address to the House of Commons, following the King's decision to abdicate.

been tested. The Government was further accused of wishing to be rid of a King who did not accept their ways of dealing with unemployment, or adapt himself to their pace. The view is still held, by many people, that the Government looked upon King Edward as a young eagle, beyond their control and likely to act with originality which would be embarrassing to them. There was also resentment because King Edward was not given the normal constitutional advice to try and form an alternative administration, to carry out his wishes, when the Cabinet ultimately refused to pass legislation permitting him to marry Mrs. Simpson and at the same time deprive her of the privileges of being his Queen Consort.

When the documents prepared during this time are made available to some future historian, justice will doubtless be done to both the King and his Ministers. In the meantime, until this fuller evidence is made available, it must be remembered that if Mr. Baldwin and his colleagues failed to observe the ethics of the Constitution, they also carried the country through the greatest drama concerning the authority of the monarch since the time of James II. King Edward was a distraught, unreasonable man during the days before his abdication, and negotiations with the Cabinet would have been impossible. The outcome of the crisis was dependent upon the character of the individuals concerned. Mr. Baldwin is always at his best when he is given a stimulus from outside himself, and, in the opinion of his champions, he carried off the negotiations with patience and understanding, saving the country from violent disruption and his Sovereign from as much pain as was possible.

The first interview between the King and Mr. Baldwin was the result of a request made by the Prime Minister to the Sovereign's private secretary. "This is the first and only occasion," Mr. Baldwin has said, "on which I was the one who asked for an interview—that I desired to see him, that the matter was urgent." The Prime

Minister saw the King on October 20. In recalling the interviews which he had on this day and on others that followed, Mr. Baldwin spoke of the King's manner. "Never has he shown any sign of offence, of being hurt at anything I have said to him. The whole of our discussions have been carried out, as I have said, with an increase, if possible, of that mutual respect and regard in which we stood." Mr. Baldwin explained his anxiety to King Edward, and, at the end of their talk, the King answered calmly, "You and I must settle this matter together; I will not have anyone interfering."

This, then, was the trend of His Majesty's mind. Mr. Baldwin did not press the King for an answer. He left Fort Belvedere and almost a month passed before he saw his Sovereign again.

Early in November, King Edward announced his intention of visiting the distressed areas of Wales. No phase of his English life had brought him greater popularity with the poor than his missions of compassion among them. His readiness to sympathise, his emotions, which he never seemed to hide, all showed the true value of his gentle heart. Once more he caught the imagination of the mass of the people by his efforts. The emancipation of the poor advances by reason rather than pity, and the King's dramatic declarations did not please those who know the great difficulty of reducing unemployment. He said, at a town in Glamorganshire, "Something ought to be done to find these people employment." At the end of his journey he crystallised his interest by making a promise. "Something will be done." Cynics have said that the King made this last effort in charity, to establish himself in the good opinion of the people. Political theorists said that his campaign was part of his wild intention to begin a royal dictatorship independent of the Constitution. Neither accusation seems to suit his character. But, if these were his intentions, they were cut short. *The Times* described his comments and promises to the miners as part of "a constitutionally dan-

1936. *King Edward VIII's visit to South Wales : Inspection of the Pen-y-garn Housing Estate, November 19, 1936.*

gerous proceeding." By this way he drew attention to the alleged apathy of the Government in dealing with unemployment, and if continued such actions on the part of the King would "entangle the throne in politics."

There was a fantastic anomaly in the history of these days in November. Just before going to Wales, before making his dramatic promise, "Something will be done," the King had sent for Mr. Baldwin once more and he had said, "I am going to marry Mrs. Simpson and I am prepared to go." Five days after the King's return from Wales, while the poor of Glamorganshire were still repeating his promises and taking hope from them, Mr. Baldwin was sent for once more. Up to this time he had obeyed the King's wish. He had not reported the first interview to the Cabinet. He had perhaps hoped that there was still time for the King and himself to "settle the matter together." During this interview, the King's mind apparently played with compromise. He desired the Prime Minister to consider whether he could marry Mrs. Simpson and, by Act of Parliament, enable her "to be the King's wife without the position of Queen." An important point of change thus came to the conversations between the King and his Prime Minister. Up to this moment the King had consulted him as his private adviser, a rôle which Prime Ministers have usually played; a rôle distinguished by Melbourne, Peel and Disraeli. When the King asked if the Government would pass legislation permitting a morganatic marriage, he made his problems into a constitutional issue, and, in his report to the House of Commons, Mr. Baldwin showed that he was immediately aware of this moment; immediately aware of the moment in which he ceased to be private adviser and became Prime Minister, with his duty to his Cabinet. He said to the King that he would have to place the suggestion "formally before the whole Cabinet" and that he would also be obliged to seek the opinion of the Dominion Prime Ministers before he could give his Sovereign an answer. The King told Mr. Baldwin that it was his wish that this wider, constitutional field of opinion should be sought; it was his wish to know the will of the British and Dominion Governments.

On December 2 Mr. Baldwin went to the King with his answer. He was certain that no such legislation as that sought by the King would be acceptable. The plan was, in Mr. Baldwin's word, *impracticable*. King Edward received the news quietly, without protest or complaint. Mr. Baldwin said that "he behaved as a great gentleman; he said no more about it." This moment was perhaps the most poignant in the crisis as far as the King was concerned. He had in his hands the last opportunity of using his prerogative as a monarch. If he had acted wildly he might have dismissed his Ministers. This was constitutionally open to him, but in this, the last act of his little reign, he acted wisely and unselfishly towards the country. The King seemed to see that to throw the issue into the arena of politics in a way that would have involved a general election was unthinkable. It would, indeed, have prejudiced the future of the Crown. He withdrew, and he wore his defeat with dignity. He stayed at Fort Belvedere so that he would not stir popular feeling, an action which made Mr. Baldwin say, "I honour and respect him for the way in which he behaved at that time."

On December 1, the day before Mr. Baldwin's third interview with the King, the Bishop of Bradford spoke to his Diocesan Conference of his Sovereign's tardiness in religious observance. "The benefit of the King's Coronation depends, under God, upon two elements," he said. "First, on the faith, prayer and self-dedication of the King himself—and on that it would be improper for me to say anything except commend him, and ask you to commend him, to God's grace, which he will so abundantly need, as we all need it—for the King is a man like ourselves—if he is to do his duty faithfully. We hope that he is aware of his need. Some of us wish that he gave more positive signs of his awareness."

The King had been criticised for his unconscious condemnation of Government methods in going to Wales. Now he was criticised as a Christian and therefore as Head of the Church. It was strange that after the long silence of the newspapers the first breaking of the rule should come from the provinces. The London newspapers reported the Bishop's words without comment. The Diocesan address and the knowledge that a secret meeting of the Cabinet had been held loosened the tongues of all. The Stock Exchange showed the growing fears in a fall in the price of Consols, insurance companies increased the premiums for Coronation risks, and manufacturers of souvenirs bearing King Edward's head hurried to protect their investments with policies drawn up against his abdication. This commercial nervousness spread quickly, and the word *crisis* was used in the newspapers for the first time, to describe the country's anxiety.

On Thursday, December 3, Fleet Street lifted the ban which had weighed it down for perhaps too long. The sensational newspapers spread the news of the crisis across their pages, and when England stirred to its duties on this exciting day, revolution in Spain, anger among nations and all world problems were forgotten. Domestic anxiety held the minds and hearts and tongues of Britons captive for many days. The newspapers expressed their concern, each in its own way. *The Times* talked of the " paramount importance " of reaching a decision which would " proclaim afresh the fundamental harmony of all elements of the State." The *Daily Mail* said that abdication was " out of the question " because of the mischief that would ensue, and the *Daily Express* asked, " Are we to lose the King or keep him? He knows the answer that the people want to hear." The *Daily Herald*, the newspaper of the working people, declared, " Either the King is bound to accept his Ministers' advice or else the British democratic Constitution ceases to work."

In the new countries, comments were loyal but frank. A Melbourne newspaper said, "Only the King can relax the tension. His sacrifice might be unreasonable, but it is necessary for the sake of the monarchy." A Canadian newspaper hoped that the King would find "duty more appealing than personal inclinations," and some of the Indian journalists wrote wildly of his trying to "render a distinct service to British democracy." New York reminded England of her "inexhaustible" gift for compromise, and hoped that it would "avail in this case."

In the British Parliament, Mr. Attlee, Leader of the Opposition, asked a question of the Prime Minister. He wished to know "whether any constitutional difficulties" had arisen, and whether he had "a statement to make." The ensuing conversation was guarded and inconclusive, but the day ended in gloom and the events of the night made people wait beside their wireless sets or congregate before the newspaper offices. London was dazed. The dark façade of Buckingham Palace seemed to fascinate hundreds of people who stood still, staring at nothing. Great Britain suddenly declared itself into two camps. The smaller was all for licence and freedom, at the expense of security and judgement. The greater was sympathetic, willing to be patient, but certain that the throne was of more importance than any one man who could sit upon it. The leaders in the drama lived through a busy and anxious night. The King saw Mr. Baldwin once more, and he also waited upon his mother. He had seen the Duke of Gloucester and the Duke of Kent during the day. When he went to Marlborough House he saw also the Duke and Duchess of York.

Whatever tide of criticism there was welling up against the King, his courage was not at fault. He was perhaps incapable of conquest within himself, but he did not avoid the frightening interviews: those with his Minister, which must have tortured his reason beyond common understanding, and those with his mother and his brothers, which must have tried his affections. He blundered on, fiercely loyal to his poor ideal, and if the scope of his conflict seemed small and unworthy, there was no doubt of his honesty or his

Photograph by Fayer of Vienna, Dorland House.

Mrs. Simpson.

sincerity. "He told me his intentions, and he has never wavered from them," Mr. Baldwin said.

The sensation of the next day, December 4, was the departure of Mrs. Simpson for the South of France. The night before, after his distressing interviews with his mother, his brothers and Mr. Baldwin, King Edward had bade Mrs. Simpson good-bye. In the morning she was already out of England and her car was hurrying south, pursued by reporters. The newspapers were full of her photographs, and millions of people saw for the first time a likeness of the woman who had helped to bring such pain to the country. The public view of her was not wild or unkind. It would have been easy to heap derision and cruelty upon her, but there was acknowledgement of her talents and a concession that she had helped the King, in less important ways, to overcome some of the faults of his behaviour. She did not emerge as a great character or personality, but it was human to hope that she deserved the devotion which she had let loose. There was disappointment, a few days afterwards, when she posed for the Press photographers. It seemed then that she was insensitive. People examined her oval face and wondered over the hardness of her mouth. Englishmen loved King Edward, no matter whither his twisted reason led him, and they were anxious lest he should destroy himself instead of finding the emancipation and inner peace which he needed.

Mrs. Simpson's journey towards the South of France gave a new field to the public imagination. It was hoped, for an hour or two, that she had withdrawn upon the strength of her own pride from a position which was afterwards described, in her name, as "unhappy and untenable." But it was not to be. As the hours of Friday, December 4, passed by, attention moved once more towards Westminster. In the afternoon, Mr. Baldwin was to make his first considerable statement upon the situation. He was to tell the House of Commons that neither the British Cabinet nor the Dominion Governments could accept the suggestion of special legislation to permit Mrs. Simpson to become the King's wife and not assume the full dignities of being his Queen.

The behaviour of the responsible members of the House of Commons during these alarming days is one of the happy signs left over from a time of great national humiliation. Mr. Attlee, Leader of the Opposition, showed sensitive consideration for Mr. Baldwin's repugnant duty, and neither his questions nor the comments which followed the Prime Minister's statement were harassing. When the Leader of the Opposition questioned the Prime Minister on Friday, Mr. Baldwin answered:

> ". . . . Suggestions have appeared in certain organs of the Press of yesterday and again to-day that if the King decided to marry, his wife need not become Queen. These ideas are without any constitutional foundation. There is no such thing as what is called a morganatic marriage known to our law. . . . The King himself requires no consent from any other authority to make his marriage legal, but, as I have said, the lady whom he marries, by the fact of her marriage to the King, necessarily becomes Queen . . . . and her children would be in the direct line of succession to the throne."

The Prime Minister then told the House what he had told his Sovereign two days before. The only possible way in which Mrs. Simpson could become the King's wife, without a consort's prerogatives, was through special legislation. "His Majesty's Government are not prepared to introduce such legislation," said Mr. Baldwin. The Commons cheered for so long at this announcement that Mr. Baldwin had to pause before adding that he was satisfied that the Dominions would be equally steadfast in refusing their assent to such a solution.

Friday closed with little more to add to the story, except a statement from the Archbishop of Canterbury which was designed to guide the clergy in preparing their sermons for the coming Sunday. Dr. Lang hoped, he said, that they would "refrain from speaking directly" on the matters "which had arisen" affecting the King himself and his subjects. He added, "Words spoken with imperfect knowledge of an extremely difficult situation can give no helpful guidance, and may only mislead or confuse public thought and feeling. Silence is fitting until the ultimate decisions are made known."

The Church has since been criticised because it gave no guide to public thought during the crisis. The reason is not far to seek. The Archbishop had been a close friend of King George V, and from the beginning, the King had called on him to help in trying to persuade the Prince of Wales that his friendship with Mrs. Simpson was an error. The Prince rejected the advice of both his father and the Archbishop, and when the crisis came, all hope of his being influenced by Dr. Lang was exhausted.

The Archbishop rightly judged that the Church should be silent upon the question of the marriage, as it was fully known that the Government and the Press were opposed to it. There was no need for the Church to emphasise this objection. If the Government had legalised the King's marriage, the Church would have been forced to speak, as the entire constitutional relationship between the Church and the Crown would have been involved and altered. In such circumstances the Church would doubtless have been obliged to demand her disestablishment.

The sensational week ended in indecision. Mr. Baldwin had his fifth audience with the King, and, during these negotiations, he had to reconcile himself to a fresh kind of attack from some of the newspapers. The accusation that he was forcing the King's hand went on, and those journals which were usually opposed to his policy, described the crisis as an opportunity for keeping "a good King" and discarding "a bad Prime Minister." But these opinions were not general, and the *Herald*, which showed repose and good judgement all through the conflict, said, "Sad as the consequences may be, we cannot see how the Cabinet could have done other than tender the advice which seems to it right." One more interesting voice was raised before the day closed. Mr. Winston Churchill pleaded for "time and patience." In a statement to the newspapers, he criticised the Cabinet for prejudging the question "without having previously ascertained at the very least the will of Parliament." "Parliament has not been consulted in any way, nor allowed to express any opinion." Mr. Churchill drew public attention to the circumstances of the divorce, which, if made absolute, would not free Mrs. Simpson until April of 1937. "Why cannot time be granted?" he asked. "Surely, if he asks for time to consider the advice of his Ministers, now that at length matters have been brought to this dire culmination, he should not be denied. Howsoever this matter may turn, it is pregnant with calamity and inseparable from inconvenience. But all the evil aspects will be aggravated beyond measure if the utmost chivalry and compassion is not shown, both by Ministers and by the British nation, towards a gifted and beloved King torn between private and public obligations of love and duty."

He used the words, "If an abdication were to be hastily extorted," but the accusation lying behind them was unjust. King Edward was no longer "torn between private and public obligations of love and duty." He had made up his mind and he had declared his decision, in favour of love and against duty. For him to have imagined, for one moment, that the traditions of British respectability could withstand the union he proposed showed how far he had wandered from knowledge of his people.

The leisure of the week-end gave many people the opportunity for demonstration in the streets. They had been fed with surprises in the morning newspapers, and the reporters, hiding in the laurel bushes about Fort Belvedere, told of strange comings and goings. Mr. Baldwin passed through the gates, in the darkness, for still another interview with the King. In the London streets, women walked with banners bearing the words, " We want our King " and " God save the King from Baldwin." A newspaper announced that the King was leaving England immediately for Cannes, and Mrs. Simpson was reported to have said to a correspondent of the Paris *Soir*, " I have nothing to say except that I want to be left quiet. . . . I have no plans. The King is the only judge. While waiting for his decision I am going to withdraw into silence and rest." These were the outward signs, but it was significant that most of the churches in the country were heavily attended. The day of suspense was quiet in most places.

On Monday, December 7, a member of the Commons put a question to Mr. Baldwin which contained the phrase, " the fatal and final step of abdication." The unanimous protest against the word showed how Mr. Baldwin had gained and held the confidence of the House. When Mr. Atlee asked him whether he had " anything to add to the statement which he made on Friday," the Prime Minister answered some of the accusations which had been made against him and his Government; mainly the accusation that they had pressed the King for a decision. He again declared that no advice had been given to the King except upon the question of a morganatic marriage, and that this had been at His Majesty's wish. The conduct in the House continued to be quiet, and it was significant that when Mr. Baldwin expressed " deep and respectful sympathy with His Majesty," the Leader of the Opposition added his agreement. A question from Mr. Winston Churchill was abruptly nipped in the bud with cries of " Sit down! " and " Shut up! " Never in his career had the Prime Minister been attended with such respect and consideration, and on this occasion the Socialists joined in the cheering. The imagination of politicians no doubt played about the dramatic interviews in the modest country house in which the King was now alone. Most of them trusted Mr. Baldwin not to misuse the frightening opportunity which had come to him.

Fort Belvedere had never been described in fullness to the people of England. It was the King's independent home, upon which he had spent much affection. Now the thoughts of everybody turned upon the house, in which his fatal love had matured. The knowledge of his unhappiness was painful to all sensitive people, but emotion could not drown the certain knowledge that there was only one way to nobleness for him and that through renunciation. In the days that followed, when returned soldiers talked over his abdication, they sometimes murmured against him. He had always promised them so much. "I want all ex-Service men . . . . to look on me as a comrade," he had said to them, and it had not seemed possible that he could turn from his vows. They said, with simple truth, "We had to give up our girls and leave our wives for our country." The magnitude of his world compared with the simplicity of theirs made no difference to the issue on the basis of character.

The King's life had been a pathway of promises from the day when he walked in Carnarvon Castle to vow to his father that he would always be a "husband" to his people. These pledges were recalled during the early days of the last week of his reign. Business men in Manchester were able to remember the day when he leaned across a table and said, "I shall always pull my weight." Even the dusky Maoris in New Zealand were able to think of the day when he said to them, "I will ever keep before me the pattern of Victoria, the Great Queen." In almost every land of the earth, over a period of twenty years, he had frowned, with the earnestness which had always made his utterances attractive, and had promised that his heart and his talents belonged to the people. It did not seem possible that he would turn from this good history to embrace the smaller needs of his heart.

Chapter Twenty-six

THE ABDICATION

This is the state of man; To-day he puts forth
The tender leaves of hope, to-morrow blossoms,
And bears his blushing honours thick upon him:
The third day, comes a frost, a killing frost;
And, when he thinks, good easy man, full surely
His greatness is a ripening, nips his root,
And then he falls, as I do.

"King Henry VIII,"
Act III, Scene 2.

Chapter Twenty-six

THE ABDICATION

KING EDWARD announced his decision to abdicate on Thursday, December 10. The preceding Tuesday and Wednesday gave no fresh themes to the drama. There had been faint hope when Mrs. Simpson's statement was published—that she "wished to avoid any action or proposal which would hurt or damage His Majesty or the throne." She said that she was willing, "if such action would solve the problem," to withdraw from the situation. But nothing would shake the strength of King Edward's purpose, and the world waited, excited and anxious, to know the outcome of the hurried meetings between members of the Royal Family, the meetings of Dominion Ministers and the continued interviews between Mr. Baldwin and the King. The signs were increasingly grave, and renewed gloom settled upon financiers and members of the Stock Exchange. On Wednesday a note of impatience was in the air. Mr. Baldwin added nothing to his previous statements in the House, but he hoped to be able to do so "to-morrow." This last day was a maze of anxious talk, and the members of the Cabinet sat for two and a half hours. The leaders of the country were busy and silent: they did not share the confidence which some of the newspapers drew from the statement which Mrs. Simpson had made. As the Parliamentary correspondent of *The Times* wrote, the Ministers had been merely embarrassed by the "very confident assurances" which some of the journalists built upon her message. "This was never the view of those of them who realised that the final decision rested with the King and with the King alone." It was expected, said *The Times*, that a message from the King would be read in the

House during Wednesday afternoon, and it was "generally anticipated" that it "would indicate the monarch's desire to relinquish the throne."

It was with this melancholy announcement that the last day of the crisis began. The King remained at Fort Belvedere. His health and his reason were said to show the strain of his unhappy state, but the will within remained firm; firm enough for him to withstand the touching appeal of his mother's visit to him on Wednesday afternoon. When the letters and diaries of this time become historical documents, posterity may know the extent of this appeal. We can know only that if it took the form of words it was calm and wise. King Edward was wrapped in his own stubbornness and he did not change his mind.

At the Cabinet meeting on Wednesday, Mr. Baldwin reported the conversation of the day before, when the King "communicated to him informally" his "firm and definite intention to renounce the throne." In a letter written after the meeting, the Prime Minister made his last appeal to his Sovereign. "Ministers are reluctant to believe that Your Majesty's resolve is irrevocable, and still venture to hope that before Your Majesty pronounces any formal decision, Your Majesty may be pleased to reconsider an intention which must so deeply distress and so vitally affect Your Majesty's subjects."

On Wednesday night King Edward answered Mr. Baldwin. The end had come and his pledges of twenty years died upon the wind. The King wrote, "His Majesty has given the matter his further consideration, but regrets that he is unable to alter his decision."

This was the news with which the Prime Minister faced the House of Commons on Thursday afternoon. The hushed, strained morning ended. Thousands of people stood outside the Houses of Parliament, but they made little sound. The day was cold and it added to the gloom; the sense of anxious meditation which spread over the capital. London seemed to be stunned into silence, knowing that hope was past. When it was almost four o'clock, Mr. Baldwin rose from his seat and walked to the Bar of the House, carrying three sheets of typescript which bore the royal coat of arms in red. He turned quickly and bowed to the Chair, and then, in a clear, unhesitating voice, he said, "A message from His Majesty the King, sir, signed by His Majesty's own hand."

He handed the three sheets of paper to the Speaker and then walked back to his seat. There was one break in the strained silence as the Speaker began—there was a movement in one of the galleries. The word *Order* was cried and then, with the return of silence, the Speaker read the King's message.

> *After long and anxious consideration I have deter-*
> *mined to renounce the throne to which I succeeded on*
> *the death of my father, and I am communicating this,*
> *my final and irrevocable decision. Realising as I do the*
> *gravity of this step, I can only hope that I shall have*
> *the understanding of my peoples in the decision I have*
> *taken and the reasons which have led me to take it.*
> *I will not enter now into my private feelings, but I*
> *would beg that it should be remembered that the*
> *burden which constantly rests upon the shoulders of a*
> *sovereign is so heavy that it can only be borne in cir-*
> *cumstances different from those in which I now find*
> *myself.*

There was also the sentence which revealed his own wretchedness: ". . . . I am conscious that I can no longer discharge this heavy task with efficiency or satisfaction to myself." Later in the message occurred the phrase, "But my mind is made up," and at the end he directed his Ministers to avoid further injury to his people by giving effect to the "instrument," without delay, so that his brother should ascend the throne.

We are close to the terrible week preceding King Edward's abdication and unable to view it with the perspective of the historians and dramatists of to-morrow. But we have emerged far enough from the events of December to realise that the authors of the future will not write upon the romantic theme of a King who gave up his throne for love, so much as upon the theme of a man of promise who came to disaster through the slow disintegration of his character: disintegration which was hastened by the perpetual frustration which he suffered. That the circumstances of his life contributed to this end, circumstances often beyond his own control, will be conceded, but people of the future will doubtless comprehend Mr. Baldwin's mind when he said, after the King's message had been read, "Sir, no more grave message has ever been received by Parliament and no more difficult, and I may almost say repugnant, task has ever been imposed upon a Prime Minister."

Then began the long, simple record of the preceding days. When the story was ended, Mr. Baldwin was cheered. There was no protest yet, and no criticism. The Leader of the Opposition asked that the sitting should be suspended until evening, in view of the gravity of the King's message. Little more than half an hour from the time when Mr. Baldwin rose from his seat and took the King's message to the Speaker, the House rose and withdrew in silence.

King Edward remained in England one more day. In London, the Commons closed the formalities associated with the Abdication Bill. The House had met on Thursday evening, when the Leader of the Opposition said, "This occasion does not, in my view, call for long and eloquent speeches." He spoke with sympathy for the King and with understanding for Mr. Baldwin. The Leader of the Opposition Liberals and Mr. Winston Churchill followed, and it must have solaced Mr. Baldwin to hear the latter speaker withdraw his early suggestion, that the King had been harried into making his decision. "I accept wholeheartedly," Mr. Churchill said, "what the Prime Minister has proved—

namely, that the decision taken this week has been taken by His Majesty freely, voluntarily and spontaneously, in his own time and in his own way."

The day in the House ended with the speeches of those who were openly opposed to monarchy. The most interesting address was from Mr. Maxton, who revealed the danger which the King's abdication was likely to let loose among Communists. Mr. Maxton spoke with quiet appreciation of the opposite view. "'I am speaking in a House in which an overwhelming proportion of the membership is under feelings of very strong emotion. I respect these emotions, although I do not entirely share them. . . . I share the same sympathies with the Prime Minister, who has to shoulder a task which few, if any, of the occupants of his office has ever had to shoulder before, and, in the nature of the case, has had to shoulder it alone." There Mr. Maxton's sympathies ended. He moved to the theme of the damage to the cause of monarchy. He spoke for men of his own opinion. "We therefore intend, however it may be against the general run of opinion in this House, to take strongly the view that the lesson of the past few days, and of this day in particular, is that the monarchical institution has now outlived its usefulness." There were other speeches, but they did not affect the general tide of thought. Through the great sadness which pervaded the country, two or three scenes and figures could be seen clearly. Mr. Baldwin had become one of the celebrated Prime Ministers in English history. Never an inspiring figure, sometimes attracting derision and stirring discontent because of his apparent lethargy, he had suddenly emerged as a distinguished statesman, and it was not possible to imagine any other man in the land who could have nursed both the country and its King through such a disaster with satisfaction and so little hurt to them both. From this view of Westminster the thoughts of the people moved back to Fort Belvedere. There was the King, still alone. The simple truth was already spreading over the country and into the world. It was better that he should go; better in every way, despite the affection which was still strong for him, and despite his good history. The anxiety had passed and the general feeling was of resignation and relief.

The British public react calmly and with speed in times of crisis. As the night of Thursday came, people began to talk of the new King. The sense of history in their loyalty was strong, and crowds gathered outside the Duke of York's house in Piccadilly, as a sign of their curiosity, but also of their devotion.

King George VI began his reign at 1.52 p.m. on December 11. The business of the country went on. It seemed that the strange, persistent machine of English life was strong enough to withstand any accident to the State. It was said that the world looked on with admiration because of the public calm; the dignity in a time of alarm and pain. They knew the closing words Mr. Baldwin had used in the House on Friday morning in speaking of the ex-King. "Like many of his generation, he was flung into the war as a very young man, and he has served us well in trying to qualify for that office which he knew must be his if he lived. For all that work I should like to put on record here to-day that we are grateful and that we shall not forget. There is no need in this Bill to say anything of the future. It deals with the fate of him who is still King, and who will cease to be King in a few short hours. . . ."

The few short hours passed. In the afternoon Queen Mary addressed a message to her son's subjects. She spoke of the sympathy which had been given to her. "I need not speak to you of the distress which fills a mother's heart when I think that my dear son has deemed it to be his duty to lay down his charge, and that the reign which had begun with so much hope and promise has so suddenly ended." Queen Mary did not embrace her disaster or her grief. She went on: "I commend to you his brother, summoned so unexpectedly and in circumstances so painful, to take his place. . . ."

1936. *King Edward VIII broadcasting to the British Empire from Broadcasting House.*

Life never stays upon the tragedy of an individual, and the integrity of the throne is in its own existence rather than in that of any man who sits upon it. Before the day ended King Edward said his last words to those who had been his subjects. At ten o'clock he was within Windsor Castle, ready to broadcast his farewell.

It is not difficult to understand why kings have sometimes gone mad with the unnatural weight which life puts upon them. It was amazing that King Edward had lived through the days at Fort Belvedere with any remnant of his reason left. But it was disturbing to realise, as one sat beside an English hearth, nursing all the comfort of British life, that he was going out into a wilderness in which he will never know what it is to be other than alone. For his busy mind and his interest in life, his sympathy and his training as a prince will never fit into the little space of desire.

As one waited for the striking of ten o'clock, the hour when the farewell was to begin, there were many agitating thoughts for those millions of people whose chief sensation was of disappointment; not only disappointment in an individual, but disappointment in the vagaries of human nature. We like to believe that kings and princes and priests and statesmen are better than ourselves, against all our logic and our information about life, our knowledge of history and our cynicism. One remembered that kings had ruled in Windsor Castle from the days of the Norman Conqueror. One thought of the earlier story, of Edward the Confessor lisping his prayers in the same forest through which his namesake of the twentieth century had driven a little time before. There was John to recall, climbing the Windsor hill on the way back from Runnymede, giving "vent to rage and curses against the Charter," and there was the White King, being carried within the shadows of St. George's, where the Cavaliers found a place for him beside the body of Henry VIII. It was not reasonable to suppose that these ancestral voices would be audible to Prince Edward in such an hour. One remembered also that the only King of England, since the Conqueror, who never slept in the Castle, as a Sovereign, was George IV.

At ten o'clock a voice announced, over the air, "This is Windsor Castle. His Royal Highness Prince Edward."

Then came another voice, thick and tired, and one was aware of the Prince's will summoning its strength: trying, along the way of sorrow and self-pity, to explain his intimate tragedy to the world. He had always been sincere. He said, "I have never wanted to withhold anything. . . ." And this was true. He pleaded then, "But you must believe me when I tell you that I have found it impossible to carry the heavy burden of responsibility and discharge my duties as King as I would wish to do without the help and support of the woman I love."

Later came the quickened sentence, "I now quit altogether public affairs, and I lay down my burden. . . ."*

From Windsor Castle, Prince Edward travelled to Portsmouth, where a destroyer was waiting to carry him across the water. Midnight had passed when he came to the coast. Fog had settled on the land and on the Channel, and H.M.S. *Fury* moved cautiously towards Boulogne. With the Prince went an equerry and a detective, but none of his servants. The train carried him from Boulogne to Vienna. One incident on the railway station made people wonder still more over the intricacy of his character. All the way across Europe the train had been overrun by reporters and photographers, but the Prince had evaded them. In the distress and hurry of arrival at Vienna he paused on the railway station and said to the British Minister, "I want you to let the photographers come along. They have had a very tough journey and they deserve some results."

On Sunday, December 13, the Archbishop of Canterbury preached a sermon in the Concert Hall of Broadcasting House in London. Dr. Lang depended upon moral indignation for his theme, influenced, no doubt, by the long

---

* The full text of the farewell speech is given in the appendix on page 293.

months during which he had watched King George suffering great bitterness because of the wilfulness of his son. It was not unnatural that he should have had resentment in his heart, but he was out of sympathy with the general feeling of the nation, however true his words may seem when they are considered at a distance of time. The mass of people had watched the young King passing through a crisis, and they had been deeply sad when he chose to go out, a solitary figure, into the night. Dr. Lang said:

"Seldom, if ever, has any British Sovereign come to the throne with greater natural gifts for his kingship. Seldom, if ever, has any Sovereign been welcomed by a more enthusiastic loyalty.

"From God he had received a high and sacred trust. Yet, by his own will, he has abdicated—he has surrendered the trust. With characteristic frankness he has told us his motive. It was a craving for private happiness. Strange and sad it must be that for such a motive, however strongly it pressed upon his heart, he should have disappointed hopes so high, and abandoned a trust so great.

"Even more strange and sad it is that he should have sought his happiness in a manner inconsistent with the Christian principles of marriage, and within a social circle whose standards and ways of life are alien to all the best instincts and traditions of his people.

"Let those who belong to this circle know that to-day they stand rebuked by the judgement of the nation which had loved King Edward. I have shrunk from saying these words. But I have felt compelled for the sake of sincerity and truth to say them."

Many people regretted the condemnation in these sentences. British people still loved the Prince and they had no wish to give him new pain.

It was strange that Prince Edward should have chosen the country of lost causes for his exile. It seemed to give the final air of gloom to his story as a monarch: that he should have hurried across Europe to the little, crushed country where the Habsburgs flourished and died. One could not help reflecting on the pathos of the Prince's state when news came of his walking through the vast, empty rooms of Schoenbrun Palace, free of the "golden yoke of sovereignty" and alone with his failure.

Appendix

Appendix

King Edward VIII's Last Speech

"At long last I am able to say a few words of my own.
"I have never wanted to withhold anything, but until now it has not been constitutionally possible for me to speak.

"A few hours ago I discharged my last duty as King and Emperor, and now that I have been succeeded by my brother, the Duke of York, my first words must be to declare my allegiance to him.

"This I do with all my heart.

"You all know the reasons which have impelled me to renounce the throne, but I want you to understand that in making up my mind I did not forget the country or the Empire, which as Prince of Wales and lately as King I have for twenty-five years tried to serve.

"But you must believe me when I tell you that I have found it impossible to carry the heavy burden of responsibility and discharge my duties as King as I would wish to do without the help and support of the woman I love.

"And I want you to know that the decision I have made has been mine and mine alone. This was a thing I had to judge entirely for myself. The other person most nearly concerned has tried up to the last to persuade me to take a different course.

"I have made this, the most serious decision of my life, only upon a single thought—of what would in the end be best for all.

"This decision has been made less difficult to me by the sheer knowledge that my brother, with his long training in the public affairs of this country and with his fine qualities, will be able to take my place forthwith without interruption or injury to the life and progress of the Empire.

"And he has one matchless blessing, enjoyed by so many of you, and not bestowed on me, a happy home with his wife and children.

"During these hard days I have been comforted by Her Majesty, my mother, and by my family. The Ministers of the Crown, and in particular Mr. Baldwin, the Prime Minister, have always treated me with full consideration. There has never been any constitutional difference between me and them, and between me and Parliament.

"Bred in the constitutional traditions by my father, I should never have allowed any such issue to arise. Ever since I was Prince of Wales, and later on when I occupied the throne, I have been treated with the greatest kindness by all classes of people, wherever I have lived or journeyed throughout the Empire. For that I am very grateful.

"I now quit altogether public affairs, and I lay down my burden. It may be some time before I return to my native land, but I shall always follow the fortunes of the British race and Empire with profound interest, and if at any time in the future I can be found of service to His Majesty in a private station I shall not fail.

"And now we all have a new King. I wish him and you, his people, happiness and prosperity with all my heart. God bless you all. GOD SAVE THE KING!"

INSTRUMENT OF ABDICATION

I, Edward the Eighth, of Great Britain, Ireland, and the British Dominions beyond the Seas, King, Emperor of India, do hereby declare My irrevocable determination to renounce the Throne for Myself and for My descendants, and My desire that effect should be given to this Instrument of Abdication immediately.

In token whereof I have hereunto set My hand this tenth day of December, nineteen hundred and thirty-six, in the presence of the witnesses whose signatures are subscribed.

EDWARD R.I.

SIGNED AT
FORT BELVEDERE
IN THE PRESENCE
OF

ALBERT.

HENRY.

GEORGE.

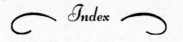

Index

ABDICATION, King Edward's, first mooted, 277; decision announced, 281 et seq.; message read in the House, 283; instrument, text of, 294-5

Abraham, the Heights of, 92

Accra, 170

Acorn, H.M.S., 62

Addison's Walk, Oxford, 35

Aden, 141

Adriatic, King Edward's cruise in the, 261-2

Aire, 72

Albert, H.R.H. Prince, now King George VI, *see* George VI

Albert, Prince Consort, 12; administration of Duchy of Cornwall, 23; visit to Rome, 67; comparison with George V, 215; on the Constitution Hill incident, 259

Aldershot, O.T.C. manœuvres at, June, 1914, 49

Alexandra, Queen, 14, 72

Alice, Princess (Countess of Athlone), 171

Allahabad, 153

America, Prince of Wales's first visit to, 92, 93; second visit to, 226-7

American criticism of Mr. Baldwin, 266

American Nation, The, quoted, 95

Andes, the Christ of the, 195

Antigua, 123

Antiquities, Edward VII and Edward VIII both indifferent to, 38, 63, 64

Argentine, the Prince in the, 192-4, 223

Argentine meat trade, Prince's interest in, 193

Army, Prince of Wales's training in, 49

Art, the Prince's attitude to, 211

Arthur, Sir George, *quoted*, 52, 53

Ashanti, 169, 170

Athlone, Countess of, *see* Alice, Princess

Athlone, Earl of, 171

Attlee, Major, M.P., 272, 274, 277

Auckland, N.Z., 105

Australia, particular character of, 115, 116, 120

Australia, Prince of Wales's visit to, 115-122

Australian and N.Z. soldiers, Prince's first meeting with, 63, 67; impression made on him, 80, 81

Aviation, beginnings of, 44; Prince of Wales's interest in, 218-223

Baldwin, Rt. Hon. Stanley, 137, 246, 265-285

Balfour, A. J. (afterwards Lord), 129

Ballarat, 118

Balmoral, King Edward's economies at, 258

Baltimore, 94

Banff, Canada, 90

Banjo, the Prince of Wales as performer on, 37

Bantus, the Prince addresses the, 176

Barbadoes, the Prince of Wales in the, 99

Barker, Canadian airman, 70

Baroda, 148-9

Baroda, Gaekwar of, 148

Baroda, Resident of, *quoted*, 148

Basuto chiefs greet Prince, 176, 177

Benares, 153

Bendigo, 118

Bengal, Chief Secretary to the Government of, *quoted*, 155

Berlin, Prince of Wales's visit to, in 1913, 45

Bermuda, the Prince's reception in, 124

Bethune, 60

Bharatpur, Maharajah of, 151-2

Bhopal, Begum of, 158

Bikaner, 151

Blue Mountains, Australia, 122

Boers, the Prince's reception among the, 172, 173, 177

Bombay, 145, 146, 147

Botany Bay, legends, 115

Bradford, Bishop of, 270

Brazil, British railway contract with, 111

Breteuil, Marquis de, 29

Breteuil, Prince of Wales at, 29 *et seq.*

Brighton, Prince dedicates memorial to Indian soldiers at, 139

Brisbane, the Prince in, 121

Britannia, George V on, 12, 13

British Industries Fair, 1929, Prince's speech at, 71, 212

Brittain, Sir Harry, 219, 222

Broadcast, Archbishop of Canterbury's, 288, 289

Broadcast, King Edward VIII's last, 287, 288; text of, 293-4

Brontë, Charlotte, 109

Brown, Charles Armitage, 108

Browning, Robert, 108

Bruce, Colonel, 68

Buckingham Palace, crowd scenes at, on Peace Night, 83; during King George's illness, 1928, 215; during Constitutional crisis, 272

Buenos Aires, the Prince's welcome in, 192-4

Bulawayo, 185

Burma, Prince of Wales's visit to, 155-6

Butler, Sir Harcourt, 152

Butler, Samuel, 109

Cadogan, Major, 34, 43, 70

Calais, 62

Calcutta, 154

Calgary, the Prince buys a ranch at, 91

Cambridge, Prince's speech at, on receipt of honorary degree, 128, 129

Canada, Prince of Wales's visit to, 1919, 89-92

Canning, George, 195

Canterbury, Archbishop of (Dr. Lang), 243, 247, 250, 251, 274, 275, 288

Capetown, the Prince's reception at, 171-2

Carnarvon, Investiture of Prince of Wales at, 21, 22

Castries, B.W.I., 123

Cavan, Field-Marshal Earl, 58, 70

Ceylon, the Prince in, 163-4

Chancellor, Sir John, 185

Charles I, 7, 11, 249

Charles II, *letter quoted*, 111

Charlotte, Princess, memorial to, 249

Cheetah hunting in India, 149

Chesterton, G. K., *quoted*, 214, 231

Children, the Prince's understanding of and popularity with, 110, 217, 218

Chile, the Prince in, 194-5

Christchurch, N.Z., 109

Christmas in New Zealand, 108

Church of England and King Edward, 270, 271, 274, 275, 288, 289

Churchill, Rt. Hon. Winston S., 44, 60, 137, 276, 277, 284

Clayton, the Rev. P. T. B. ("Tubby"), 72, 73, 74

"Colonial goose," 87

Colonial loyalty, 87, 88 *et seq.*

Colonial tours of King George V as Prince, 79, 80

Columbus, Christopher, 123

Commons, House of, and constitutional crisis, 265 *et seq.*

Constitutional crisis of King Edward's reign, 265-286

Cook, A. J., 201, 202

Cook, Sir Thomas, 200

Cornwall, Duchy of, 22, 23, 24, 212, 221

Coronation of King George V, 19

Cotes, Everard, *quoted*, 100, 121, 122

Crisis, Constitutional, of King Edward's projected marriage, 265-286

Cromwell, and the Duchy of Cornwall, 23

Crown, strength of, in 1914, 57, 58; in 1935, 231 *et seq.*

Curtis Bennett, Sir Noel, 202, 203, 204, 205

Cymbeline, quoted, 70

Daily Express, quoted, 111, 239, 271

Daily Herald, quoted, 247, 271, 275

Daily Mail, quoted, 271

Dartmouth, Prince Edward goes to, 13; first public speech of Prince at, 15

Davis, D. L., American Ambassador, 128

Deakin, Ralph, 176, 187, 193

Dehra Dun, 162

Delhi, Prince of Wales at, 159, 160

Democratic manners of the Prince, 11, 36, 37, 163, 210, 211, 225-6, 255, 258

Denmark, visit to, 222, 223

Deutsche Allgemeine Zeitung, quoted, 257

Devonshire, Duke of, Governor-General of Canada, receives Prince, 1919, 90

Dhar, Maharajah of, 158

Divorce, the Simpson, 265

Domett, Alfred, 108

Dominion comment on Constitutional crisis, 269, 271-2

Dominion loyalty, nature of, 87, 88

Dominions' response to the war, 88, 89

Don, Squadron-Leader D. S., 220, 221, 222

Down Under with the Prince, cited, 100

Dudley, Lord, 111

Durban, 178

Dutch reception of Prince in South Africa, 172, 173, 177

Edinburgh, Duke of (great-uncle of Edward VIII), 175

Edward I, 21

Edward VI, 22

Edward VII, accession, 8; his Court, 8, 9; relations with his grandson, Prince Edward, 9, 13; death of, 14; dislike of the Emperor William, 20; at Oxford, 33; attitude to scholarship and antiquities, 38; letter to William II, *quoted*, 43; as a father, 50, 210; and Dean Stanley, 63, 64; American visit of, in 1860, 92, 93; contrasted with his grandson, 225; appreciation of his son, George V, 232

Edward the Confessor, 287

Egypt, Prince of Wales's visit in 1916, 63

Empire tours, their effect on the Prince, 110, 111, 127-9

Energy, the Prince's physical, 27, 28, 45, 46, 204, 205

Englishman, The, on the Prince's Indian visit, 162-3

Enterprise, H.M.S., 215

Equator, the Prince first crosses the, 101

Escoffier, M. Maurice, the Prince's French tutor, 29, 30

Eucalyptus tree, 117

Ex-service men, Prince of Wales's work for, 129-131

Fiedler, Professor, the Prince's German tutor, 43, 44, 238

Fielden, Wing Commander, 223
Fiji, the Prince of Wales in, 101, 122
Fisher, Admiral Lord, 44
Flameng, François, portrait of Prince of Wales by, 30
Flying, *see* Aviation
Ford Motor Works, Prince's visit to, 13
Fort Belvedere, 240, 245, 265, 267, 274, 275, 276, 278, 285, 287
Fortune, American magazine, *cited*, 137, 232
Forward, *quoted*, 247
Fourteenth Corps, Prince of Wales with, 70, 72
France, Edward VII and, 20, 28, 29; Edward VIII as student in, 29-30; war service in, 57-62
Frederick, the Empress, 20, 55
French, Sir John (afterwards Earl of Ypres), 60, 61
Frogmore, Royal mausoleum, 8
Frustration of Prince's desires and ambitions, 223, 224, 225, 261
Fury, H.M.S., 288

Gambia, 169
Gandhi, 145, 146, 147, 149, 152, 153, 154, 155, 157, 159, 160, 161, 162, 178
Garter King of Arms proclaims new Sovereign, 250
Gaskell, Mrs., *quoted*, 115
Gathorne-Hardy, General, 71
General Strike, the, 200
George I, 6
George IV and Duchy of Cornwall, 23
George V, stay with Queen Victoria at Windsor, 1897, 5; as a midshipman, 12, 13; succeeds to the throne, 14; Coronation, 19; character, 19, 21, 137, 138, 163, 231, 232-6; relations with tenantry, 23, 24, 233; as a father, 34, 50, 138, 153-8, 236; complete identification with England, 19,

20, 57, 58, 136, 137, 231-4; bans alcohol during the war, 61; accident at Hesdinguel, 71, 72; Imperial tours when Prince of Wales, 79, 80; widening gulf between Prince and, 199, 209, 210; comparison with Prince Consort, 215; illness of, 1928, 215, 216; reluctance to allow the Prince to fly, 220, 221; Jubilee of, 231-6; estrangement from Prince, 236; death, 243; lying-in-state, 245; burial, 247-251
George VI, H.M. King, birth of, 7; youthful anecdotes, 7; connection with aviation, 219, 223; accession, 286
George, Rt. Hon. D. Lloyd, 137
Germany, Queen Victoria's partiality for, 20; King Edward VII and King George's dislike of, 20; the Prince's pre-war visit to, 43-6
Gibbs, Sir Philip, *quoted*, 59, 60
Gibraltar, 139, 140
Gladstone, W. E., on Edward VII, 38
Gloucester, H.R.H. Duke of, 214, 272
Gold Coast, the Prince on the, 169-171
Golf, the Prince at, 210, 217
Grand Cerf, Hôtel du, Paris, 61
Gray, Thomas, poet, 247
Grenada, B.W.I., Prince's visit to, 123
Gwalior, Maharajah of, 158, 159

Ham, 81
Hanno, 169
Hanover, King of, memorial to, 249
Hardy, Thomas, 122
Hartals, planned against the Prince in India, *see* India, Gandhi
Hawke, Mr. Justice, 265
Henry VIII, 249, 287
Hercules, air liner, 222

Hesdinguel, King George V's accident at, 71, 72

Hindustan, Prince Edward as midshipman on, 14, 15

Hinkler, Bert, 219

Hofmeyer, Mr., Administrator of the Transvaal, 183

Honolulu, Prince of Wales in, 100, 123

Horne, General, 60

Hookupu gathering, the Prince at at, 100

Hughes, the Hon. W., Australian Prime Minister, 117

Hunting, the Prince's interest in, 34, 35, 216, 217

Hyderabad, 158

Imperial questions, growing importance of, in twentieth century, 79; great services of Prince of Wales to, 80 *et seq.*

India, the Prince of Wales's visit to, 145-163

Indore, 158

Ismailia, 63, 141

Isolation, beginnings of Prince's, 199

Italy, Prince's war service in, 67, 70

Italy, traditional friendship with England, 68, 69

Jagersfontein, 177

Jammu, 161

Japan, Prince of Wales in, 164-5

Jews mourn George V at Wailing Wall, 244

Johannesburg, the Prince in, 184

Jones, the Rev. Llewellyn, 58

Jubilee of King George V, 231-236

Kaffirs, 173, 175

Kandy, 163

Kano Plain, Durbar on the, 170-1

Katanga, Governor of, 186

Keats, 108

Kennington estate of Duchy of Cornwall, 23, 24

Kent, Duchess of (mother of Queen Victoria), 153

Kent, Duke of (father of Queen Victoria), 123, 139

Kent, H.R.H. Duke of, 214, 272

Kindersley, A. F., *quoted*, 148

King William's Town, 176

Kitchener, Field-Marshal Lord, 51, 52, 53, 60, 61, 62, 69

Kitchener College, Delhi, 160

Kitzbuhl, the Prince's holiday at, 239

Labour leaders, Prince's growing sympathy with, 200-204

Lahej, Sultan of, 141

Lahore, the Prince in, 160

Lang, Most Reverend C. G., *see* Canterbury, Archbishop of

Lansbury, Rt. Hon. George, 256

Latorre, Chilean battleship, 195, 196

Laurent, Marcel, French novelist, *quoted*, 61-2

Laxmi Vilas Palace, Baroda, 148, 149

Lee, Sir Sidney, *quoted*, 8, 9, 29

Le Jour, *quoted*, 234

Lifeboat Association, Prince's address to, 128

Liliuokalani, Queen of Hawaii, 100

Lindbergh, Colonel, 259

London Chamber of Commerce, Prince's address to, 212

Lovie Château, 70

Lucknow, 152

Lyon, C. A., *quoted*, 239

MacDonald, Rt. Hon. Ramsay, 137

Madras, 156-7

Magdalen College, special character of, 35

Magdalen, President of, on the Prince of Wales, 38, 39

Malta, the Prince's reception at, 140

Mandalay, 156

Maoris greet Prince at Roturua, 106, 107

Marco Polo, 139

Marlborough House, 52, 53

Marriage proposal, King Edward's, 265 *et seq.*

Mary, H.M. Queen, 7, 27, 68, 69, 118, 135, 136, 225, 244, 245, 249, 250, 251, 256, 270, 286

Matabele War, 175

Matapos, Prince visits Rhodes's tomb on, 185

Maude, General, 71

Maxton, James, M.P., 285

Maxwell, Donald, 149, 150, 151

" May," Princess, *see* Mary, H.M. Queen

Mayo, Katherine, 147

Medina, voyage of King George V in, 68

Melbourne, the Prince's visit to, 116, 117

Miners, Prince's appeal for, 1923, 201-2

Mining areas, Prince's visit to, 1929, 202-5; King's visit to, 1936, 268

Monro, Sir Charles, 58

Mons, 80, 219

Montevideo, 191

Montreal, Prince of Wales addresses French Canadians at, 91

Moore, George, 211

Mother India, quoted, 147

Mountbatten, Lord Louis, 109, 140

Mysore, the Prince in, 157-8

Nagpur, 158

Napoleon, 191

Natal Indian Congress, attempts to boycott Prince, 178

National Press Club (U.S.), Prince's speech to, 94

National Relief, Prince of Wales's appeal for, 81, 82

Native States, Prince of Wales in Indian, 148-152, 157-8, 160-161

Navy, Prince Edward's service in, 10-15

Nawanagar, Maharajah of, *speech quoted*, 159-160

Nepal, 154

New York welcomes the Prince, 1918, 93; criticism of, 226, 227

New York Times, quoted, 233, 234

New York World, quoted, 227

New Zealand, particular character of, 87, 88, 105; Prince of Wales's visit to, 105-112

Nicolas II, Tsar of Russia, visit to England, 12

North-West Frontier, Prince of Wales on, 161-2

Norway, the Prince's holiday in, 46

O.T.C., Prince of Wales with, 49

Osborne, Prince Edward at, 10-13

Osborne, Queen Victoria's villa at, 10-11

Oudtshoorn, 173, 174

Oxford, Prince of Wales at, 33-9; return to, 127

Oxford, quoted, 35

Pacific Islands, the Prince in, 100, 122, 123

Paris Soir, cited, 274

Patiala, Maharajah of, 160

Pegoud, the airman, 44

Perth, W.A., 121

Peshawar, 161-2

Phillips, Sir Percival, 164

" Piccin, King," African nickname for the Prince, 170

Pinafore, H.M.S., Prince Edward in, 13

Pioneer, The, quoted, 146

Popularity of Prince of Wales after the war, 82, 83, 163; possible ill-effects of, 226, 227, 236, 237

Port Elizabeth, 175, 176
Post-war conditions and effect on the Prince, 74-6, 127, 209, 233
Poverty, the Prince and the problems of, 129, 199-205
Prince of Wales's Feathers, 22
Privy Council, King Edward VIII's first speech to, 256
Probyn, Sir Dighton, 52, 53

Queen Mary, the, 255

Rangoon, 155, 156
Rawalpindi, 162
Rawlinson, Lord, 156, 157, 159
Reading, Lord, 159
Religion, importance of, to King George V, 21, 138
Renown, H.M.S., voyages of Prince of Wales on, to Canada, 89-92; to Australia, New Zealand, the Pacific Islands and the West Indies, 99-124; to India, Burma, Ceylon and Japan, 139-165
Renown Magazine, *cited*, 90, 92
Repulse, voyage of Prince of Wales in, 169-196
Restlessness of Edward VIII developed by continual tours, 135-8
Returned soldiers, *see* Ex-service men
Revolver incident on Constitution Hill, 259
Rhodes Scholars, influence of, at Oxford, 34
Rhodesia, the Prince in, 185-6
Roberts, Field-Marshal Earl, 7
Rotorua, Maori festival at, 106, 107
Royal Air Force, Prince's interest in, *see* Aviation
Royalty, Australian view of, 120
Russian Royal Family, 12, 57

St. George's Chapel, Windsor, 7; burial of King George V in, 247-251

St. Helena, 191
St. James's Palace, 9, 10
St. John's, 90
St. Omer, 60
Salisbury (Rhodesia), 185
Sallust, *quoted*, 88
Samoa, the Prince in, 122
Sanders, Miss, *quoted*, 216
San Diego, 100
Sandringham, 9, 10, 19, 232, 233, 258
Santiago, Chile, 195
"Sardine," the Prince's nickname at Osborne, 11
Schoenbrun Palace, 290
Seddon, Mr., Premier of New Zealand, 79
Segontium, Roman camp at, 21
Sheldrake, H.M. destroyer, 62
Sierra Leone, the Prince in, 169
Simpson, Mrs. Ernest, 238-240, 243, 255, 259, 260, 262, 265, 266, 267, 269, 273, 281
Sims, Admiral (U.S.), 129
Snowden, Viscount, 202
South Australia, the Prince in, 121
South Oxfordshire Hounds, 35
Southward Ho!, 176, 187, 193
Spectator, The, quoted, 228
Stanley, Dean, 38, 63, 64
Stanley, Lady Augusta, 210
Statesman, The (India), quoted, 146, 160, 161
Stationers and Newspaper Makers, Company of, 212
Stellenbosch, 174
Stenning, Colonel, 49
Stevenson, R. L., 123
Stoke Poges, 247
Storey, Mr., Australian Minister, 117
Stuttgart, visit of Prince of Wales to, 44, 219
Suez Canal defences, the Prince reports on, 63
Sydney, reception of Prince of Wales at, 119
Sydney Sun, quoted, 116

Takoradi, 169
Talbot House, Poperinghe, 72.
    See also Toc H
Taranaki, N.Z., 108
Taylour, Mary, 109
Thomas, Sir Godfrey, 202, 204
Thomas, Rt. Hon. J. H., 200, 201
Thompson, G. Patrick, *quoted*,
    202, 203, 204
Thuringia, the Prince in, 45, 219
Times, The, quoted, 33, 35, 36,
    259, 266, 268, 269, 281
Times of India, The, cited, 152
Toc H Movement, foundation of,
    and Prince's interest in, 72-4,
    193, 194, 201
Togo, Admiral (Japan), 164
Toheroa soup, 111
Tokyo, 164
Trade, the Prince's interest in, 89,
    110, 111, 112, 127, 128, 211, 212
Transvaal, the Prince in the, 179-
    183
Travelling, effect of, on the Prince,
    199, 209-11, 236, 237
Trenchard, Lord, 220
Trinidad, Prince's visit to, 123

Udaipur, 149
Udaipur, Maharajah of, 149, 150,
    151, 216, 217
Udine, 67
" Untouchables," the Prince and
    the Indian, 160
Uruguay, Prince's welcome in,
    191-2
Uspallata, 195

Vaea, Mount, 123, 261
Vailima, 123
Valparaiso, 195
Verney, Major, *quoted*, 13, 37, 38
Vickers, Ltd., contract with Cen-
    tral Railway of Brazil, 111
Victor Emmanuel I, King of
    Italy, 67, 68
Victor Emmanuel II, King of
    Italy, 69, 70

Victoria, Queen, last days at
    Windsor, 5-7; death, 7; atti-
    tude to Germany, 20; physical
    stamina, 27; anxiety over Ed-
    ward VII's visit to Rome, 68;
    indifference to Imperial ques-
    tions, 79; indulgence to ser-
    vants, 237; attempt to assassin-
    ate, on Constitution Hill, 259;
    loneliness of widowhood, 249;
    Journal, quoted, 5, 6, 7
Vienna, King Edward VIII in,
    261, 288
Virginia, tribute to King George
    V in House of Delegates, 244

Waikiki, Hawaii, 123
Wales, King Edward's last visit
    to, 268-9
Wales, Prince of, history of title,
    22. *See also* Carnarvon
War, outbreak of European, 1914,
    51; Prince of Wales's early ser-
    vice in, 51 *et seq.*
Ward, Major Dudley, 71
Warley, training camp at, 51, 52
Wellington, N.Z., 108
Wells, H. G., *quoted*, 213
Western Australia, Lieutenant-
    Governor of, *quoted*, 80
West Indies, the Prince in the,
    123-4
Westminster Hall, King George's
    lying-in-state at, 245
White House, Prince's visit to
    President Wilson at, 94
White Lodge, Richmond, birth-
    place of Edward VIII, 6, 7
William II, Emperor of Germany,
    13, 20, 43, 45, 213
Williamson, David, *quoted*, 46
Wilson, Woodrow, President U.S.,
    94
Winchester, Bishop of, 249
Windsor, Prince of Wales is made
    Freeman of, 96
Windsor, St. George's Chapel, 7,
    247-251

Index

Windsor Castle, 5, 6, 7, 8, 287, 288
Wolferton, 245
Wood, Sir John, 156
Worcestershire Regiment, Prince presents colours to 3rd Batt. of, 153
Würtemberg, King and Queen of, 44

Yeta, Barotse chief, 186

York, H.R.H. Duke of, see George VI
York House, St. James's, the Prince makes his home in, 80-83
" Young Thunder," Indian chief, 90
Yule, Lady, 261

Zambesi, Victoria Falls, 186
Zeppelin, Count, 44, 219
Zulus and the Prince, 178-9